Regime Change You Can Believe In

The Minimalist Joy of Opting Out

Jack Perry

Regime Change you can Believe In: The Minimalist Joy of Dropping Out

STAIRWAY PRESS—LAS VEGAS

Cover Design by Guy D. Corp, www.GrafixCorp.com

STAIRWAY⹀PRESS

www.StairwayPress.com
848 North Rainbow Blvd #5015
Las Vegas, NV 89107 USA

Dedication

Thanks be to Jesus Christ. To my wife who believed in me, all my eternal love and thank you for guiding me in the light of your love. Your faith in me is a treasure beyond price. To Ken Coffman, my publisher at Stairway Press, Keith Ougden, my editor, and Linda Bustabade Coffman, my transcribist, a thousand thanks for all your hard work and making this book breathe its first published breath. Thanks to Lew Rockwell for opening the door to my articles. May God Bless the Sisters. And to all people of the world, peace be upon you.

INTRODUCTION

I'M NOT JOKING when I tell you that I wrote this book with pen and paper while sitting at my kitchen table. Why? Because this is just how we'd discuss these things, you and I: seated around the table with a cup of coffee.

That's what's missing in America today: honest dialogue with common sense based on wisdom derived from having lived the issues we're talking about. Discussions from the actual people that live in the neighborhoods Senators and Congress people don't even drive through. Politicians pay other people to write about their supposed experiences. Ask a Senator when the last time was that he had to go to the food bank because his paycheck didn't go far enough. Who was the most recent president who buried a son killed in a war fought by the United States? When was the last time Congress had to meet to decide if they'd buy food and do without medication, or buy medication and get by on one meal a day, because there wasn't money enough for both?

Not to mention this: if corporate CEOs had to live on what they pay their employees, they'd march on Wall Street en masse—demanding higher wages and economic justice. If politicians struggled to pay their bills and buy groceries, then were told that our most important problem right now is climate change, you'd hear outrage a billion miles into space.

You won't find endless footnotes referencing various scholarly books thicker than the Pentagon budget. I know all this stuff because I read lots of books and I pay attention. I find out what I wish to know without being led into what others wish me to see. Yes, I know this stuff off the top of my head because before coming to a conclusion, I carefully investigate the facts. And so should you.

We need to return to frank, blunt and truthful discussions without splitting ourselves out into "sides" dominated by two political parties. That's partially what got us into this mess. People will say about me: "How is he qualified to speak on these things? He's not an expert!" It doesn't take an expert to see that the United States, since 1945, enters into unwinnable wars that accomplish nothing except costing lives for no genuine goal. It does not take an expert to see that our economic system favors Wall Street, impoverishes the nation as a whole and does so in conspiracy with the government. It does not take an expert to see the government jails people for breaking laws that it does not itself follow.

In fact, it's often the "experts" who, like the Pied Piper, lead us into disasters while playing songs of patriotism or free money, and we go right along into another war or huge recession. The "experts" told us the Iraq War would pay for itself and lead to the creation of secular democracies throughout the Middle East. The "experts" told us the Housing Boom was the greatest thing for the economy since World War Two. The "experts" tell us that the Pentagon and Wall Street know best—because the Pentagon and Wall Street are staffed with experts.

When the Pentagon knowingly gives covert military aid to terrorists who then become Al-Qaeda and ISIS, where are these experts then? When Wall Street "experts" engage in behavior more risky than professional gamblers, where are these experts when the Great Recession happens as a result? When foreign policy "experts" say the elected leader of Syria must be deposed by force, where are these "experts" to explain themselves to the hundreds of thousands of people who die as a result? These are the same "experts" that told us the Vietnam War could be won? "Experts" are largely responsible for creating these problems and many of them have innocent blood on their hands.

The experts wrote the Obamacare bill. There they sat, consulting endless numbers of other experts, and Obamacare is what they came up with. They presented us with Obamacare and gloated as if they'd just discovered a cure for cancer and hadn't just written the Vietnam War of social programs.

We simply cannot afford any more experts.

If some think I should be one of these experts to have written this book, they'll certainly be disappointed. As I said, I wrote this with pen and paper seated at my kitchen table. I wasn't sequestered away in a lavish study with four walls holding thousands of books I've never actually read. I didn't need to consult "experts" because the trail of the "experts" is easy enough to follow. Just follow all the futile wars and economic policies that resulted in failure. There you will find the experts at the end of the trail. The experts are going to blunder us right into the Third World War and another Great Depression—probably at the same time.

It seems as if we're in a permanent loop of repeating the same mistakes, over and over. Chasing the same flawed policies and ideas, over and over again. Nobody has any new ideas and when they say they do, we soon see it's the same old idea with a new wrapper to convince us it's new. We went through Bush's "regime change" idea right into Obama's "change you can believe in" and yet nothing at all has actually changed. And no one who ran for president in the 2016 election offers anything remarkably different from anyone else before them.

We couldn't win World War Two today if the future of the country depended upon it. We couldn't build the Panama Canal today for all the advances in technology we've made. We couldn't build the Transcontinental Railroad today with all the money the government prints. But, if we were fighting the Civil War today, it'd go on for the next fifty years so the government would have a way to keep Americans fighting each other so we won't notice the government is collectively screwing us all.

This book doesn't play favorites. Everyone owns responsibility for this mess. Republicans, Democrats, conservatives, liberals: all have played silly games that have cost the lives of real people and are rapidly plunging the nation into poverty. These people couldn't work together to put out a fire in a locked room if one side was given a hose and the other had access to the spigot. They'd all perish together, arguing over who'd get the blame for starting the fire and who'd take the credit for putting it out. It's ridiculous, but this is what they're doing. The nation is on fire, but instead of working together to put out the fire, they tell one another that if there is a fire, it must be the fault of the other. That's if there is a fire in the first place, because they haven't yet formed several committees to do an investigation over a ten-year period to see if there *is* a fire, despite the fact everyone can see it.

A room full of corporate CEOs would do no better. "Well what's our margin if we put out the fire? I mean, we can't just put out this fire for anything less than a 20% profit margin. The fire itself is growing by 30%, which is impressive growth, to say the least. A smarter move might be to feed the fire rather than try to put it out. But we can't do anything until we have a few staff meetings. Put out an email requesting a meeting. If we're still alive after the meeting, we'll see if we can obtain a government grant to put out the fire. I mean, we can't just eat the cost of the hose and the water bill. We've got to watch the budget."

It might all be funny if it wasn't all of us suffering from the actions of these people. But, at the end of the day, if we adjust and restructure our lives and return our priorities to where they belong, we can laugh at it. When we realize the only regime change we can believe in begins within us, we won't blindly follow charlatans into disaster after disaster after disaster.

We can't do much about the government and Wall Street, but there's a lot we can do with regard to our lives and isolating ourselves from the government and Wall Street as much as possible.

The ultimate truth is this: we don't need them.

They need us.

What if we remove ourselves from the equation? Impossible? No, it is not. But we must wake up to the truth.

That's what this book is about.

Chapter One: The divisions in the country between Republicans and Democrats / Liberals and Conservatives; neither are good, bad, right, wrong. Both act hypocritically across the board, never learn from the past and engage in personality politics. American voters do not think through issues and are at fault for allowing the divisions to continue.

Chapter Two: Five great American beliefs: America is based on the Rule of Law; American Exceptionalism; America is the Greatest Nation on Earth; America has Freedom; America is a Democracy. The conclusion is that all of these are myths.

Chapter Three: The profound influence the media has on the election process. The media has caused American society to become obsessed with violence both real and virtual.

Chapter Four: "Celebrity Government", where candidates are not chosen for ability but for electability; where "Celebrities" have unwarranted influence on the political process.

Chapter Five: Detailed explanations of how America's involvement in World War One has led directly to all subsequent wars which America has initiated, or wars in which America has participated. The causes of Al-Qaeda and ISIS are charted. America has never learned from its mistakes and is unprepared for World War Three; yet America's actions seem set on starting World War Three.

Chapter Six: The scam known as the American Economy. How the economy went from self-sufficiency to the boom-time industrializations of World War Two and the Cold War, to subsequent loss of jobs and the several failed "booms" created by Wall Street.

Chapter Seven: The American health-care system; the over-powerful Food and Drug Administration and Drug Enforcement Administration; the prescription scam; Big Pharma. A Community Based system for health care is proposed.

Chapter Eight: Corporate greed and incompetence and how Big Business lacks a moral dimension. Corporate calls for "privatization" of true national assets must be resisted.

Chapter Nine: The terrible consequences for Americans of failed economic policies, yet how Americans are caught in the myth of "good times to come". How an amoral Wall Street perpetuates the myth. How employees have an equivalent claim to profit as do employers. Local, "underground" economies could bring Wall Street to heel.

Chapter Ten: Scams are everywhere, from corporate retail pricing scams to government scams about immigration, Islam and so on. "Jack's Three Rules" about scams are offered.

Chapter Eleven: The ills of America can be bypassed by *Opting Out*—from consumerism, the accumulation of possessions, political lobbying. The difference between "wealth" and "prosperity" is examined. Opt Out of politics above the local level. Don't enlist for military service. Refuse to prop up the system.

Chapter Twelve: Has technological "progress" brought the benefits it promised – more leisure time, a better quality of life; or has it tied us to a treadmill of more "progress" and more government intervention? But—there is a way off of the treadmill.

The Epilogue summarizes the arguments put forth in the book and points the way towards a better life for individuals, families and communities.

CHAPTER ONE—POLITICS

WHEN I LIVED in Los Angeles, my apartment building was a small, rather bohemian enclave. We had regular parties just for ourselves. But, one night, someone invited a bunch of people who didn't live there. They took over and made themselves the center of attention. Finally, one of the tenants in our building, Dave, stood up and shouted: "Who _are_ these people?! Why are they here? Who invited them?!"

Have you ever felt that way about the strangers we call the United States government? Perhaps people you voted for, once they were in office, became unrecognizable compared to how they were on the campaign trail.

You're not alone.

Many, if not most, Americans ask those questions. Who are these people who turn up in our elections? Who decided to keep running certain candidates? Or, if new ones, who told them to run, or gave them the idea? Obviously, it isn't all random chance or a fairy tale where a pizza delivery boy becomes the president. The democratic election process is not in any way true. A lot of money is spent to make it appear so, but, as I will demonstrate later, the links between politicians and entertainment celebrities are so close, the election process is all but a scripted movie.

But before we can touch on that, we need to understand who we're talking about—along with the ideologies they allegedly represent. As everyone knows, American politics are firmly divided into two exclusive groups that are antagonistic to one another. Or, that is the script that's read to convince us to believe in the roles they play. On one side, we have Republicans who represent the Conservatives for the most part. On the other side, we have Democrats who represent Liberals—to the point where Conservatives consider them one and the same. And, of course, the same can be said as to how Democrats view Republicans. Both sides represent what appear to be two sides of a textbook-perfect conflict: good versus bad. Each side portrays itself to its followers as the "good" ones and their opponents as the "bad" ones. Therefore, no side can actually be realistically quantified as "good" or "bad" since there is no neutral method that can be used for judgment.

Be that as it may, there is a method by which both sides at once can be determined as "good" or "bad." The actions of both must be investigated as a whole and not merely the actions of one party while absolving the other. If I were to look at the use of military force without a true need for self-defense, I can successfully judge both parties as bad. Both have used such force without restraint since the end of World War Two. Since the end of World War Two, over 90,000 Americans have died in wars the United States had no justification to enter or start. Both political parties, Democrat and Republican, entered wars or started them. What's more, wars entered or started by Democrat presidents were continued when a Republican president took office, and vice versa. Again, over 90,000 Americans died in these wars and for no tangible result that carried on beyond the conflict.

Even worse, most of these wars were not won. The United States became bored and abandoned them. Often, chaos and humanitarian disasters occurred in the wake of these wars after the United States had washed its hands of them. There was one relevant thing that occurred after the United States signed the 1973 Vietnam War cease-fire. In 1975, North Vietnamese forces took over South Vietnam, thus uniting all of Vietnam under a communist government. Previously, the United States claimed such a thing would create a "domino effect" throughout Southeast Asia and every nation in the region would fall to communism. In fact, this did not happen in the way the United States said it would. The "domino theory" was the reason the United States entered the Vietnam War under a Democratic president with a Republican president continuing the fighting.

You would think this massive error would cause the United States to refrain from entering more wars where it was not directly threatened, because the fall of South Vietnam disproved the United States' "domino theory." But you would be wrong if you thought the Vietnam War taught anything whatsoever to either political party. Both parties now use military force with little or no restraint and virtually no public discussion or authorization.

Thus, if I assign a value of "good" or "bad" for the parties, both have justified the killing of other human beings for no justifiable reason. Both parties sacrificed Americans in wars it had no desire to actually win. Therefore, on this basis alone, both parties are bad and neither can claim itself to be good. Nor does one or the other have moral credibility to point fingers at the other side. If anyone thinks one party is more warlike than the other, that's a serious mistake. This is how wars begin. People vote for this or that candidate, believing that person to be against war. Yet, that candidate will support any war if his or her party supports it. Pay attention to that. These people do not vote for what is right or wrong, they vote for what their party tells them to. This brings me to my next point.

When determining the difference between "good" and "bad," the values of "right" and "wrong" come into play. How do these two parties adhere to doing what's right, even if it goes against party ideology?

That question can be answered.

Think of Donald Trump when he was a Republican presidential candidate for the 2016 election—he made several anti-Muslim comments on the campaign trail, many expressing the desire to engage in unconstitutional actions should he gain the presidency.

On the hot seat for these bigoted remarks, the other Republican presidential candidates soundly condemned Trump.

They said his ideas were wrong.

However, when asked if they would vote for Trump if the Republican Party nominated him, they said yes! This is a textbook-perfect example of what's wrong with our election process. Not to mention the entire government. The Republican presidential candidates will vote in favor of what they know and admit to be wrong if the Republican Party tells them to. Again, the Republican Party candidates will depart from what they know to be right—and do what they know to be wrong—because their party status is more important than doing what they know to be right.

It's a serious mistake if anyone thinks this behavior is unique to the Republican Party. How many Democrats voted in favor of the Iraq War and then later half-heartedly admitted they thought it to be wrong? How many Democrats voting in favor of Obamacare actually read the entire bill to make sure it was right and fair? How many Democrats spoke up against the Obama Administration arming terrorists in the Syrian Civil War?

And, why was *that* justified, whereas Reagan having done the same with the Nicaraguan Contras in the 1980s was wrong? Certain Obama Administration members were present in the House and Senate during that time and soundly condemned Reagan. Yet, when Obama did the same thing, they approved it!

Why?

Because the Democratic Party told them to. Both parties do what they know is wrong when party ideology tells them to. Neither party has a moral stance preventing them from wrong-doing. In fact, the reverse is true. Their ideology is more apt to excuse doing the wrong thing rather than insist on doing the right thing. Thus, we see, rather obviously, that both parties are bad.

If we're going for two out of three reasons why we can state that both political parties are bad, they've both already lost. But to be fair, let's present a third experiment. This third investigation is about the selection of political candidates and, especially, presidential candidates. If we imagine there is actually a difference between the two political parties, and one is "good" while the other is "bad," then we should see it reflected in whom they select to run for office.

An entity that is "good" self-regulates and weeds out the "bad" from amongst them. Or, at the least, knows enough about a member's character to ascertain whether or not that person knows right from wrong and is trustworthy enough to hold a public office. Not to mention whether that person does what's right and does not do what's wrong. But that is not what political parties look for in a candidate. What they actually look for is this: can the person win? As I've already shown, right and wrong are irrelevant to the parties.

The parties will tell you they have to select winning candidates in order to get their political ideas fielded and in place. But, on the face of that, even then they admit to manipulating the American people. What if the political agenda the party wants to advance is not at all what the candidate says on the campaign trail? In other words, the candidate is an actor reading from a script in a movie with an unknown plot.

They select the candidate because he can win, not because he'll do what he says on the campaign trail. He'll do what it is the party wants done, as I also demonstrated earlier. Take, for example, Obamacare. What the American people understood Obama to be promising during the 2008 Presidential campaign was a national health care system along the lines of the ones European nations have. That's what people wanted. What was delivered was a byzantine, mandatory health insurance program that was still private insurance just as before. Now, if private health insurance actually worked in the first place, why did Barack Obama claim it to be broken during the 2008 campaign to get elected? Then, when the Democratic Party agenda could be implemented, the resultant Obamacare came from collusion between party officials and private health insurance corporate officers. Anyone with eyes can see that.

Before anyone thinks I'm singling out the Democrats, let's

talk about his predecessor, George W. Bush. Could he have been elected after promoting a disastrous, no-win war in Iraq?

Of course not.

Yet, people within his administration were deeply involved with a group called "Project for a New American Century" which lobbied for taking over Iraq long before 9/11 happened. The tragedy of 9/11 was not a justifiable reason to invade Iraq—Iraq was not involved in the 9/11 attack. I examine this further in Chapter Five.

As I said, the candidates are selected because they can win, not because the party actually intends to do what the candidate says to get elected. The party hires consultants to coach the candidate about what to say. Speeches and sound bites are rehearsed like a script for a movie. The candidate is groomed to win based on personality, appearance and saying the right things.

Think about it for a moment. Would the American people vote for Bush if he promised to start a war with Iraq without any plan on how to actually win it? Would the American people vote for Obama if he told them he'd create a health insurance system they'd be forced to buy into? And if they didn't, they'd be penalized on their tax returns?

Of course, neither would have been elected. But they *were*, because their parties thought they could win. Then, afterwards, the party agenda could be implemented. It is the same with Congressional and Senate candidates. Therefore, it's clear that both parties are bad. Good entities do not engage in this kind of dishonesty and deception, particularly when it results in cataclysmic wars and financial hardships for the people the parties allegedly serve. Thus, on all three counts, the only logical conclusion we can arrive at is that both parties are bad and neither one nor the other is good.

How do these parties continue to exist, win elections and deceive the American people? It is because both use the theatrics of their ideologies to divide the Americans into Conservative and Liberal camps.

Truth be told, people that are staunchly conservative or adamantly liberal are not in a majority. As a whole, the American people fall somewhere in the middle. If this were not so, you wouldn't see a Democrat elected president after a Republican, and vice versa. But everyone has one or two issues that matter the most to them and they vote strictly according to that. People should start thinking beyond that, because that is exactly how the parties manipulate them. Often, manipulating them into voting against their own long-term interests.

As one-issue voters go, consider this scenario: Bob votes for strictly pro-gun candidates. But one of Bob's pro-gun politicians he helped elect votes to close a recreational area owned by the government in order to "limit big government." Bob works at the recreational area and, thus, loses his job. In order to pay his rent, Bob is forced to sell his gun collection. How, therefore, was Bob served in the long-run by voting for one issue that, in the end, ultimately became irrelevant for him?

Or, consider Sally, who votes strictly for what she is told are "pro-women" candidates. However, some of the "pro-women" candidates Sally helped to elect are also "social justice" advocates who vote to overturn strict mandatory sentences for felons. As a result, some serial rapists serve short sentences and are released. A few years down the road, Sally finds herself afraid to go to her city park anymore due to a serial sexual predator that attacks women there. Sally wasn't afraid like this before the activist politicians decided on lesser sentences for felons and, oops, included violent felons in that equation. Therefore, how was Sally served in the long run by being a one-issue voter on an issue that, in the end, ironically caused her fear as a woman? Because if those politicians really were "pro-women," why did they not see women that would be victimized by their voting actions?

But Bob and Sally were not entirely deceived by a hidden party agenda. In fact, on the campaign trail, Bob's favorite candidate vowed to "cut government spending" on "unnecessary programs such as parks and recreation centers..." But he also vowed to protect gun rights and that's all Bob heard and cared about. And had Sally paid closer attention to those "pro-women" candidates, she would have heard them state they were on a mission to restore "justice and fairness in sentencing" and favor "probation over incarceration." But by being one-issue voters, they blinded themselves to the genuine reality of those candidates. And in so doing, they became perfect suckers for the hidden agendas of their political parties that the candidates didn't mention.

Often, the issues are blatantly presented by candidates exactly for the purpose of capturing one-issue voters, sometimes luring voters who would not otherwise support the candidate. How many times have we heard from friends, "Well, I held my nose and voted for Skunky Shylock because he's pro-gun." Or, "I know Cindy Simpleton is a crook, but I held my nose and voted for her because she's pro-choice."

What these people are saying is they did the same as politicians do: they voted for what they knew to be wrong because they felt there was something in it for them. People say, "Well, that's just how politics is!" Right, and so is crime. Do we justify that, too? Settling for the lesser of two evils is still settling for evil.

Keep in mind that you're voting for what the candidate's speech writer wrote—as instructed by the party and its strategists. Also, if the candidate has written a book, it was written by a ghost writer in most cases—often, one employed by the party to make the candidate look good or heroic. Everything from the issues presented to the speeches that are written are geared toward making sure the candidate wins. Delivering on the promises isn't necessary. Failing to deliver on promises can be blamed on "obstruction" by the other party which will carry a politician past a term where he failed to deliver on promises and now faces reelection. Once he is reelected, he can be counted on to not deliver any promises at all. Or worse, to deliver things he said he wouldn't, such as military interventions or new taxes.

There's also the "see-saw effect." This is also known as

"throw the bums out" effect, where people become disillusioned with one party and elect the other in response or protest. This was evident in 2000 when people, disillusioned by two terms of Bill Clinton, elected (as we are told) George W. Bush. In the middle of two simultaneous wars, America reelected Bush in 2004. But, by 2007, people were extremely disillusioned by Bush and in 2008, voted for "Change You Can Believe In" and Barack Obama. Obama was reelected in 2012 and it was in his second term that America finally recognized the disasters of Syria and Obamacare.

See the pattern?

In the second term, the other shoe drops. After 2004, we saw the true disaster of the Iraq War. After 2012, we saw the disaster of Obamacare and the unfolding disaster of Syria. When a two-term president leaves, the other party gets in with promises to "fix" what the other party broke.

Except it never does.

This began when people imagined Reagan to be a great president. After his two terms, they elected his vice-president George H. W. Bush who ran the country as it fell into a deep recession unseen since before Reagan. That's what catapulted Clinton into two terms after Bush. But since then, it's been a different party elected after a two-term president. This is because getting re-elected gives the party the opportunity to do a lot of things they wouldn't want pinned on a president facing reelection. That, of course, infuriates the American people. So, they "throw the bums out" and vote for the other party.

The scenario goes like this: President Shmoe is in his second-term as president. He's a Democrat. He signs an executive order banning certain guns. He also creates three new government agencies, increases taxes by signing an authorization bill and does other things seen as "liberal, nanny-state government" actions. Therefore, the Conservatives rally behind the Republican Party to get rid of the now-hated liberals. The Republican presidential candidate, Bucky McDoofus, wins the election. By his second term, he's gotten the United States into two no-win wars and the economy has crashed into a brick wall. Now the Liberals rally behind the Democratic Party to get rid of the now-hated conservatives. The Democratic presidential candidate, Goody Two-shoes, wins the next election. It's nearly as predictable as weather: a cycle that goes on and on. Throw these bums out, bring these bums in. Those bums disappointed us, so throw them out and bring back in the previous bums we threw out.

Excuse me, but has anyone noticed we've been throwing out and bringing back the same sets of bums for over 40 years now? It actually goes back further than that, but I'm being nice here.

How is it all tied to their ideologies? That's easy. Each party has things the majority loves and things the majority hates. No party has even 70% of what the majority loves. The ideologies are as follows:

DEMOCRATS/LIBERALS: Favor social programs such as welfare and food stamps. Supports minority rights, gun control and/or gun bans, and "Green" energy and programs. Generally favors more versus less government spending. Perceived as "soft on crime" and often is, to some extent. Pro-choice, mostly secular, challenges conservative social values, claims to be anti-war and favors less military spending in theory. Allegedly favors civil liberties.

REPUBLICANS/CONSERVATIVES: Favors cutting social programs such as welfare and food stamps. Supports gun rights and the right to self-defense. Does not tolerate or seek to understand criminal behavior. Generally favors less and not more government spending except where the military is concerned. Often pro-life, often influenced by conservative Christian values, seeks to uphold traditional social values, willing to use military force whenever felt necessary and supports private property rights.

Now, espousing several of those values will endear a candidate to some and alienate him from others. However, what the American people don't realize is that both political parties overlap and do the same thing on the following issues:

a.) Both parties will not hesitate to use military force to accomplish whatever they deem necessary. Both parties have done so. Both parties engage in "regime change."

b.) Both parties will not hesitate to create more government agencies even if a virtually identical agency already exists. Both parties have done so, creating redundant government agencies.

c.) Both parties will enter or start wars they have no genuine intention of winning, nor any concise plan of how to win. Both parties have done so, throwing lives away for nothing.

d.) Both parties will spend more, cut social programs and curtail civil liberties when they wish to do so. And raise taxes after saying they would not. Again, both parties have done so.

Those four things are critical to understanding that despite their alleged differences, both parties are actually two sides of the very same coin. Each party uses "lightning rod issues" such as abortion and gun control to leverage an election. In reality, neither party is serious about the lightning rod issues. Their real and actual concern is gaining and maintaining power. Both parties are funded behind the scenes by the same banks and corporations.

The struggle between the parties is not truly a struggle between competing ideologies, but actually a fight to see who'll gain the primary attention of Wall Street. In that, the two parties are closer to one another than anyone imagines. The entire system is co-opted and both parties vote in favor of what benefits the banks and corporations behind both parties. The ideologies are used to lend legitimacy to the charade or assert control over a certain aspect of American life.

How does this work? I shall explain.

Where I grew up, there was a small, volunteer community

melodrama that produced plays. They were always understaffed, so it was typical to have one actor play three parts/characters in a play. He'd play a part as a good guy, run backstage, change costumes, and re-emerge as a bad guy for the next scene. In the next play, he might play nothing but all good guys. And the bad guys in one play will be good guys in the next.

Have you not noticed this very same melodrama playing out in our elections? In late 2001, George W. Bush was a good guy. By 2007, he was a bad guy. Why? He was the same guy he was in 2001, doing the same things even the Democrats said he should do after 9/11. But by 2007, the Democrats were saying he was a bad guy, even though they themselves had voted to give him that role.

In 2009, Barack Obama was such a good guy, you'd swear he walked to the White House across the Potomac without using a bridge. But, by 2015, his policy of "regime change" in Syria caused an unprecedented disaster in world history and Obamacare proved to be the Vietnam War of social programs. Definitely a bad guy. What happened? It's the same guy America re-elected!

To be fair, the Republicans were never behind Obama as Democrats were behind Bush after 9/11. But you would think— after seeing the mess Bush left behind in Iraq—they wouldn't go along with Obama in getting us involved in Libya and Syria! Yes, you would think that, but you would be wrong. They're not there to learn from history and avoid repeating mistakes. They are there to support whatever the party says even if it means making mistake after mistake after mistake—no matter how many lives it costs. If the party needed you to do something unpopular, well, just go backstage and put on the bad guy costume. Don't worry. You can be a good guy in the next play. Why do you think another Bush and another Clinton ran for president in 2016? What have we got here, a dynasty?

No, it's a melodrama.

It is not a question of the Right or the Left or whose policies are best. Both are dead wrong, even on the lightning rod issues. Nothing is ever as simple as they make it out to be. To prove that,

I will examine a lightning rod issue from each side.

First: gun control. In the late 1960s and the 1970s, up into the 1980s, most states did not issue permits for the concealed carry of handguns. In the 1970s, it looked as if handguns might be banned altogether. Most states did not have a specific law guaranteeing a right to self-defense. What also happened during this time period was a series of liberal judges were literally letting dangerous violent criminals loose after a "slap on the wrist."

American cities became very dangerous and criminal activity soared everywhere. The reason people demanded the right to carry concealed handguns for self-defense is because the police could not protect them and judges refused to keep violent criminals in jail. People were tired of being assaulted, raped and having family members murdered as they stood by helpless. That is why states passed laws allowing people to carry handguns for self-defense.

Gun owners didn't just wake up one day and decide to lobby for those laws. Nothing happens all by itself—a series of causes and conditions leads to it. In this case, a series of liberal decisions to unleash violent criminals on an unarmed population led to concealed-carry laws. If liberals want to know who is responsible for the re-appearance of armed citizens in public, they need to go find a mirror.

Next, let's examine the flip side of the coin, food stamps. This one seems to infuriate Conservatives more than anything else. Every one of them has a cherished "food stamp story" to tell. "I saw this man buy steaks and beer with food stamps and he then got into a Cadillac that was brand-new!" Right, except you can't buy alcohol with food stamps.

They're actually a type of debit card now, not stamps. Yes, you can buy steaks with food stamps. But smart people don't. The food stamps have limits. Once you spend that month's allotment, that's it—no more until next month. The Conservatives who think everyone should work for a living are also the same jokers who think a company has the right to do whatever they want and fire anyone at will.

If Acme Widget Factory is the only employer in Townsville and they lay off everyone and move the factory to China, the Conservatives support Acme's "right" to do so. And when the former employees of Acme collect food stamps, the Conservatives blame the employees for being "too lazy to work."

Excuse me, but those people did work, they had jobs. The blame belongs on greedy Acme for moving the factory to China. People drawing food stamps cannot be accused of "greed" while simultaneously absolving the corporation whose greed caused those people to have to apply for food stamps to begin with. But, because both Liberals and Conservative follow the ignorant, knee-jerk reactions of the politicians, no one takes the time to actually investigate these issues. Therefore, the politicians use these issues to divide Americans against each other and keep them bickering and fighting. In the end, politicians of both parties screw everyone equally. You wanted equality? You got it!

Things are never as simple as these parties claim. Will one law suddenly change 5,000 years of human history overnight? Nothing is ever as simple as "pass a law and, presto-o change-o, instant results."

Banning guns will not stop or deter crime. Cutting food stamps will not make people without jobs find jobs that don't exist. Bombing another country will not convince them to love America. Banning abortion will not mean the children born as a result will all be adopted into loving homes. Excusing violence because of people's skin color is tantamount to saying they deserve to live that way because they don't know any better. Saying Christian businesses should be allowed to refuse service to gay people but we need to pass laws to ban Muslim Sharia law is an apt definition of hypocrisy.

All this and more are misguided and woefully ignorant ideas regularly discussed in the Senate and the Congress. Nothing is ever as simple as these charlatans make them out to be. You're against anyone owning and carrying guns until your wife is shot to death in a robbery because she didn't have enough money. What changed your mind is the robber was shot by an armed citizen at his next score. You think no one should be allowed to get food stamps until it's you that loses your job and your kids are hungry. You think gay people are all sick until it's your beloved daughter that comes out and tells you she's gay. You see, that's who politicians are turning you against: your family, your friends and your neighbors.

Why?

To seize power and assert control over you, your family, your friends and your neighbors. Is it so cut-and-dried as Left and Right, Liberal and Conservative, Democrat and Republican? How long will we continue to play this ridiculous game? This country is divided against itself thanks to these political parties and their insane gambits for power. Again, fundamentally, there is no significant difference between these two political parties. There is more difference between two football teams than between the Republicans and the Democrats. In a football game, one team wins. But in American politics, no matter which party wins, the American people ultimately lose every time.

Essentially, both parties have a trust or a monopoly in our political system. No third party can win an important election because they are locked out by the political monopoly. In other words, they've created a Big Box Government that locks out the Mom-and-Pop Government the American people actually want.

If a Mom-and-Pop political party tried to win an election (as they have in recent past), they lose the "price war" with Big Box Government. They can't compete with the high-dollar advertising and marketing Big Box Government has. Wall Street will never fund Mom-And-Pop parties because, for all intents and purposes, they own Big Box Government. What's more, when Gore lost the 2000 presidential election, the Democratic Party blamed the third-party Mom-and-Pop presidential candidate for "siphoning off" critical votes. Thus, it is pretty much said that, "Yes, it's a Big Box Government, but you can't afford to shop anywhere else."

Just like Big Box superstores across America that put the Mom-and-Pop stores out of business.

Both of these political parties amassed power and answer to nobody. It was unforeseen at the founding of this country that, in time, two political parties would arise and gather tremendous power to themselves. Nor was it foreseen that there would be such great power to gather in the first place. It cannot be said that those who founded this nation had our current system in mind. For indeed, it is worse than the system they fought against. For example, the military is used to advance the aims and goals of the two political parties and not the defense of the American people, as was intended by the founders of this country. The founders of this country would have been horrified to see the way our military is used today.

The American people are never told what the end game of the political party goals are in various military operations. Actually, it is kept secret—by federal law, it's illegal for us to know. Without oversight, how will such power not be abused? We don't know if these military operations are a goal of the political party or a Wall Street goal the party was ordered to achieve. We simply do not know. Nor are we allowed to know. And if anyone dares to try and tell us, he is jailed and silenced and that is also an action both political parties are in firm agreement on.

The actual goal of political parties in this incessant wrangling is to keep Americans divided and fighting. Thus, the public will never unite and challenge the government. Throughout time, this has been a favored tactic of kings and despots. Presidential elections are nothing more than a gigantic "dream team" match as one sees on faked television wrestling. Is it any wonder that when a presidential candidate seeks his vice-presidential running mate, it's referred as a "dream team"? Television wrestling is where that term came into modern usage. What's extraordinary is that many Americans are unable to see the fraudulent nature of the political parties and the elections. However, what's truly remarkable is that even when they do, they continue going along with it.

People act as if these political parties are not manipulating them. "Oh, no, they can't fool me!" Oh, really? People who say that never fail to find one or two social issues or problems that can be laid upon the doorstep of "liberals" or "conservatives." Meaning, blaming one another for those things. People fight, failing to see that it is the political parties pitting them against each other like handlers at a dogfight.

People act like their own neighbors are some foreign invader or enemy that must be stopped at all costs. They endlessly battle to force their ideas and beliefs upon one another. We don't need another civil war because we've already got an ideological one going on. "We can't let the Democrats win!" "We've got to get rid of these Republicans!" What they are talking about is the gay couple down the street or the avid hunter around the corner. They talk about one another as if these aren't their own neighbors.

Why?

Because the parties put them up to it.

Obscene amounts of money are thrown down a rat hole in political campaigns and elections—while average Americans struggle to pay the rent. If the time and money squandered on political campaigns and elections were directed to non-political getting out there and doing what needs to get done in regards to social problems, there wouldn't be any. Instead, we spend a decade, billions of dollars and two presidential elections to keep talking while nothing gets done.

If we were building the Transcontinental Railroad, it'd be like it was 1957 and all they'd agreed on so far was what color the locomotives should be—without having laid a single rail or driven a single spike. The parties profit from American suffering and exploit it to get elected. Together, they are two fleas on the body politic, parasitizing the American people. Both of them, not one or the other.

How can one pick a side in this battle? There is a constant

need for strife, discord and fighting between them. Nothing gets resolved. Only unjust laws are passed and only what benefits Wall Street comes into being. Yet, we are told it is our civic duty to elect these charlatans and scam artists. Why is it my "duty" to make a choice between two people no different from the last two we chose between?

Be that as it may, what's killing us is not the infighting between the two political parties. That's just theater and showmanship to avoid doing anything of genuine value, the same way a toddler throws a temper tantrum to avoid going to bed. What's killing us is where the two parties agree and do the same things. The use of military force and the intimate relationship the parties have with Wall Street. The parties recklessly endanger American lives by consorting with terrorists and through covert military operations that the American people did not approve of or even have any knowledge of. Each party, once elected to the presidency (because we're now basically electing a political party, not a president), has the ability to wage wars and use military force as a matter of party politics. Each has the ability to order the assassinations of people, including American citizens, without a trial, and under parameters the American people are not allowed to even examine. This isn't one party or the other doing this. It's both of them.

Both parties engage in criminal behavior such as illegal wars, extra-judicial killings and extortionary laws such as Obamacare. At no time does either party admit to a mistake, correct an error or reform themselves. Therefore, the only logical conclusion that can be reached is that both political parties should be disbanded and not allowed to merely continue under a new name. It should be understood that both parties threaten the long-term survival of the United States. But unless disbandment happens, these parties will have a monopoly on the government and there is no point to thinking anything of value to the American people can be accomplished.

Both political parties have promised that things will get

better for decades. "Vote for Dummy MCorkle! He'll bring prosperity back to America!" Not one of them has been able to make good on that promise. When more Americans fall into poverty than rise out of it, we can conclude that these buffoons cannot deliver on their promises to bring prosperity to America.

Some, realizing that, distract us with campaign promises of bombing raids on Iran. They don't bother mentioning to the American people that's an act of war against a nation that soaked up 600,000 dead in an eight-year war against Iraq. Iran has a navy and an air force. Right, but let's get into a war with Iran. Why not just cut to the chase and sign a cease-fire with them now and avoid the rush later?

Yes, they've been promising "better" for decades.

Have we gotten it?

Where is this prosperity? Where are the secular democracies we were going to create in the Middle East? Where are the stunning battlefield victories that built nations worth every American life spent in pursuit of them?

Where are the good jobs where we can work long enough to use a 401K as retirement and not an unemployment insurance supplement plan?

Isn't it time to dump the political parties in the trash can of history—along with all the other broken things that don't work?

If the American people stood up and demanded the political parties to step down, that would truly be regime change we can believe in.

CHAPTER TWO—FIVE AMERICAN MYTHS

AT THE TIME of writing this book, there is a very curious nation on this planet. This nation belligerently threatens other countries it feels are humiliating it or are not showing enough respect. As far as that goes, the respect it feels it deserves is that questions should not be asked by other countries. They must obey the orders of this country without asking those questions. Failing to obey this country can carry serious consequences. This country can launch military attacks without warning and has done so several times in the past and continues to do so.

What's more, if this nation accuses another of something, no matter how strongly that other nation denies the allegations, it will not be believed. This can also lead to an attack without any prior warning, even if that other nation proved the allegations false.

This nation, if it accuses a person of certain crimes, can assassinate that person without a trial or any warning whatsoever. Even citizens of this nation can be assassinated, despite the founding documents of this nation forbidding that type of extrajudicial punishment. Now, this nation refuses to say who is on its list to assassinate or even how, exactly, one gets on that list. For that matter, revealing how one gets on the list is a crime punishable by a long prison term. This nation has amassed a fleet of aerial robots to carry out these assassinations, even if innocent bystanders are killed in the process. And we don't even know that the target wasn't innocent, as well, because this nation stubbornly refuses to identify these on the list.

The person assassinated might or might not be guilty of the crimes this nation has accused him or her of. But also, even if that person is guilty, the crime might not carry the death penalty as a punishment a jury could hand down. However, there's no jury in the first place, so this is all irrelevant to the discussion. That this nation could assassinate political opponents, gadflies, protestors, activists, or whistleblowers and then accuse them of crimes afterwards goes without saying.

This nation can also send covert teams anywhere in the world to kidnap anyone they want without an arrest warrant handed down by a legitimate court of law. This team can cart that person off to a secret prison and hold him indefinitely without an arraignment or hope of a trial. While they have that person in custody, they can torture him and use that torture-extracted information to justify more kidnappings and even assassinations. This nation will obstinately refuse to put these captives on trial because revealing the evidence against them would allegedly endanger national security.

This nation insists it has the highest standard of living yet, each year, the number of its citizens falling into poverty is increasing, not decreasing. It is also dropping behind several other countries in terms of infant mortality and average lifespan. Its high school graduate students cannot spell proficiently or read beyond a grade school level. Yet, it will tout itself as having one of the best educational systems in the world, despite the fact many of its citizen cannot find on a map countries their nation has attacked. It has one of the highest rates of people in prison per capita in the world. Many of its prisons are privately owned and benefit from prisoner labor, which most countries call "slave labor." Many, if not all, of the police forces in this nation are heavily militarized to the point they are virtually identical to the army with the sole exception being uniform insignia.

This nation spies on its own citizens, monitoring their Internet, email, and cell phone use. Air travel is strictly controlled and passengers must submit to humiliating body scans that basically unclothe them. In some cases, passengers have been sexually groped by government security officers during a "pat-down." The government even monitors what books people check out of public libraries.

This nation claims to uphold democratic principles. Yet, the president of it has the power to create new laws by his decree and not through any democratic process whatsoever. His direct orders thus become the law of the land and, thus, must be obeyed. The nation's government itself demonstrated the power to create an insurance program everyone has been ordered to buy. If citizens refuse to do so or do not wish to, they are financially punished with penalties that skyrocket each year. Yet, this nation repeatedly boasts of its commitment to "freedom" and "liberty."

Now what nation is this I am talking about? Is it North Korea? No. Is it some regime in the Middle East? No. Some of you have already guessed. It is the United States I am describing here. All of these things I mentioned (and I left out quite a few) are actions and policies of the United States government and/or state and local governments within the United States.

What? I'm not being fair here? Consider this: you have four levels of government and at any one level, or two or more, or all of them you can be convicted of crime and be imprisoned. What might be legal in your county might not be legal in your city, for example. And you can't plead ignorance of the law. It's your responsibility to know—even if the legal codebook is five inches thick. And that's just the county laws.

Now, I said quite a bit, so let's backtrack a little. I said the United States is a very warlike country that hypocritically engages in what it has successfully prosecuted in the past as war crimes. Oh, yes, the United States government is very good at writing laws everyone else had better follow. But the government itself does not follow them. For example, after World War Two, the United States successfully prosecuted Japanese Imperial Army officers for war crimes against Allied POWs. What was the war crime? That they tortured POWs. How did they torture them? They water-boarded them to extract information they felt was vital to their war effort. Where have we recently heard about water-boarding? Oh yeah! The CIA was water-boarding detainees at secret prisons since the 9/11 attacks. Gosh, I had no idea that a torture technique could go "retro" and become a fad like 1950s kitchen appliances! Who knew?

Right, who knew these guys were water-boarding people, which is a war crime? Everyone high up in George W. Bush's Administration. And not one has been prosecuted for war crimes that they probably ordered in the first place. I bet Japanese and German war criminals are rolling over in their graves, saying, "They hung us for that but then they get away with it? How is that fair?!"

And they have a valid point.

They basically rode Richard Nixon out of town on a rail and forced him to resign in disgrace or face an impeachment—for the Watergate Scandal, which amounts to the same eavesdropping the government now does every day with citizens' email. Actually, it amounts to less because Nixon wasn't looking at the personal papers of everyone in America.

But the Bush Administration tortured human beings and not one of the administration went to trial for it, despite having also lied to the American people about having knowledge of torture going on. Not one indictment, not one resignation over it, not any impeachment proceeding. But Nixon was badgered out of offices as if the dude had bombed the Vatican or something. These same Republicans wanted to impeach Clinton over playing patty-cake with a not-his-wife in the Oval Office. But the Bush Administration tortures people and gets away with it? What everyone is forgetting here is this: they broke the law! Okay?! Torturing people is against several laws, not just in the United

States but all over the world. Are we to believe that the entire Bush Administration didn't know torturing people was against the law? Nixon never said that he didn't know that burglary was against the law. But the Bush Administration lied to the American people and said the United States does not torture people. Because they did not consider water-boarding to be torture!

Yet this is the same government (federal) that successfully prosecuted Japanese military officers for the war crime of torture because they water-boarded allied POWs! Remarkable! Not one person has been held accountable from the Bush administration officials that ordered the water-boarding to the CIA officers that carried it out and knew it to be a crime just as did the officials that ordered it. But Nixon they lectured and badgered for what was, compared to torture, some nickel and dime B-and-E rap.

Now, kids, what Great American Myth have we just ridden out of town on a rail here? The Great American Myth that the United States is a nation based on law and the rule of law. Malarkey. If it was, George W. Bush, Dick Cheney, Donald Rumsfeld and several others would all be cooling their heels in a federal penitentiary somewhere or facing international war crimes tribunals up in The Hague or someplace. Instead, they hired ghost writers to scribble out a few books and made a few bucks off of it. This is one of the first Great American Myths we'll deflate, along with others such as American Exceptionalism, the Greatest Nation on Earth, Freedom and Democracy. But let's continue with Rule of Law myth.

When Rule of Law governs a nation, the law is enforced impartially. Be you the President or a store clerk, if you break the law, you are arrested. You go to trial and if convicted, pay a fine or go to jail or both. But what happened when Obama took office? Did he try and prosecute the Bush Administration officials it was now commonly known had ordered the torture of people? No! His attitude was basically, "Let bygones be bygones and move on. Let's just put that behind us now." Can anyone imagine what the reaction would have been had the Allies said that about the Nazis after World War Two? "Well, we guess they shouldn't have had all those death camps and mobile firing squads, but let's move on. That was then and this is now."

The entire world would have become unglued had they not held war crimes trials after World War Two. People had to answer for that, and rightfully so. That's why there are laws. And laws are useless unless they are upheld and violations of them prosecuted. But the reaction of the Obama Administration to ongoing revelations that the Bush administration had broken the law was more akin to a bad relationship ending. "Well, we're moving on. You guys can't stay stuck in this war crimes thing. It won't help anyone to enforce the law now. So let's move on, okay?"

Excuse me, but this is international law against torture we're talking about here, and not a prenuptial agreement. We're not looking for alimony here, we're looking for justice. But, see, the federal government is above the law. When an entire presidential administration can walk away scot-free from having committed and ordered numerous war crimes, then it can readily be seen that the rule of law does not apply to them. And if they can break that major law and get away with it, they've broken every law under it and gotten away with that too.

A political system allegedly based on the rule of law does not work and is not moral if it does not obey those laws itself. And if that political system refuses to enforce Rule of Law against its own fellow officials, it is also unjust. Especially so when they will gladly jail anyone else who breaks those laws but is not a politician or has no political connections. They can deny that all they want, but the truth is as plain to see as the sun in the sky.

There are multiple opportunities for a citizen to go to jail or pay a fine in this country. That's because we have so many laws at so many levels of government and government agencies. Yet, as I have shown, the top level of government—the federal—got away with violating a most basic law of humanity. We have criminal law, civil law, tax law, environmental law, building codes, zoning codes, food laws, and on and on it goes. Four levels of government—federal, state, county and city—and they all have their own laws unique to them. For example, you could buy a certain kind of knife legal to carry in Arizona. Cross over into California with that knife and you just broke the law. Unless you can prove you're passing through to another state, you're in violation of the law.

In some places, what's legal in the county may not be legal in a city within that county. Or a county might ban things otherwise legal in the state. There are also laws that make absolutely no sense. For example, in the city where I live, there's a law that says weeds in your yard can't be higher than your ankle. I'm not making this up because a city enforcement officer came out to try and cite me for it. However, they weren't "weeds" but cultivated plants. So the city officer went away. They were responding to a complaint from a busybody neighbor who seems to think plants in someone's yard is a more urgent issue than the fact we had an entire presidential administration literally walk free after committing multiple felonies. But this is the problem with American society as a whole. They'll worry about some "weeds" in their neighbor's yard, but ignore the fact they had an entire presidential administration composed of war criminals.

Here are some points I'd like to make. Okay, number one, we've got too many laws. Paying a government agency to enforce proper lawn care is about as wasteful of taxpayer money as you can get on a local level. But on laws we all agree are right, such as torturing people being a crime, the government refused to follow their own laws! Or prosecute those amongst then who break them! But the biggest point here I wish to make is that the statement "our government is based on Rule of Law" is absolutely untrue.

The government enforces laws against us. Not against themselves.

The laws are often there to control us, not to control them or limit their behavior. When they need to break a law, they will do so without consequences. Therefore, we can conclude that "Rule of Law" is a great American Myth that belongs in a book of Mother Goose tales for children.

Next up out of nursery rhymes, we have American Exceptionalism. This is the idea that American can do great things other countries can't accomplish. I tend to think the genesis of this idea is in the building of the Panama Canal. See, before the United States managed to do it, the French tried it. They died by the droves because they didn't understand the nature of the tropical disease they were up against. That's really why America pulled it off. We happened to have some good medical personnel who understood what needed to be done to limit the effects and spread of tropical diseases. That said, lots of Americans still died building the Panama Canal, but we were able to finish it. So this created this myth that America can do great things other countries can't. Excuse me, but the Ancient Egyptians constructed the Pyramids and American intelligentsia to this day still cannot explain how the Pyramids were built.

Another thing, and the major thing, that created this nonsense about American Exceptionalism is World War Two. They call the people that fought this war, the Greatest Generation. As if the 600,000 or so Americans that died in the American Civil War was just a blip on the radar or something. Americans only like to reenact that war and collect tchotchkes and memorabilia commemorating it, they don't like to remember how many actually died in it. Well, for one reason, we don't actually know how many died in our Civil War. It could be as high as 750,000 according to some books. And we pulled that off with single-shot, muzzle loading muskets and cannon! How's that for American Exceptionalism?

But getting back to World War Two, to hear America tell this story, you'd think we won that war with one hand tied behind our backs. As far as the Pacific theater goes, that is mostly correct. And it was us that nuked them. However in the European Theater, we forget that the British and Free French forces helped us out quite a bit.

But the biggest thing we forget is that the army that did the most damage to the Germans was the Red Army of the Soviet Union. The Soviets soaked up ten million dead in military casualties alone and still took Berlin. America might have been signing an exceptional cease-fire with the Germans had the Soviets not been in the war. American Exceptionalism did not win World War Two. American industrial power and cooperation with allied nations allowed America to help win World War Two. This was a joint effort.

Let's also not forget the United States has not won a war hands-down since World War Two. "What about Grenada?! What about Panama?!" America knocking off two bush-league banana republics is the same as D-Day now? I'm talking about major wars. "What about the Gulf War?" We left Saddam in power (after saying he was another Hitler in order to justify to the American people using their sons to save the Kuwait Theocracy) and came back in 2003 to allegedly finish a job Bush's dad left undone thirteen years prior.

We didn't have a true victory in that war either. Are you kidding me?! We couldn't win World War Two today if our fates literally depended upon it. We'd refuse to ally with the Russians, then sign cease-fires with both Germany and Japan and leave Britain swinging in the wind. About twenty years later, American corporations would be doing business with both of them and outsourcing American jobs there. American corporations would say, "Gosh, we've sure been able to save a lot of money on labor outsourcing those jobs to the Third Reich. Gee, I wonder how they do it?" Americans that were outraged by those jobs being outsourced to Nazi Germany would be called "anti-business socialist liberals." Have I now exceptionalized you, America? But wait, there's more.

Imagine trying to build the Panama Canal today. The United States couldn't pull off something like that today if it had twenty years, twenty trillion dollars (borrowed from China, of course) and a hundred no-bid contracts out there to do it. They'd probably never get past the environmental impact assessment report. "Gosh we can't build the canal here! It'll harm the habitat of the South Panamanian Warbling Mosquito!" "Yes, but that's the mosquito that carries malaria." "Makes no difference! It's endangered species! We'll have to run the canal though Mexico. We can probably get away with it there."

Not to mention the no-bid contract that goes to a construction company in which the Vice President of the United States owned a lot of stock. Twenty years later, they'd have it finished only to discover no ship can fit through a canal only three feet wide. "Well, the CEO of the corporation got through it on his Kayak, so we don't see what the issue is. We finished ten years ahead of schedule, so we are owed a bonus." No, we couldn't build the Panama Canal today. But we thought we could "nation build" in Iraq and Afghanistan. Why? Because of the Great American Myth of American Exceptionalism.

Understand this. When you hear the government start to talk about "American Exceptionalism" they're talking about another war to ship your kids off to. And not a war they intend to win. That's what cease-fires are for. These days, American Exceptionalism just fills body-bags.

American Exceptionalism is the Great American myth that invokes the holy relics of the Panama Canal and World War Two. "We can do anything!" (Except win a war.) "We can build anything!" (Except bridges that don't collapse later.) Then they'll equate American Exceptionalism in World War Two with getting into a sectarian war involving five different armies all fighting each other. There is nothing "exceptional" whatsoever about the United States government. These clowns can't hang a picture of George Washington in the White house without securing a permit, obtaining an environmental impact assessment, and calling a press conference to boast that they're going to hang the picture soon. It'll be American Exceptionalism in action. Oh, and by the way, we need to invade three Central Asian republics at once...to build nations. The only thing exceptional about our government is they've managed to keep this scam going for decades.

I'll give them that.

But as long as people keep falling for the "American Exceptionalism" myth, they'll believe anything else the government says. Like a war they started being justified, for example. It's a fine piece of propaganda to tell people they're so much more special than everyone else in the world. Hey, it worked for Hitler.

That brings us perfectly to the next Great American Myth: We're the Greatest Nation on Earth. Hooray! You can tell that to the foreign countries we owe trillions of dollars to. You know, I bet the Roman Empire thought this about themselves, too. "We just put down a slave revolt and crucified a thousand men! We're the greatest nation in the world."

And then their emperor declares himself a god. Almost like our presidents created presidential libraries as their legacy. The Roman emperors built temples dedicated to worshipping themselves, but our presidents build libraries for that purpose. Excuse me, but how is it that the Greatest Nation on Earth has more people falling into poverty than rising out of it? How is it that the middle class that pretty much built this entity called the "Greatest Nation on Earth" is disappearing? How is it that what were once cities with thriving industries now look like cities in Germany bombed by the Greatest Nation on Earth during World War Two? How is it that name brands always associated with the Greatest Nation on Earth are now manufactured overseas? How is it that the American family, once strong and cohesive, is now fractured and dysfunctional in the Greatest Nation on Earth?

When the government rolls out the "Greatest Nation on Earth" myth, it's usually to provide cover for another woefully flawed economic policy—one that will favor Wall Street fat cats and the return of the Robber Barons from the late 1800s. "Greatest Nation on Earth," is a phrase the government uses to excuse the collective screwing of the American people by Wall

Street and their banks and corporations. It's an old brainwashing technique whereby if a lie is told often enough and with enough conviction, it will come to be accepted as truth and no one will question it or remember where it originated. "We live in the Greatest Nation on Earth!" Really? Says Who? "Uh…well…everyone?"

No, not everyone.

It's the government that says that. Usually Republicans are so deeply in bed with Wall Street that if two fat cats fart, it'll smother ten Republican senators. You should walk into a dollar store in an inner-city neighborhood where all the jobs have been outsourced and ask them, "Hey, any of you guys realize you live in the Greatest Nation on Earth?" They'll probably think it's a new gentrification project where wealthy hipsters buy their apartment buildings out from under them and they end up homeless. But if you tell them you're talking about the United States, they'll swear you made it up. And honestly, someone did make it up.

I'll tell you someplace you can hear this phrase regularly. On some country music stations in the Southwest, they play the national anthem at twelve noon. It's creepy, because it's almost like they've given this some type of religious significance the way Catholic and orthodox Christian monasteries have mid-day prayers at noon.

Anyway, at twelve noon, an announcer comes on the radio and says: "let's all pause for a moment, and give thanks that we live in the Greatest Nation on Earth." Then they play the Star Spangled Banner. See what I mean about how it has this religious nature to it? "Let's all pause for a moment, and give thanks…" Yeah, I bet the mother who can't afford shoes for her kids is really thankful to be living in a country where that happens and yet still calls itself "great." I bet the kids who'll lose their school lunches if Republican politicians have their way will appreciate the benefit of living in the "Greatest Nation on Earth." "Sorry, kids, we can't afford funding the school lunch program anymore. We needed to buy cruise missiles to kill kids elsewhere on the planet." A nation

31

is not great because it calls itself so.

A person who congratulates himself for honors he hasn't actually earned is living a delusion of his own mind. To be called the "Greatest Nation on Earth" would require a worldwide vote and every other country awarding that distinction to the United States. That's not likely to happen, considering how many people we've angered or whose relatives we've killed. Even countries we've bailed out in the past will say, "Well, they do have a problem controlling their temper. So, great? Well, maybe not. In fact, no." But the reality is: "Greatest Nation on Earth" is not what our government tells other countries about us.

No, it's what the government tells us to try and get us to believe that we actually are. Lots of gullible people believe it too. There are guys that could lose their jobs to outsourcing, then lose their homes to the banks and have the government come after them for a grand in back taxes, and they'll still swear, up and down, they live in the "Greatest Nation on Earth." There they'll be, standing in line at the food bank without a pot to piss in, saying, "Well, at least I live in the Greatest Nation on Earth." Hey, sport, if it's so great, how come you're over there at the food bank?

Right, ask that guy how it is that the Greatest Nation on Earth has so many people going to food banks just to get enough to eat. Or has so many people unemployed. Nine times out of ten, they'll say, "It's the darn liberals! They're anti-business! Their liberal environmental protection laws put good companies out of business and there go those jobs!"

Right, let's scrap the environmental laws so we can build another grade school atop a toxic waste dump. Just like at Love Canal. Or we can watch with glee and cheer as the Cuyahoga River Bursts into flame each month. Hey, genius, it was Republican Richard Nixon, yes, President Nixon, that signed the bill creating the Environmental Protection Agency. No one can point to any corporation that said, "Well, we can't dump benzene into the river anymore or bury drums of dioxin and PCB's in the woods. Looks like we'll just have to shut the door and go out of business." But there are several corporations that said, "Well, we're paying Americans twelve dollars an hour. We can pay people in Southeast Asia twelve cents an hour to do the same job. Looks like we'll have to shut the doors here in America and then open them back up again in Southeast Asia. And we'll blame it on the liberals, environmental laws, and high corporate taxes on top of that so Americans will continue buying our products."

Before the liberals think I'm taking their side, let me remind them that their all-wise, all-knowing President Obama bought into the "Greatest Nation on Earth" crap, too. And, also, so do they. "No we don't!" Oh, really? So what, then was this all about meddling in Libya, Egypt, and Syria? Right, the all-wise, all-knowing Greatest Nation on Earth wants to bring the oh-so-special secular democracy theory to three dictatorships that will teeter toward—or fall to—Muslim radicals once the dictator is gone.

Libya will, Egypt got saved by another strong man leader, and Syria may yet fall to the Muslim fundamentalists attempting to install a caliphate there. But, oh no, you were going to make secular humanist democrats out of these folks that would all do yoga five time a day instead of prayers. And read various Squishy liberal magazines instead of the Quran. Pardon me, but what were you people thinking?! This is the "Greatest Nation on Earth" thinking at its finest among liberals.

Just like you clowns didn't learn a thing in Somalia where Bill Clinton thought warlords would be rather impressed by the "Greatest Nation on Earth." They weren't. And neither is any nation in the Middle East that isn't getting U.S. military weapons at cost plus ten. Not even Israel genuinely likes the "Greatest Nation on Earth" anymore, but they can't find quality helicopter gunships anywhere else, so they're stuck with us for now.

If your oh-so-great President Obama hadn't played "Greatest Nation on Earth" in the Middle East, this mega disaster over there in Syria would have never blown out of proportion as it has. And we'll be paying for this mess in blood and treasure for decades to come. Blood debts are not forgotten or forgiven in that part of the world. Look how long Osama bin Laden had to wait to settle his with America. And so you Democrats created even more?! On top of the ones that Dubya created?! How exactly was Obama any better or smarter that George W. Bush?! I think he's only better spoken than Bush, but aside from that, they darn near even dress the same! If I didn't know better, I'd swear it was like Charlie's Angels and Charlie was actually Bush telling Angel Obama what to do! There's Charlie (Bush) on the old-time speaker phone telling Angel Obama to topple Bashar al-Assad over in Syria. Syria was on Bush's old "Axis of Evil" list, after all.

Therefore, we can arrive at the only sane conclusion: we certainly do not live in the "Greatest Nation on Earth." Most Warlike Nation on Earth, yes. Most Economically unjust Western nation on Earth, probably. But "Greatest Nation on Earth"? No. This is, again, the government telling us this to justify their shenanigans and the economic crimes of their Wall Street pals. It's basically them saying: "Stop complaining! You live in the 'Greatest Nation on Earth'! Why are you complaining? You're ungrateful!" Need I say more? Well, I will.

Nothing stokes the fires of American mythology more that the word "freedom." You see this word plastered all over the place, everywhere, and all the time. It makes the Stalin personality cult where they plastered his face everywhere seem pretty small-town. Truthfully, the "Freedom" cult dwarfs the Stalin personality cult, hands down. "Freedom" is also another Great American Myth: one of the largest of them all. And a lot of people don't even know or remember where it began. No, it did not begin after 9/11. That's where it got widespread traction but that's not where it started. The whole "Freedom" mantra was the brainchild of the gun rights movement that began in the 1980s but really gathered steam and followers in the 1990s.

What started it was the liberal movement in the 1970s to ban handguns in the entire United States. The liberals couldn't have picked a worse time to attempt that because their crime-lenient social justice policies and revolving door liberal judges had effectively turned American cities into crime-infested hell holes.

But, by the early 1980s, they attempted to ban handguns by going state-by-state with handgun ban ballot initiatives. These were all defeated and what was once just a small-time association for firearms enthusiasts, the National Rifle Association, soared in membership and power. If the liberals think the NRA is a "monster," they should know they created that monster with foolish gun ban initiatives. The NRA would have never gained the membership and the political power it has today if not for the attempted handgun bans of the early 1980s. People saw those as an attempt to disarm them and leave them as sitting ducks for the criminals that were pretty much overwhelming the ability of police to control.

People rallied to keep their handguns and flocked to the NRA by the droves. What's more, the NRA began a political counter-attack to not just keep handguns legal, but to legalize concealed carry of them for self-defense. And they were successful in doing so in several states.

In the 1990s, a new type of firearm got the attention of liberals. This is the semi-automatic, military-style rifle that liberals call "assault rifles." Liberals were successful in getting these weapons controlled during the Clinton Administration, but that law has since expired. The reason liberals wanted to ban this firearm was due to several mass shootings where these weapons were used. But paradoxically, all the liberals really accomplished with the so-called "Clinton ban" (which, as I said, has now expired) was to swell the ranks of the NRA even more and increase the membership of the Republican Party.

You can do a lot of things in America, but don't try banning guns. You might get the vote through Congress and Senate, but a voting majority of people don't really support gun bans. Too many people remember the lawless period of 1970s when they were unarmed and unsafe. While they are horrified by the recent epidemic of mass shootings, they're not willing to return to the 1970s either. So, the liberals once again unknowingly increased the power of the NRA in the 1990s.

Now, the main argument the Gun Rights Movement used since the 1980s is that owning, and even carrying, a firearm is a Constitutional Right. That reason being The Second Amendment. I'm sure we're all aware of that. Therefore, the Gun Rights Movement picked that up, broadcast that, and said this was all about "freedom," not guns. This was about a Constitutional right, not what type of gun a person should be allowed to own. You would see bumper stickers in the 1990s with the American flag and the word "freedom" alone and you knew that was about gun rights.

Gun owners universally hated Clinton. It was probably that one issue alone that lost Gore the 2000 election, if that election was legitimate. But the whole use of the word "freedom" was started by gun owners and popularized by the NRA.

In the immediate aftermath of 9/11, the Bush Administration was looking for a battle cry to rally behind. Something with the panache of "Remember Pearl Harbor." But saying "Remember the World Trade Center" didn't have the same gravitas.

Well, Republicans in the Bush Administration were very close with the NRA and were quite familiar with the "freedom" battle cry. The NRA had been using it for years to define what they saw as a quintessential American Struggle against tyranny. So that one word—freedom—came out as the *ne plus ultra* of what defined us in this conflict.

Remember what Bush said of Al-Qaeda? "They hate freedom." Everyone accepted that explanation, as preposterous as it was. No, it wasn't that they hated freedom. They hated America. Not because we were free, but because we kept on meddling over in the Middle East. Lots of countries after about 1960 hated America with a passion. And every time, it was not because we were a free country, but because we had meddled in their country or propped up a regime that oppressed them.

Take the 1979 Iranian revolution, for example. They didn't become so vehemently anti-American because they hated Freedom. They were angry because we had toppled their democratically elected government in a CIA backed coup. Then we installed a brutal dictator to run Iran and keep oil prices down, which was the reason for the coup. You can't run around trumpeting how much you love "freedom" when you're installing and propping up dictators all over the world. Or, when people angered by that attack you, start whining that they attacked you because of some hatred of freedom.

Then, in 2003, we decided to bring "freedom" to Iraq, remember that? They even called the war by that name: Operation Iraqi Freedom. Let's not kid ourselves here. It was a bloodbath. It became obvious no one in the Bush Administration had a clue as to what needed to be done after Saddam Hussein was gone. They thought they'd off Saddam, wave the magic wand, say "freedom," and they'd have an instant democracy over there.

Then the entire Middle East would say, "Gee, isn't that swell? Let's copy them." And the whole Middle East would become secular democracies. Except for the theocracy/monarchy of Saudi Arabia, of course. We support their right to put down protest with gunfire and floggings. But what happened was that all of Iraq collapsed into a civil war that the Bush Administration denied was a civil war and stubbornly refused to treat as a civil war. As a result, tens of thousands of Iraqis and thousands of American military personnel died in what the Bush Administration wanted us to believe was a well-organized drive-by shooting.

Why?

Because the Bush Administration was afraid of hearing "I told you so!" from nations he had ridiculed as basically cowards for not joining the war. Right, and one by one, the countries that did join, quietly left the war like people leaving a party that had gotten out of hand. The Administration was also afraid that an anti-war movement would begin to gather steam in America and they'd have another Vietnam War on their hands. And that is exactly what they had gotten us into. I can't see how Iraq will remain out of the hands of Islamic fundamentalists in the future. Why did we get into this quagmire again? Oh, yeah! "For Freedom," one of the deadliest of the Great American Myths.

Even more astonishingly ignorant was the thinking we could bring this "Freedom" concept to Afghanistan. People say, "Well, we had to get bin Laden!" Fine, go in there and get him. But don't stay there! If your neighbor is hiding a football that went into his yard, and he won't give it back, does it make sense to take over the mortgage on his house and start paying on it?

Even worse, we have seen this all before in Vietnam where the French fought North Vietnam communist forces in the 1950s and lost that war. It was a humiliating disaster. So what does the United States do? Decide to fight North Vietnam in the 1960s. My gosh, that's like buying a failure-prone used car from a neighbor after you've seen it break down on him several times! But here we go into Afghanistan, right on the heels almost of the Soviet army retreat after their defeat there! During the 1980s, we sat there and boasted that Afghanistan was going to be the Soviet Union's "Vietnam War" and we went right in there, eyes wide open, a little after a decade after the Soviets left. You could start a series of "No Win Wars" trading cards based on U.S. military operations alone.

But, it gets even better.

The United States needed to find a puppet to run Afghanistan after the Taliban were gone. Well, they found that the old king of Afghanistan was still alive and living in Europe. He had abdicated and left in the 1970s. So the United States approached the Afghan king and asked him if he'd like to return and be the king of Afghanistan again. He said no! He didn't want the job! That should have tipped the United States off right there that we were getting in way over our heads. Their own King doesn't want to run the place! Most people, if approached with an offer to be the King of a country, will scramble for the pen to sign on the dotted line. But this dude says no, and can you please shut the screen door on your way out. And you can see why. We're still stuck over there and the Taliban we swore to eradicate is just as lively as ever, some fifteen years later. Evidently, "freedom" hasn't made a very big impression on them. Only the Afghan King treasured his life enough to refuse the job.

Two quagmire wars aren't the only "freedom" we garnered after the 9/11 attacks. We also got the great, wonderful, Dear Freedom police state provisos of the Patriot Act.

Now, before I get into that, I need to digress for a moment and explain this whole "patriot" phenomenon. This is another word dredged up by the Republican Party, but not from the NRA. No, they got this word from the Mel Gibson movies of the same name: *The Patriot*. The movies came out before 9/11, but not *so* long before that it wasn't on the radar anymore. This movie showed the typical reluctant warrior that, if it was in modern era, would be a Vietnam vet. As it was, the movie was about the Revolutionary War that the Mel Gibson character, Benjamin Martin, wants to stay out of and argues against. But when his family is attacked by a rogue British cavalry officer, well, of course he joins the war. Very interesting movie, because 9/11 happened only a bit over a year after this movie came out.

Why do I think the government channeled this movie when naming the Patriot Act? Well, in the movie, Benjamin Martin is disillusioned by the death of his son in the war and wants to quit. But this colonel tells him, "Stay the course!" Those were the exact words in the movie. And when the Iraq War had descended into a bloodbath and the government was on the ropes in the press over it, guess what Bush said? "Stay the course!" Yes! Those were Bush's exact words, obviously lifted from the movie. So, the image the government wanted put into everyone's mind when they named the Patriot Act were the images from the movie *The Patriot*. Images like the reluctant warrior, staying the course, making the sacrifices no matter how painful and how it'll all be peaches in the end. Except it wasn't and hasn't been in real life.

All we've done by passing the Patriot Act is create a plug-in police state. The government can declare a "national emergency," invoke the Patriot Act, and we'll be living in what will be a police state in reality, no matter how many times the word "freedom" is invoked.

Equating freedom with the Patriot Act makes as much sense as an atheist attending church. The government basically told us: "If you love freedom, you'll support our need to have a police state on stand-by." But another reason they named it the Patriot Act is because if you didn't support it, then you were unpatriotic. Thus, the government told us that we needed to give up our freedom in order to have freedom. We need to protect freedom by taking it away. Or, at least, having the power to take it away in the event of anything the government deems to be a "national emergency."

The Patriot Act will not go away. Because, understand this: The Global War on Terror has not ended.

Nor will it end.

How do you end such a war? Terrorist entities will exist for the rest of human history. Thus, the Patriot Act will remain until the United States government collapses. Right now, the government does not have a good reason to invoke certain parameters of the Patriot Act that would, in effect, plunge us all into a police state. But with the rise of ISIS and small scale terrorist attacks occurring within the United State, it will only be a matter of time before the Patriot Act measures are plugged in.

Here's what'll happen.

If a Republican President enacts it, as long as he targets Muslims for the most part, all the flag-waving, freedom-loving Republicans will support him—even the ones who nominally claim to be against the Patriot Act. But if a Democrat enacts it, it'll spur a small-scale armed resistance from various militia groups which will reinforce the "need" to have invoked the Patriot Act. Thus the democrats, who are also nominally against the Patriot Act, will support it having been invoked. Because they think the militia groups are all "gun nut wackos."

By the time anyone figures out there's a much larger game afoot, be it the Patriot Act plugged in by a Republican or Democrat, it'll be too late. However, terrorism will only be the excuse used to authorize implementing Patriot Act parameters. The genuine reason won't become apparent until afterwards. Plugging in the Patriot Act will precede a major economic crisis. Such a crisis would create civil unrest and disorder. That such a crisis is more than possible should be readily apparent to everyone who saw the Great Recession of a few years ago. Nothing that triggered that economic collapse has been fixed.

The government will know some weeks in advance that the economy is about to go into a crash worse that the Great Depression. That will be when they "discover" a "terrorist plot" that is so deep, they "need" to use the Patriot Act to "keep us safe." Then the economy will crash sometime after that. But unless the economy crashes, the government has little or no reason to plug in the Patriot Act. With the government, everything is about money and Wall Street. Even the two wars in Iraq and Afghanistan were about money: defense contractors and no-bid contracts. But to understand the peril, it is imperative to know that the conditions and causes that led up to the Great Recession still exist and have not been remedied.

However, one thing is sure. When the Patriot Act is turned on by the government, the majority of Americans will just go along with it, just like they do with TSA security checks at airports, which are closer to in-processing procedures for inmates at the labor camps of dictatorships than genuine security measures.

Speaking of the Transportation Safety Administration, the TSA, this provides us with an excellent opportunity to demonstrate the "false-face politics."

What are "false-face politics?"

This is where you put on a public face as being against Big Government, but actually aren't and actually help create more Big

Government. And that describes the Republican Party perfectly. At least the Democratic Party isn't touting themselves as the party of "limited government." Ever since Resident Ronald Reagan went around mumbling several phrases advocating limiting the government, the Republicans have claimed themselves the party of limited government. They ran around quoting Reagan on it. But when they say they want to limit government, what they mean to say is that they want to abolish social programs such as welfare and food stamps. And also privatize Social Security and place it into the hands of Wall Street.

But as far as trimming the myriad rolls of fat from the Pentagon or cut some of the duplicated and redundant defense agencies, the answer is no. To even suggest cutting the defense budget and eliminating redundant defense agencies is tantamount to treason as far as the Republicans are concerned. See, to them, school lunch programs for poor kids is "Big Government." But multiple defense agencies and intelligence agencies all with the same mission, but none know what the others are doing? Right, that's not Big Government to the Republicans.

Knowing that, it is wholly understandable why the Republican Bush administration created two megalithic federal government agencies right after 9/11. The biggie was the Department of Homeland Security. Now bear in mind we already had every single government agency under DHS already there, including FEMA. And FEMA had been created to take over what was called Civil Defense during the Cold War. Supposedly, the Department of Homeland Security would better coordinate interfacing and cooperation between multiple government agencies under their authority.

Excuse me, but wouldn't it make sense to only have the Department of Homeland security alone and then abolish all the other agencies under them as obsolete? Not to the government. No, they'd rather keep this Byzantine network of multiple redundancies that answered to a redundancy itself. Brilliant! But wait! There's more! Also created was the Transportation Safety

Authority, a federal agency now universally hated by a majority of Americans, and rightfully so. The TSA is in control of airport security.

However, this "airport security" has been taken to such an unreasonable and unwarranted extreme, it has created the perfect environment for thugs and sexual predators that made it past the TSA's hiring and screening process. Evidently, their employee screening process is not as stringent as the one airline passengers are forced to endure. Because several TSA employees were caught and convicted of using pat-searches of airline passengers to sexually grope and fondle people. Now, let's be clear as to what that is. Those are federal government employees—security personnel—using the government security apparatus to sexually assault a captive group of people—who have no choice but to submit. And this is all that "Freedom" and getting rid of Big Government the Republicans sat there and bragged about!

Countless examples exist of passengers sexually assaulted by TSA personnel. People have died in TSA custody—people who did nothing but protest the brutal way they were being treated. The TSA treats airline passengers the way guards treat inmates at prisons. We are not inmates! We are supposedly free citizens attempting to use public transportation!

But not to the TSA. Or to the government, for that matter. We were told we had to accept this. Why? You guessed it. "To protect our Freedom!" That's what we were told. The Department of Homeland Security and the TSA are gifts to us. From the brains of the Republican Party. The party of limited government. Yet they created the DHS, which runs a bunch of redundant agencies under them including the TSA. And we have the TSA itself, a group of wanna-be cops and sexual predators who found the perfect place to exploit innocent people for their perverted fantasies of dominating others. And they call this "Freedom"? I call this a travesty.

The government will defend itself by saying "yes, but you have the freedom to speak out against the government here." So?

Nearly all the countries in Western Europe have the same right. What's more, if the government doesn't want you to protest or demonstrate in an area they don't want you to, such as in front of a hotel where the president is staying, they won't let you. Instead, they will force you to hold your demonstration in a "free speech zone" miles away from that hotel.

If you try to get close to the hotel with your protest, in come the police with batons and tear gas, and to jail you go. Usually from orders that came down from the Department of Homeland Security that would see a terrorist threat from Buddhist Monks Against War. A protest against the president has no value if the government can move it to where the president doesn't have to see it. I bet dictators around the world slapped their foreheads and said, "Gosh, now why didn't I think of that?!"

Plus, the government can set a limit on the amount of time protestors are allowed to use the "free speech zone." If they refuse to leave when their time is up, again here come the riot police and buses with chain link over the window to haul everyone to jail. Maybe they should just put parking meters in the "free speech zones" and call them Freedom Meters. "Hey, Tom, have you got a quarter for the Freedom Meter? Bill isn't through with his speech denouncing the war yet." I probably just gave the government an idea on that one. The Department of Homeland Security apparatchik tasked with reading subversive literature will see that and go, "Say, that's not a bad idea! Freedom Meter! I bet I can sell that idea as my own to the boss!" They could create a whole new government agency to administer the Freedom Meters. Basically, federal meter maids.

Anyone caught talking in the Free Speech Zone when the Freedom Meter is expired gets a ticket. "But I was just asking my friend, if he wanted to go get a coffee!" "Makes no difference, pal. Speech is speech, You want to talk here, you have to put in a quarter!" The government will say we value our free speech so much, we've managed to arrive at a price for it: Twenty-five cents per five minutes. The Free Speech Zone idea was thought up by the government when they were looking to cut expenses for tear gas and rubber bullet. "Let's just move them where the president can't see them. Then if they don't get bored in a couple hours and go home, we'll move in and tear gas them and shoot them with rubber bullets."

But, let's try to watch the budget and save a couple of bucks first, okay guys? Seriously, this is how the government thinks. Plus, when they move in with the riot police and start bashing in the heads of old people and nuns, it won't be seen on international news. The foreign camera crews will all be over at the hotel where the president is giving a speech about his approval ratings. Then he'll tell them how horrible it is that some Middle Eastern country used tear gas and water cannons to break up a protest. "That's why we've got Freedom here in America! Where people are free to criticize their government!" Right, as long as it's not within five square miles of the president. "Okay, folks, you've had your freedom! Now go home or you're under arrest!"

At the end of the day, using a word doesn't make it true. Communist dictatorships during the Cold War all called themselves "democratic republics," after all. But it didn't make it true. The word "Freedom" is no different.

The United States government uses that word in the exact same way old communist dictatorships used the word "democratic." It is not in the interest of freedom that a government creates a police state in the snap of its fingers because they wrote a law giving themselves that power and authority.

It is not freedom to treat airline passengers like inmates being processed into the forced labor camp of a dictatorship. It is not freedom to lie to the American people into two wars it had no coherent plan to win, or administer government to the two nations it allegedly sought to build. It is not freedom to create government agencies out of thin air, inventing the reason why as you go along. And then giving those agencies the same power and authority over American citizens as the Gestapo had over the Germans. The government acts as if this is just another postal services or park ranger outfit they've created and not what is, in truth, an apparatus of secret police agencies.

You cannot create secret police agencies to spy on the American people and call that "freedom." Well, you can, but then you're no different than any of the other police states in history that did that. Also, and this needs to be said, you cannot just write executive orders as president in order to bypass the alleged democratic process and then call that "freedom." That alone is one of the most dangerous things to arise in government. Executive orders, in truth, are dictatorial power with no oversight. So when the government uses the word "Freedom," what they actually mean is its opposite.

Every year, all levels of government from city, to county, to state, to federal, pass more laws. Thus, each year, every American becomes less free. Many people don't even know what these laws are, or that they now exist. Any American, at any given place or time, is in violation of probably at least five laws he or she is wholly unaware of. When there are literally thousands of laws in this country, and people within a given local area can be subject to several hundred at once, it is impossible not to be in violation of some at any given point. Yet the government continues to pass more.

The government creates more police, more enforcement agencies, and more government agencies that will lobby for the need for more laws unique to their sphere of operations. And they will do so, all the while telling us that this is "Freedom." Pardon me, but if we get any more "freedom," we'll need a government permit just to sneeze. Plus an air quality impact assessment, including a parts-per-billion count of particulates from the sneeze. We live under the illusion we live in "Freedom." But it is merely a Great American Myth that older people can look back on and remember there was once some truth to that word here.

Lastly, let's examine one of the greatest and noblest of Great American Myths, the myth of Democracy. America did not invent Democracy, even though it seems to imagine that. No,

Democracy was an idea of Ancient Greece, you see. The so-called Founding Fathers of this country were classical students. That is, they studied the writings of Ancient Greece and Rome, the languages of both, and so on. That's where they happened upon this idea of Democracy.

However, it was not without its perils, as the Ancient Greeks had discovered. A rule by majority can be a tyranny of majority where the rights of the individual and or minority are not protected. Therefore, we have a government that is actually a representative republic based on democratic ideals. And a Bill of Rights that spells out clearly what the individual rights of each person are that the government may not take away. There are people to whom those rights are temporarily suspended to some degree, such as prisoners and military personnel. But, for the most part, the Bill of Rights protects the individual and minority from the majority and the government That is, it guards people from the application of pure, majority-rule democracy.

Pay attention to what I just said there.

The Bill of Rights does not just protect against some government force, it also protects against the even democratic application of majority rule by the people themselves.

Why is it important to pay attention to that? Because the founding Fathers knew that in Ancient Greece, Democracy was used by the majority to quash the individual and minority. Therefore, they wrote the Bill of Rights as an ultimate law of the land no one is allowed to circumvent. Or, at least, they couldn't in the past. Why is that important? What does this mean?

What if a majority of Americans could vote to make Islam illegal? Muslims are in a minority, so they might not be able to outvote such a ballot initiative. There are Americans right now that wish they could make Islam illegal here. Ironically they say Muslims are threatening our "Freedom." I think I made my point about that word quite clearly. Okay, but what if that happened and Islam was banned in America? To supposedly keep us safe. Then, later it was decided to ban the Mormon faith, then

47

Buddhism. What then? Now we have a situation where there is no right to practice religion unless the majority allows it. That is pure Democracy. Yes, it's a tyranny. But not all tyranny comes wearing a military uniform and party ideology. Some of it comes dressed like, well, everyone on the street.

Of course, someone like our president—Donald Trump—can make the case that Muslims are threatening our safety. Let there be no doubt, Islamic terrorism is a very real threat, but if one carefully considers banning or restricting an entire religion based on the actions of a minority of its followers, you make it that much easier to do the same to another religion down the road.

Far-fetched? Consider this.

Say Trump somehow succeeded in some kind of government restriction of Muslims. Then he leaves office, and a very liberal Democrat is elected president. While he is in office, a fundamentalist Christian bombs an abortion clinic, killing several people. Therefore, people call for action when it is revealed several people in the bomber's church were involved. So, the executive decision by the president comes down in the form of an executive order that restricts any church deemed "fundamentalist" or anti-abortion. Now all of those fundamentalist Christians that supported Trump in restricting Muslims have found themselves in the very same situation as the Muslims. This is not far-fetched. This can happen. It's already being discussed. This is the danger of misinterpreting what "democracy" is in this country, and enshrining it as a myth.

Here's another way the American misinterpretation of Democracy has created a disaster: The Middle East. America wanted to bring "Democracy" to the region. Excuse me, but do you understand that you are talking about bringing majority-rule to countries with religious minorities? Why didn't anyone see what a disaster-in-the-making it was to promote this idea of "Democracy" in the Arab Spring protests? They couldn't have picked a worse idea to promote than majority rule. They didn't necessarily know what the United States government really meant by that any more than the American people truly understand what the government hides behind the word they use.

What the United States really meant was toppling leaders it didn't like and installing men it thought it could control. This created a cataclysmic war, an out-of-control terrorist movement the West cannot stop, and a humanitarian disaster not seen for ages. This was all because of trying to spread what the United States government told them—and us also—was "Democracy."

In fact, with less historical knowledge of the region than a high school history student, what it turned out to be was another poorly-planned exercise in toppling governments. The American people were told that we were creating "Democracy" over there. But we know exactly what would happen here if we had true "Democracy" majority rule. Why were we then surprised when guerilla armies in Syria tried liquidating entire populations of religious minorities?

When it comes to foreign policy, "Democracy" is the word used to cover up what were illegal coups against legitimate governments. The United States has a long history of doing this and still does it. And it calls out "Democracy" even when installing despots, dictators, and incompetent provisional governments in countries it seeks to control. In other words, the definition of the word "Democracy" in the United States government is *coup d'état*.

But here in the United States, it has a different meaning. Like, for example, when the government passes a law they know to be in conflict with the Bill of Rights (such as gun bans or gun control, for example) they call it "democracy in action." The people were tired of gun violence, so the government had to act. Except the Bill of Rights doesn't define rights by what the majority wants, feels to be safest, thinks to be right or fair, or demands. There's a large number of Americans calling for banning Muslims from America too. What, will we do that also so people can feel safe? It's only a small minority of Muslims committing terrorism. The vast majority are peaceful, law-abiding people.

The exact same thing can be said about gun owners. This is where the Right and Left meet in the middle. Right-wingers will support banning Muslims, but point out the vast majority of gun owners are peaceful. The Left-Wingers will support banning guns, but point out that the vast majority of Muslim are peaceful.

The truth is: Both Muslims and gun owners are peaceful by an overwhelming number if you look at the facts. And beside all of that, the Bill of Rights forbids denying rights to both of them, period. We don't need "democracy in action" to solve problems that are social in nature. Crime and terrorism are social problems. They're not caused by guns or the Islamic faith. This is not something for "democracy" to fix. The government needs to abide by the Bill of Rights. My gosh, people were even calling for a gun ban that applied to Muslims! But people have bought into this "democracy" myth that tells them if a majority of Americans wants to deny civil right to others, they ought to be able to do so. Because it's "Democracy." And this myth comes to us from the government who uses that word to justify its own senseless actions.

You'd never hear the government use the word "democracy" in regards to taxes. As in letting the American people vote on whether or not to increase taxes in a national ballot.

No, the government would be opposed to that kind of "democracy."

Which is actually one case where it would be wholly justified. Because if the American people, not just Senators and Congress, had the power of the purse, the government would become a lot more frugal. A national vote by the people on taxes is the only place that pure Democracy should happen, aside from genuine elections. But when it comes to passing laws, if it conflicts with the Bill of Rights, it shouldn't even come up as an initiative or a bill. It isn't legitimate. Freedom has no meaning if a majority can take it away, be it a majority of the people or a majority of Senators and Congress people. And it sure doesn't have any meaning when the President can bypass any democratic procedure there is and just pass an executive order to go over the heads of the people and the Bill of Rights.

So, when people say, "We have a great democracy here," they are mistaken. And thankfully so. We have a representative republic based on democratic principles. We don't want to live in a true Democracy. We basically have a system where a majority of Senators and Congress people vote for things a majority of Americans don't really want.

We'll discuss that later.

But for now, the reason why that happens is because of corruption and the silent coup from Wall Street that owns the government, including the Congress and Senate. So what we've got is a majority of politicians voting for what a majority of them want. Or got paid off to vote for. And "democracy" won't fix that. The Senate and Congress together are already the best Democracy money can buy. Democracy was already a Great American Myth before the government discovered its value in justifying senseless military operations and wars. I'm not saying we should abolish democracy. I'm saying we need to return it to its rightful place where it belongs behind the Bill of Rights. And it isn't a foreign policy, either.

Therefore, did I just spend an entire chapter just to tell you that the government lies? Of course not. We all know that, and if we don't, we've been living under a rock for quite a long period of time. Actually, we are living under the very real rock of a fossilized government that is, in truth, no longer alive to the needs of the people.

Be that as it may, it is important to understand the jargon and the code words the government uses to deceive us. That way, we are not trapped into blindly following along with dangerously flawed ideas because we believe the words being used to deceptively describe those ideas. We should never allow ourselves to become so rigidly attached to any idea, even those we may agree with, that we resort to fanaticism to uphold and defend them. Both political parties, both the Right and the Left, use these words and phrases as well as others to cloak their true intentions behind a false wall of patriotism. It is of the utmost importance to understand that if you blindly follow along with whatever your political party tells you then you have just surrendered your ability to think for yourself. How, exactly, is that freedom?

Basically, the government—and both political parties that control it—are selling a product. They are selling you a candidate, a law, a tax, a new government agency, or a war. They cannot, in truth, sell you "Freedom" no matter what they say. We already have (or rather, had) that via the constitution and Bill of Rights. The next time the government talks about "more Freedom," someone needs to stand up and ask them why the government took it away in the first place.

But, like any product sold by advertising, it is necessary to have deceptions and omissions of facts. By now, everyone should be aware that an advertiser will not tell you the bad things about a certain product but only the good things. And that's fine when it comes to a can of baked beans. But, where this isn't fine is in selling the American people war. If you purchase a can of baked beans that doesn't live up to the advertiser's promises you just don't buy them again.

If enough people have that experience people stop buying that brand altogether.

It is far different with a war sold to the American people using false and deceptive advertising. With a war, tens of thousands or more may die, tens of thousands more maimed for life, entire cities destroyed, and entire regions of several nations may be destabilized. That's not "freedom", that's slaughter. And the United States government has always obstinately refused to own up to mistakes, thus it will continue to wage a war it knows it cannot win merely to avoid embarrassment. It did so during the Vietnam War, continuing that war some years after it knew that war to be unwinnable. Thus, the government never tells us the "bad" aspect of the product it is trying to sell us, but only the "good" sides.

Imagine, for a moment, if there was a real "truth in advertising" law for the government where, as with prescription, medicines, they had to list all the possible side effects of their actions when selling them to us. How would the Iraq War "side effects" list have gone after the Bush Administration sat up there and told us this war would pay for itself and create secular democracies across the Middle East?

Like this:

"The government has no clear or concise plan for how to win this war if it falls into a civil war fueled by sectarian violence. This war could cost up to a billion dollars a day and the claim it would pay for itself has not been proven by an independent lab. This war can create an epidemic of suicides among returning vets as well as disfigured and maimed vets. Thousands of Americans will die, and tens of thousands of Iraqis will die for no apparent reason that the United States government can coherently explain. This war will lead up to the creation of the most dangerous terrorist organization seen in decades some years after the United States abandon the war. Ask your doctor if the Iraq War is right for you."

Now, if the government said that, would anyone of good sense support such a war? Oh, they were told all of this, but only by writers, pundits, and politicians without any real credit up in Washington. The government itself never told us any disaster was possible. They stubbornly refused to admit the war and all of Iraq had plunged into a civil war.

And so even more people died, so the government could avoid confessing the truth a little while longer. All that time, they trotted out the "Freedoms," American "Exceptionalisms" and the "Greatest Nation on Earths" the whole time the civil war was in progress. Because Americans had no wish to be involved in some other country's civil war. That's what the Vietnam War was—a civil war between North and South Vietnam. So there we were, in yet another civil war the government was desperately trying to call anything but that.

Words applied to describe ideas are like dangerous, venomous snakes. They must be handled carefully and skillfully or one can be bitten and suffer great harm from them.

Words and ideas start wars and cause unjust laws to be passed. When we become attached to the false patriotism our government embodies in these words and phrases we are holding that poisonous snake by the tail. It keeps right on biting us, but we refuse to let go of it.

Why?

Because we have become trapped by the concepts we think exist because the government says they do. But if we refuse to believe those words at face value and carefully investigate the facts, we can detect the swindle. We can pin the government down with their own words.

That is like using a forked stick to hold a snake's head down with their own words so the snake can be picked up without biting us. The forked stick is careful investigation to examine the words of the government safely. That is, when the government tells us our "freedom" is at stake in the war we ask them if their own children will help fight this war. If not, then we can see our "freedom" is not at stake because the government will not permit their own children to possibly perish in that war.

This is but one example. Again, anything the government says should not be believed or acted upon until a careful investigation of the facts is done and proof that they are telling the truth is presented. If the government refuses to show or demonstrate the facts, then it can be known they are engaging in deception.

Certain high-profile business people like to parrot the phrase "knowledge is power." This is false. Knowledge is not power; correct and true knowledge is the road to empowerment. But it must be handled skillfully and wisely. Power in the wrong hands is evil. Even if it were true that "knowledge is power," this would be a bad thing if that knowledge was in the wrong hands.

Our government proves this to be so. They have gained the

ability to be the sole authority in control of the knowledge the American people are allowed to see.

They then spin and adulterate that knowledge to fit the agendas they wish to engage in. That false interpretation is what they present to the American people as "knowledge" using the words and phrases I described here, as well as others. The government selects words and phrase that stir the American's heart and sense of patriotism. And the American people fall for the charade again and again.

We'll examine why in the next two chapters.

CHAPTER THREE—THE MEDIA

RECENTLY IT'S BEEN a topic of discussion in the government as to how to get more people to vote. Offhand, it's like saying they need more people to buy into the scam, believe the illusion and help perpetuate the madness.

That people are disillusioned with voting is rather obvious. That's why they don't.

You don't fix that by enacting a law to compel them to vote by force of law, which is what the government sees as a solution. Indeed, nearly all of their so-called "solutions" involve a law that forces citizens to do something they don't want to do. No, you fix voter apathy by fixing the government itself. For one thing, as I have already said, we have two corrupt and dishonest political parties that control the voting, election, and the government in what amounts to a political monopoly.

That's one reason people don't vote.

Another reason is because, for example, Obama got elected promising a national health care system like European nations have. What he ultimately delivered, thanks in no small part to the corrupt and dishonest political party he is a member of, was the same private insurance system he said was "broken" during his 2008 campaign. Except now, the government uses the law to force you to buy that insurance or be punished if you don't. That message isn't lost on people. Things such as that create voter apathy. Yet another reason is the "quality," such as it is, of the candidate these political parties select. Obviously, one has to have money and influence to run.

They can deny that all they want, but if money is not a factor, why does it cost millions of dollars to run for office? The average American cannot afford to run for federal offices. Most couldn't even afford to run for governor of the states they live in. If political influence is not a factor, why did we have another Bush and another Clinton in the 2016 presidential elections arena?

And, even when "new, fresh faces" are elected, either they are co-opted and become as corrupt as everyone else, or they were corrupt all along but no one knew it. This is another reason why the people become disillusioned and just stop voting. It seems no matter who gets elected, the wrong things occur. Another war, more broken promises, more government, and more laws that nobody wanted.

People say, "My vote won't make a difference." They are correct. When the choice is between two corrupt party members, then either choice will deliver bad decisions and wrong action. Even the voters that actually vote who say, "If you don't vote, don't complain," also say "I have to choose the lesser of two evils." Therefore it is admitted that both choices will deliver evil.

People also say, "Men died for your right to vote!" In the Vietnam War? How was North Vietnam threatening to stop voting in America? Men may have died in the distant past for our right to vote, but not in recent history. If that was the case, we'd have lost the right to vote in 1975 when South Vietnam fell to North Vietnam. The men that died in the distant past for our right to vote might have been rather reluctant to do so for this current system we call "the right to vote." Because what it happens to be is a runoff between two wealthy career politicians who pay security personnel to keep average Americans far away from them.

It seems pretty straightforward, doesn't it? The government took over the government. Wait! Is that really so? Not entirely. The political parties didn't wake up one day and start running candidates not fit to supervise volunteer trash pick-up programs.

The American people, in no small part, collectively abdicated their responsibility to hold the government accountable. The American people also collectively abdicated their responsibility to think for themselves. That's why the public is so easy to control and we-the people go along with whatever the government fancies. The government knows how to sell it agenda.

People registered as Republicans won't go to their party and demand better. They'll go along with whatever their herd master tells them. "We all need to get behind Doofus McDorkle for the good of the party." And the allegedly more intellectual of the two parties—the Democrats—are no better. All the so-called "freethinking" professors, writers, and activists in the Democratic Party are more like a herd of sheep than an entity composed of intelligent people. Intelligent people don't go along with what they know to be wrong just because everyone else in the party says to vote that way.

I'm not talking about party cadre here: the ones the party is grooming as candidates because they've proven they can commit crimes and not get caught. I'm talking about all the average Americans registered in these two parties. The ones that say they want better, but won't demand it if the party tells them to be quiet. The ones who criticize a war the Republicans start, but justify wars that Democrats start. "I'm anti-war! Unless a Democrat starts one."

The leader of the country we're at war with is yet another action figure in the "Hitler-of-the-month Club" that's been running a special since 1945. Rank and file Republicans will sit and whine about Big Government throughout the administration of a Democrat president. But when a Republican enters the White House and creates two new megalithic federal government agencies as George W. Bush did, they'll sit still and won't say a word.

Excuse me, but what happened to the tough guys that were against Big Government? And hey Democrats, what happened to the tough guys that were anti-war? Or have you changed that to read "anti-some-wars" while the Republicans changed their mantra to "Against Big Government we didn't create ourselves?" Because people such as this, without any ability to take a firm stand whatsoever, make up the membership of both parties, why is anyone at all surprised that this is exactly what we get?

Now I know what'll be said next: "this is how politics is!" So that justifies it? That makes it all right? What that basically says is what we know to be wrong, and in some cases criminal, is actually right and cannot be questioned.

Nor can it be changed.

Does anyone realize that's pretty much what the Nazis said at the Nuremberg War Crimes Trial? "Yes, we knew what we were doing was wrong, but that's just the way things were. We were just following orders. That's just how politics goes." That's basically what the Nazis offered in their own defense, after all. "Well, what can I do!?" say the political party defenders.

I imagine that if grass-roots petitions went around each political party, threatening mass resignations of party membership and promises to form a new political party with all those who resign, it would get their attention. Especially if the point was made that unless genuine reforms were made, everyone would renounce their membership and form a new party to actively challenge them in election. The new party might not win the election, but they'll siphon off enough votes so the opposing party would win. That's how you get their attention.

But just going along with the herd? Why should they need to do anything at all? You'll vote for them if they dug up Stalin and Mussolini and ran them. Unless you demand better from your party, you won't get better. But instead, the elections are like a football game and each side rallies behind his "team" no matter what. "I can't weaken my party. Then the Democrats will win!!"

Right, so we get into two no-win wars and two oppressive federal agencies are created. Brilliant. If it were just a football game, then it'd be fine. But is isn't and real people die because of this collective insanity. Until we demand better, no matter the cost to "our" political party, we assuredly will not get it. They have no reason to do better and no motivation. You'll vote for them anyway. You always do. For the team. And that's why a lot of people don't bother to vote, too. Because it means buying into this charade, closing your eyes, and pretending you didn't just vote for someone with the morals of a racketeer.

People in both of the political parties act like they can't reform those parties. Yet there they are with the Internet, email, Facebook and Twitter. So what do they do? Share pictures of their dogs and make badly spelled comments while playing computer games. Then act like that same technology couldn't be used to create a better world for their kids. Oh, but that's right, the television is raising their kids. Or the internet. Or computer games.

Pretty much every generation born after 1970 has been raised with, or even by, the television. Therefore, it is imperative to understand that many people have a very limited attention span. Often they don't even realize this about themselves. How many times have you heard, "I just don't have time to read a book" but that person spends two hours or more a night watching television? And television programs of little or no educational or social value at that. Many of these television programs inculcate or openly espouse the very worst of social values and behaviors.

People wonder what happened to civility? It disappeared right about the time that television made a lack of civility socially acceptable and even funny to watch. Getting uncomfortable? I haven't even begun yet.

When people have a limited attention span and get lost in any discussion beyond a television sitcom intelligence level, they make the perfect population for manipulation by political parties. Is it any wonder why Ronald Reagan used a phrase ("Where's the beef?") from a television commercial by a fast food chain in his presidential election debate? He knew everyone had seen that commercial, thought it was funny, and he'd score massive points on that alone regardless of whether or not he was right. He didn't need to be right. He just needed to be funny. And as a movie actor, he already knew that. Again, with a population getting lost in discussions beyond a television sitcom intelligence level, it should not surprise anyone as to why American politics are so fraudulent and false.

I had a co-worker who, when discussing politics would say, "It's just like this one episode of..." and he would mention some cartoon or sitcom. So, regarding real political issues, we've dumbed them down into cartoon format or a comedy all of twenty minutes long after you omit the commercial.

And people wonder how the Iraq War got started so fast. Because people didn't want to wait to see if Iraq was innocent! No attention span! And the government knew that. Didn't you wonder why all the news shows had an ominous sounding theme song and logo for the Iraq War before it even got started? Was that a coincidence?

Hardly.

They saw the Vietnam War was the first televised war. Perhaps. But the Iraq War was the first one truly started by television. That's how the government got that party started. Endless television programs and a population with a sitcom-level attention span. And a sitcom intelligence level to understand complex issues in the Middle East, far more complex than what George W. Bush was telling them.

Now if you can start a war like that, obviously you can win elections that way too. Without television, no candidate has any hope of being elected. An entire political platform, distilled into a television commercial with ominous sounding music in the background. It's not that the American people are unable to understand the issues; it's that they refuse to educate themselves as to what the issues truly are. They want it done for them. Hence, they get the politicians they complain about.

And, subsequently, wars that cost thousands of lives and without any tangible victory or reason. Hey you wanted a political system put together like a television show, you got one! They've even got make-up artists to doll up the actors, er, officials before the press conferences.

What do we have when herd mentality in both the political parties is coupled with a television culture? You have the herd mentality of doing not just what the party says, but what all the TV shows appear to indicate the most popular thing is to do. We have "fad politics" in a very real sense.

Look at the Green movement, for example. Not long did the word "Green" come out in popular usage did the Democratic Party then co-opt that word unto themselves. They all wanted to be "Green" and support "Green Energy." So much so that the Obama Administration wasted taxpayer money on "Green Energy" companies that proved to be fraudulent or seriously flawed. Was he taken to task for that?

No, of course not, because the Democrats won't criticize "their guy" and "Green" was some sacred icon right out of the TV culture that popularized it. The entire "Green" movement is a fad co-opted by Wall Street just the same as "organic food." So, if a Democrat says he's "Green," he'll garner votes because it's a popular fad. For the most part, television drives modern fads. So, again, without television modern American elections would not be possible.

How is this possible amongst the Republicans? They're subject to the same fads. Take overt militarism portrayed by Hollywood, for example. Hilariously, most of Hollywood are liberal democrats, but movies glorifying war and the military come from there. The Republicans might hate celebrities because they're liberals for the most part, but they couldn't do without them acting in the movies that venerate the wars of the United States.

Liberals say they're anti-war, but they make movies worshiping it and get rich as a result. Those movies, in turn, end up on television where everyone sees them. Thus, we become infected with war fever. The American people then support whatever wars the government deems necessary, often urging the government into military action if it seems reluctant.

Then Hollywood liberals whine about these wars and act as if the Republican Party was solely responsible. No, they are responsible and we are responsible—no one is completely innocent. And, as I said, the Republicans will complain about Hollywood liberals when Hollywood is the best military propaganda machine in the history of the world. Not even the Third Reich had the budget for propaganda that Hollywood has.

Television shapes American culture and, as an obvious result, American politics follow. Television shapes and, in many cases, creates popular opinions, beliefs, and fads. That those then enter into American politics goes without saying. In many cases, this is a terrible thing.

Television cannot, within the time of an average television program, adequately form a genuine solution to complex problems. People will often think they understand another country because they saw a one hour television show about them that was presented from one point of view. That nation might be two thousand years old as a culture, but an American can think he understands all of that within an hour—an hour interspersed with commercials, often-political candidates seeking to instill fear of that country to garner votes.

Americans seem unwilling to think for themselves anymore, or go find out things for themselves. They want the television to do that for them and then relay that information to them in an hour or less. Is it any wonder both political parties exploited this? Both parties are populated by people who consider themselves intelligent. But there they go, each election cycle, voting as their parties tell them and as the television tacitly tells them.

A television show might say a certain country is bad and they'll accept it as truth. They won't bother to go to the library and investigate for themselves. They probably won't even use the internet in their own home to look it up. Politicians know that. That's how the Republican Party can continue beating the drum to attack Iran.

The American people allowed the television to dominate politics. As a result, only the wealthy can get elected because only the wealthy can afford television airtime and commercials. Perhaps it was easier for Americans to just "watch it all on TV" rather than read it in the newspaper or a political pamphlet.

But there was and is a price to pay for this convenience. The average American has effectively locked himself and herself out of the political system. Only the wealthy can afford it. The average American watched it all happen on TV and didn't realize he was watching the loss of his own voice in politics. Politics became about what corporation would pay for advertising for which candidate. But also about what candidate looked good on television or said things that had a certain appeal when televised.

It is literally impossible to fully ascertain which countries pose a genuine threat to the United States versus those the government, via the television, is telling us pose a threat when they actually don't. As a result, we attack nations that have done nothing to us while a country that might actually be plotting an attack could go unnoticed. In truth, there probably aren't any nations plotting to attack the United States now or in the future. But the story of "The Boy Who Cried Wolf" ought to be remembered, even though it probably is not aired on television.

The effect television has had and does have on our political system cannot be over stated. Nor should it be underestimated. To quote old George W. Bush, I think we all "misunderestimated" the ability of television to radically change American politics. This was not all a bad thing. Television has had the ability to, in the past, inform the American people of political issues that might otherwise have gone unnoticed.

It is also clear that the Vietnam War was "lost in American living rooms" as televised images of that war were broadcast into American homes on the news. Reporter Walter Cronkite, standing in Saigon in the aftermath of the Tet Offensive, famously declared the Vietnam War "unwinnable' on national television.

However, the government quickly adapted and now tightly controls any image of American wars carried on the news from embedded reporters. If reporters want to stay embedded with U.S. Military, he or she had better say what the military wants to be said and not show any image it does want shown on television.

Images of flag-draped caskets being shown on the news were forbidden by the government for some time after the wars in Afghanistan and Iraq began. Therefore, what we see is that television had some public value in helping to end the senseless Vietnam War. Thus, rather than the news reporting on reality of American wars, what it broadcasts is the propaganda that military censors approve of before it is shown. Because of this, Americans can think a war is being won when, in fact, it is not. There is no way to know, because the government controls the news.

Therefore, we must conclude television no longer has any true value to reporting truthful news—especially concerning military action by the government. That this is extremely dangerous to the long-term survival of the United States as a somewhat free county goes without saying. The Vietnam War was the first televised war. I would say the Iraq War qualifies as the first war started on television. The next war will literally be a reality television show the government directs and produces to generate ratings.

As long as the government depicts the war with a good soundtrack, the public will love it. Especially as individual soldiers become people's favorite characters they tune in to watch. I'm not saying they'd start a war as a television show. I'm saying they'll turn it into one in order to pump up support for it.

Anyone who attempted to report the truth would be locked out of the region, as happened during the Iraq War. You think this is far-fetched? Yes, well, people would have said it was far-fetched if, in 1976, you told them that the president would have the authority to order the assassination of an American citizen without a trial just over thirty years into the future. Probably in the future, footage from drones carrying out theses assassination will be shown on the news in the same way football scores are reported. Many Americans will cheer as another enemy of the state gets vaporized, as others see the end results of resistance to the government.

The message will not be lost on anyone.

Television news will certainly have a logo and theme song for each episode of footage from the drone strikes. By "theme song," I mean these certain little scary-sounding instrumental musical introductions that always precede certain topics on the news and are always the same musical intro when that certain topic is being aired. That way, people who are in another room know to come running back to the television when they hear that music, and then watch what the government wants them to see. Just like Pavlov's dogs, when Pavlov rang the bell.

What, you thought that the news was some independent watchdog keeping the government honest and holding them accountable? Hey, the Watergate era is over. If someone tried to publish the equivalent of the Pentagon Papers today, he'd go to jail for life—as has already happened when an insider made certain deeply disturbing facts about the Iraq War public.

News agencies on television are only concerned with ratings. Because with higher ratings go higher profits from being able to command higher prices on advertising. Now, if there's a war in progress, in order to film that war, you need to be embedded with the U.S. Military forces fighting that war. Embedded means you are attached to a military unit. No one is allowed into the combat zone otherwise. This also means that you hand over your footage and story to U.S. military censors who review it and tell you what can and cannot be shown or said. It has to be favorable the United States' "mission." There will not be another Walter Cronkite standing there telling you an American war is unwinnable. Today's reporters will tell you war is being won as it being lost. Plus a human-interest story about one of the soldiers just to tug the heartstrings.

Now, as a huge news agency, can you afford to be locked out

of the entire region as your competitors are showing footage of American tanks blowing nests of guerillas into smithereens? Everyone will flip the channel to watch those tanks blowing people away. So you can't afford to have a reporter try to tell the truth.

A Walter Cronkite would be a liability in need of being fired, because if your reporter told a truth the military did not want told, he or she would be cast out of the region and not allowed to return. Even if your reporter could produce ten witnesses to prove the war could not be won and was, in fact, being lost, no one would tune in to watch that because the scene would be well outside the combat zone.

Meanwhile, your competitors show military-approved footage of American tanks reducing alleged terrorists to atoms and you're getting eaten alive in the ratings. Everyone tunes in to your competitors. As a result, sooner or later, your sponsors abandon ship and abandon you. Not to mention they won't want to be associated with a news agency quietly labeled as "unpatriotic" because they actually told the truth if the military tells them not to. They are there to make money, not to tell the truth or even to report facts.

News is just another form of television entertainment, except it's loosely based on current events. Do people expect the government to tell the truth? If the news won't report the truth even when it knows the truth, why should the government tell the truth? Reporters in the Iraq War could see it was a quagmire. But they weren't about to end their careers by going public with that. To expect the government, and especially the military of the government, to tell the truth in an atmosphere such as this boggles the mind. People might as well believe in the Easter Bunny while they're at it.

Now, the American people themselves are also to blame for this. The TV doesn't turn itself on and change channels all by itself. The American people choose to watch news that tells lies because it has the most exciting image to be entertained by. Never mind that, watching that footage of a U.S. air strike, you weren't told they made a mistake and it killed twenty innocent women and children at a day-care center. The military edited out that part of the story. Generally, anything critical of the military comes from foreign news agencies the military had no control over. So U.S. news agencies picked up the story to at least look a little bit impartial. But overall, the American people choose to watch what the government decides they should see.

Many Americans can't even find on a map places the Pentagon is in the news gloating about having bombed. But Americans will swear up and down it was justified because the Pentagon told them so. In other words, the television told them and so this is the "truth." Yet, the American people would resent the insinuation that they're being led around by the nose though the television by the government.

I'm going to go way out on a limb here, but bear with me. A cable television network shows a program about evil and murderous government regimes. Each show is awash with violence and bloodshed. Yet this soars to the top in the ratings. What message, therefore, does this send our government? That we find such actions by government entertaining, provided it happens to someone else. Americans enjoy watching television shows that tacitly—and sometime obviously—approve of government corruption, lying, theft, murder, adultery, extortion, and bribery.

Yet, you don't want your government to do these things and don't expect the government to be influenced by these impacts upon our culture? The fact that television impacts culture is rather obvious. Children are influenced by television and act out things they see on it. When our culture is so obsessed with violence and nearly every television station carries one violent program or another, how can this not affect the thinking of the government? They rightly conclude the American people will accept violence as a solution to problems. Thus, how is it a mystery to anyone the government has gotten more warlike the more violent those television shows have gotten?

These things are all linked.

When violence becomes acceptable within a culture, violence will be practiced by it. Especially by a government with vast military resources it can use without any consequences whatsoever to itself. Why then is it a wonder to people that we're involved in one or more wars at any given time? Television ratings say you approve of violence. Television ratings say you accept violence as a solution to problems. People that don't accept violence generally have no desire to watch acts of violence on a daily basis and call it "entertainment."

In 2015, the United States nearly stumbled into a war with Russia over Ukraine.

Here were American Senators demanding America "stand up to the Russians." They didn't bother telling the American people that "standing up to the Russians" could escalate into a thermonuclear war that would virtually wipe out the entire human race. Over Ukraine, which is in Russia's backyard.

Imagine Russia telling the United States what it could or could not do in regards to Mexico. Not that the United States has any business telling any nation what to do in the first place. Who appointed us as the chaperone for every nation on Earth? Yet here were these Senators on television demanding that we pretty much start a war with Russia. Many Americans fell for it and started demanding a war also. For what?! Again, it's what the TV told them. None of them bothered looking into the facts to see how many nuclear weapons the Russians have.

No, Senators on TV told them we were being humiliated by the Russians and that's all they needed to hear. Amazingly, Americans still don't understand how these senseless wars get started. When ratings go up every time Senator Nutso screams for war with Russia, the network will be sure to show footage every time he says it, even if at a Rotary club luncheon in some tiny town in Utah.

It'll get top billing and so it'll look like war with Russian is of the utmost importance. The Senator will see he gets airtime every time he calls out for war, so he'll make sure to keep saying it, over and over. That we avoided a war with Russia was nothing short of a miracle.

Americans can't bring themselves to see the elephant in the room: television has become dangerous to our culture and political process. Television depicts what I call a "false democracy." It depicts what it says is a majority opinion when, in reality, it probably isn't. But all that television needs to do is say that it is and many people will believe it to be so without questioning it or investigating it for themselves. Television will show one Senator saying something most people don't agree with, but because he's on TV saying it, many people will come to think there's some kind of majority behind the opinion.

If he says it often enough, it'll pick up steam and followers.

No one will realize it began with him. Does anyone realize that disaster in Syria began to spiral out of control due to a small handful of people in the United States Government? They kept saying on television, over and over again, that Bashar al-Assad needs to step down in Syria. Soon, the American people began to accept that, and few were asking publicly why Assad needed to go. No one stood up and told these politicians to mind their own business. Here were anti-war Democrats, all lining up behind another covert U.S. war they'd have protested if it was a Republican war. Like they did when it was Reagan doing that in El Salvador and Nicaragua in the 1980s. But "their guy," Obama, told them on the TV that Assad needed to go, so they all tune in, ratings went up and Syria turned into a maelstrom of violence not seen for decades.

The Republicans, for the most part, spend their time whining about the "liberal news media" when television enters the discussion. As if every single network isn't broadcasting war footage the U.S. military censors have vetted and approved if it originated in an area under U.S. military authority. What "liberal news media?" Oh, yes, the big networks do run stories with an obvious liberal bias in things such as gun control and race relations. And partially so in regards to environmental issues either real or perceived.

However, we also have Fox News which has a conservative bias so overwhelming and immunized against facts contrary to its agenda, that it has garnered probably all Republican television news viewers. Therefore, how can these Republicans detect a true "liberal" bias in the other networks if they're not watching them? What the anti-Fox News Democrats and anti-liberal Republicans both fail to understand is that all of the networks overwhelmingly support the government in any military action in engages in. The actual bias that exists across the spectrum in television news is a pro-government bias that is, at times, discreet but always present nonetheless.

As I pointed out, American news crews are denied access to any area under the control of the U.S. military if they refuse to let the military dictate what can or cannot be shown or said. So you can't have that going on and claim there to be a "liberal" bias in the news. But you also cannot claim that Fox News alone is presenting a pro-war bias, either. They're all doing that. For ratings and, ergo, profits.

If television wasn't enough of a cultural wasteland, we now have computer games that kids, teens, and young adults waste several hours a day playing. How very coincidental that many of the most popular ones are "war games" that overtly glorify war and reduce the wholesale slaughter of human beings down to an entertaining game, fun to play.

I wouldn't be a bit surprised if a computer game in which the player was the commandant of a concentration camp becomes wildly popular. They could title the game *Call of Dachau* or something like that. There are computer games glorifying criminal activity and murder, so why not one glorifying genocide, too? This is what American culture calls "entertainment"—games in which the player can kill as many human beings as he or she wants to. These, as well as the overwhelming amount of violence on television and the movies, are no different than the gladiatorial games of the Roman Empire. The Roman State sponsored those to desensitize people to violence and, thus, ignore or support the wars of the Roman government.

I would say same thing is being accomplished in the United States with ultra-violent television shows, movies, and computer games. Everyone is being desensitized to violence and all that needs to be said is this or that nation doesn't respect America, and Americans will scream for air strikes to "teach" them that respect. As if air strikes are just a computer game and those aren't real human beings, including women and children, being killed. When violence is being used as entertainment in popular culture, no one ought to be at all surprised that the government will use it as a solution whenever possible.

For that matter, if the government really did want to increase voter turnout, they should just make voting a computer game. They could call it *Call of Voting* or *Grand Theft Election*. If it had the best computer graphics, voter turnout would be the highest in American history.

The government has discussed internet voting, but that's going the wrong direction unless they made it into a social media venue like Facebook. You know, cast your vote, post a photo of your dog, leave a message on someone else's dog photo like, "OMG, he so cute, lol!" or maybe twitter out your vote. Hashtag, the lesser of two evils, lol!

This is where we are now, where people value endless and meaningless discussion over the direction their country is heading. I'm not saying voter turnout will change that. I'm saying here's the same social media the Arab Spring organizers used to rally themselves, and instead of using it to create an American Spring, Americans just use it to pass silly pet photos back and forth. These same people then wonder why the government amassed the power it has.

They say in an old adage, "Give a man a fish and he'll eat for a day. Give a man a fishing pole and he'll eat for a lifetime." Yes, well, give an American a fish and he'll post a photo of it on his Facebook page. Give an American a fishing pole, and he won't know how to use it.

Back in the 1960s and 1970s, music was a powerful voice against war and for social change. Music today can barely string sentences together in a coherent pattern recognizable as language. We've been basically hearing the same beat and melody structured around the same sexual moans and groans for the past twenty years. And this they call "popular" music. A person doesn't even have to have a good voice to "sing" these days. They sing through electronic voice-over machines the same as throat cancer survivors used.

Or in some cases, the "singer" just whines in a nasal drone that would irritate a person if that was someone talking to you on the phone. But in a "singer," oh, they'll pay damned near twenty bucks for that CD. All of this is in every musical genre from pop to country. Only Classical is immune so far, because they haven't figured out how to run an orchestra through a voice-over machine.

Most of these singers lead self-destructive lives, yet they have access to the politicians in Washington DC. They go up there and lobby for this or that cause, and Senators listen to these mumbling whiners as if it's another Gandhi speaking to them. Does anyone at all see what's wrong with this picture? Anyone? Some "singer" who lives in a twenty million-dollar home and with a thousand-dollar a day heroin habit is suddenly the most qualified person to address Congress about education? Or about the plight of the poor?

It truly is pathetic especially since the average American is locked out of true political voice. Look what happens if an average American wears an anti-war T-shirt and stands up where the Congress can see that person. That person gets arrested and dragged off to jail. But some "singer" who can count all the days she'd been sober over the past month on one hand can stand up in Congress and tell them how important health care is.

These are not people who sing anything resembling the old sixties protest "songs" and it'll sound like two people having sex in the bathroom.

The government loves these folks.

No more protest songs, and plenty of celebrities for their fund raisers. And Americans will quote what these celebrities say about this or that political issue as if that celebrity is a political expert and not some ex-stripper with a recording contract.

As I said, why are Americans mystified about why the government is the way it is?

How could it be anything else?

We have a celebrity Government now…and that bring us to our next chapter.

CHAPTER FOUR—CELEBRITY GOVERNMENT

THE ONE, SINGLE, watershed event that birthed the Celebrity Government was when Marilyn Monroe sang "Happy Birthday" to President John F. Kennedy in 1962. The country should have been ashamed at that spectacle. Or at the least embarrassed by it.

But, instead, Americans thought it was cute. Sexy, erotic, and cute, the idea that the President could be "sexy" is in no small part what led to the election of Bill Clinton and Barrack Obama as President for two terms. Both of those men were directly compared to John F. Kennedy.

The "Happy Birthday" episode showed America at that time that JFK was so handsome and sexy that one of the sexiest women in America, a stunning actress, could desire him. That resonated into the future. Bill Clinton played footsie with Monica Lewinsky in the White House. Again, portraying the president as "sexy" is bound to have consequences. At a Hollywood fundraiser, actress Gwyneth Paltrow gushed about how handsome President Barrack Obama is. So it is that the President of the United States assumes celebrity status. Therefore, celebrities have the ear of the president, and all the other politicians as well.

When it comes to celebrity Government, the Democratic Party is the worst offender. When a Democrat is president, the

White House becomes Hollywood East. So many celebrities are coming and going out of there, you'd swear you're filming a movie.

Hollywood holds huge fundraisers for various Democratic Party candidates. By the way, those fundraisers are around ten grand a plate for dinner, but these people claim the Democratic Party to be the party of the working class. Poor people probably spend less than ten grand a year on food for their entire household. But here's liberal celebrities paying ten grand a pop for supper and saying "I feel your pain" to the poor. And there sit the Democratic Party candidates, smiling and grinning ear to ear like they're not all supreme hypocrites. Is it any wonder the working class has so many Republican voters? Not that they're better, but at least they're not acting in a movie they call the presidency. Well except Ronald Reagan, but we'll get to him later.

The first campaign of Bill Clinton in the 1992 presidential election is where Celebrity Government really took off. Here was this young sexy candidate who was constantly being compared to JFK. He even went on MTV! And MTV had the whole "Rock the Vote" shtick.

Clinton really went over the top when he appeared on television wearing sunglasses and playing the saxophone. I don't think JFK could've won the race against Clinton at that point. Now, it wasn't sex appeal and looks alone that won the presidency for Bill Clinton. The end of the Cold War on Papa Bush's watch was one among many factors that led to a massive recession and unemployment. We went to war against Iraq, the government telling us Saddam Hussein was another Hitler. Yet, they left Saddam in power, so the "victory" of the Gulf was bittersweet, at best. People were disillusioned and here came this energetic, young Bill Clinton. Of course he got elected.

This very same scenario led to the election of Barrack Obama in 2008—the parallels are strikingly similar. America was in a huge recession and disillusioned by a second war with Iraq still in progress. There was, again, massive unemployment. Here again came a young, energetic candidate, Barack Obama. Both men played a role in the American psyche—the role of the "good guy in the white hat" in the Westerns that occupied the "Golden Era" of television. The era when everything was good and prosperity was abundant, so people believed. The "good guy" came just in the nick of time to save everyone in the western TV shows. But it was not Bill Clinton and Barack Obama that pioneered that role. They were merely stepping into the cowboy boots of their predecessor who began all that. That was Ronald Reagan.

Ronald Reagan did not need to become president in order to be a celebrity. He already was one. He was an actor that had appeared in Westerns as a "good guy." The presidential election of 1980 was a time ripe for a "good guy," especially a tough-talking cowboy which is the persona Reagan used. The 1979 Iranian Hostage Crisis resulted from the take-over of the United States embassy in Tehran. The diplomatic personnel of the embassy were held hostage for 444 days.

Jimmy Carter was president and this was one more crisis he couldn't afford on top of the 1978-1979 Energy Crisis that had already infuriated Americans against him. In the Energy Crisis, lines at gas station stretched for several blocks, when the stations actually had gas. Carter tried freeing the hostages in a failed rescue mission that resulted in the deaths and serious injuries of several U.S. Military service members. It failed due to infighting between branches of the military as well as their own incompetence. But it was widely believed to have been as a result of military weakness and loss of strength in the aftermath of the Vietnam War. And that is exactly how Reagan sold his vision.

Reagan campaigned as the stereotypical Western cowboy who could stand up not only against Iran, but the Soviets, too. The Soviets had invaded Afghanistan in 1979 and President Carter's response to that was to boycott the Olympics. Americans belittled him for that, but what did they expect him to do? Get into a war with the Soviets over Afghanistan? A war that would certainly escalate into a nuclear war, because this was the beginning of another terrifying decade of the Cold War. But Reagan was basically saying the American military had deteriorated to the point it no longer deterred the Soviets from doing things like invading Afghanistan. Or deterred Iranian radicals from sacking a U.S. embassy and keeping everyone there as hostages. So here came Reagan playing this role as the "good guy" to save everyone. Remember, this was a frightening time for Americans. Iran was still holding the American hostages. There was an Energy Crisis and no one could count on being able to fuel their cars.

There were economic problems as a result of that. The Soviet military was on the move and several experts were claiming the Soviets had us outgunned. Of course Reagan got elected. This was the role he was born for.

Here came Reagan as the new sheriff in town to deal with the bad guys, those being the Iranians, the Soviets, and liberal economic policies. When the hostages in Tehran were released the very day Reagan came to power, everyone saw that Reagan intimidated the bad guys. At least, that's what they wanted to believe. Because the truth was, a deal had been made with Iran that basically gave Iran gold bars in exchange for the hostages. Plus, a treaty was made whereby the United States promised not to attack Iran into the future. But it was claimed, wrongly, that Iran was afraid of Reagan so they released the hostage. However, the Soviets did not pull out of Afghanistan, so that left Reagan with them to deal with.

Reagan increased military spending while cutting taxes. Obviously, there is a serious problem with that. That's one other thing that created the economic problems that plagued the George H.W. Bush Administration after Reagan's two terms. The bills finally came due, basically. In fact, serious economic problems continued from the Carter era well into Reagan's presidency. But because Reagan increased defense spending, some economic prosperity was created. Which is why, when the Cold War ended on Papa Bush's watch, the economy tanked in part due to that.

With the Soviets gone, there was no need to keep building strategic weapons systems.

Reagan, however, went down in history as a "great American president" despite the fact he'd won no major war as had FDR or defused a serious crisis as had JFK. Reagan didn't end the Iranian Crisis and his economic policies have borne no long-term fruits going into the future even two years after he left office. That Reagan was a great president is pure Hollywood. But what he did do was create the role of the "good guy" coming to save America from disaster that both Bill Clinton and Barrack Obama were able to step into. Republicans now might whine about all the "Hollywood celebrity liberals" rubbing elbows with the president, but it was one of their own that pretty much made it possible by helping to craft the image of the president as a movie character.

All of these things together led up to the Celebrity Government. Both Republicans and Democrats are responsible for this. The American people themselves can shoulder the biggest burden of responsibility because it is they who have this bizarre fascination with celebrities. Entire magazines are dedicated to nothing but following what celebrities do and say. In the year 2006, we're in the middle of two wars, yet the antics of celebrities would garner headlines over news from those wars.

You could stand in a supermarket checkout line where the magazines are and, in 2006 never realize we're in two wars because all those magazines are talking about are celebrities. A helicopter could get shot down in Afghanistan and twenty American solders die. It'd be in the news a day or two, maybe even garner a headline. But next week, it'd be forgotten. Let a celebrity die, however, and that'd be in the news and garnering headlines for a month or more. Plus live television footage of the funeral and endless television tributes.

Americans, as I have said, will quote celebrities on political topics. Excuse me, but these clowns are not elected officials, so why is it so damned important what they say or think? Americans set such great store on celebrities going up to address the

Congress as if these people are saints that live on the streets ministering to the homeless.

We created a situation where celebrities have unlimited access to elected officials but the average American has little or none. So what Americans now do is try to get the attention of a celebrity to take up a cause and carry it up to the politicians in Washington. This is truly a disgrace, because these are not elected officials, but they're being unofficially recognized as representatives of Americans who would not otherwise be given attention by the government. If Charles Dickens were alive today, he'd surely write a novel about it. But no one would read it and unless it became a movie, no one would be aware of it. Some today don't even know who Charles Dickens was.

When you have celebrities acting like unofficial politicians, we have a serious problem in our government. These people were not elected, nor do they represent even a sizeable segment of the American population. But they can carry issues up to the politicians and have those issues heard when those issues might not even be important to the American people. As a result, the issues Americans do want heard take a backseat to whatever the celebrities are up there broadcasting. Therefore, laws might get passed that were not even necessary simply because celebrities popularized the issue and carried it up to Washington.

There needs to be clear and un-crossable boundaries between Hollywood and Washington. We are rapidly creating a class of nobility not unlike that of 1700s era monarchies. These are people that have access to government because of who they are, not what they know or who they were elected to represent. The fascination with celebrities itself has a dangerous facet when Americans become mesmerized by a celebrity persona in the government or one running for office. The case in point there is Sarah Palin.

Sarah Palin was not selected to be John McCain's running mate in 2008 because she had brains. She was selected because the Republican Party knew their voters would see her as "hot." We could go into detail about that, but I think everyone can see what the Republicans were doing. They needed a woman as some minority street cred for their campaign.

After all, Hillary Clinton almost got the nomination and, had Obama not been running, she'd have gotten it. But the Republicans figured, hey, if we're going to put a woman in this race, let's find an attractive one. The sexist pigs in the party will eat that up. It became obvious that Sarah Palin was being coached in everything she said. And if she wasn't coached on something and had to speak from her own store of wisdom, it became apparent that her store had long been out of business.

Yet, the Republicans thought her to be perfect as second-in-command of the largest nuclear weapons arsenal on the planet. They, too, had bought into the cult of celebrity-government of the young and attractive (and sexy, to their eyes) candidate. McCain lost the election to someone who at least had some modicum of intelligence to go along with being young and attractive.

Yet, Sarah Palin continues to enjoy celebrity status and is regularly consulted in political matters. Now, as then, she has little to say of worth, but her status as a celebrity guarantees her a voice. That Democrats can be astounded by the Republicans selecting Sarah Palin as a vice presidential candidate while turning a blind eye to their own celebrity fascination is truly comical. Not one of them is innocent in that.

And, if the Republicans think their fascination with celebrity candidates ended with Sara Palin, they'd better remember Donald Trump. If you have not, by now, sensed the inherent dangers of celebrity government, then ask yourselves the following questions.

Should a person deserve greater access to a voice in government because he acted in a popular movie?

Should a pop singer testify as to the education your child receives?

Should unqualified people be entrusted with nuclear

weapons because they're attractive?

Should the money to fund candidates come from the entertainment industry?

What happens if a celebrity becomes president, has an image to uphold and refuses to negotiate with Russia to defuse a confrontation with them?

Do the values of Hollywood that they have off-screen truly reflect the values of the American people? And if not, why is it permissible for Hollywood to act as the de facto elected representative of the American people when they are not?

Are these presidents truly trying to serve the American people or are they seeking fame?

Are people becoming Senator and Congress members to serve their constituents, or are they auditioning for the role of president?

The access and influence of celebrities in the government needs to be cut off. Government should not do things because some celebrity endorses it or it appears to be something popular that would afford that politician some celebrity status of his or her own. Things should be done because they are right and that is not always what is the most popular. As I have said, a pure democracy can, and often is, a tyranny of the majority.

And celebrities, like television, present "false democracy" or what might appear to be a majority opinion when it isn't. Politicians court celebrities because they donate large sums of money to political campaigns. How is that different from a corporation doing that? Democrats will sit there and tut-tut a Republican candidate that took a million-dollar campaign contribution from a major corporation. But a Democrat could take a million-dollar campaign contribution from a well-known actress and they'll all applaud that actress' sense of "social justice." As if it's not the exact same political corruption the Republican opponent is engaging in. But the actress is a celebrity so that makes it okay in the eyes of the Democratic Party.

At the end of the day, people need to realize this is supposed to be a government, not a movie or a music video. This government starts wars that real people die in. They're not acting, they're actually dying.

We can't sit here and say that Wall Street funding campaigns are wrong, but Hollywood-funding elections is just fine. Both are equally bad for the same reasons. It's about some person's pet project being pushed forward in Washington because of who they are and how much money they donated to the campaign. All money and influence needs to be cut off from Washington be it a CEO, a singer, an actress, the owner of a major corporation, or the king of some Middle Eastern country. They are all the same thing—people that subscribe to the adage "It's not what you know, it's who you know."

That doesn't belong in our government. Or is that what we send men and women to die for in wars and military operation overseas? Because if it is, we need to be clear about whom they really are.

Our troops are not really fighting for our freedom—they're low paid mercenaries.

We'll discuss that in our next chapter.

CHAPTER FIVE—WAR

MY ANCESTORS HAD a proverb describing the process by which one gains the wisdom of being cautious:

He who has been burned by hot soup will blow on cold yogurt.

Unfortunately, the United States government does not appear to have heard this proverb. Or, if they have, they stubbornly refuse to practice it, getting burned by hot soup again and again.

What's more, not just burning their lips on it, but knocking the bowl of scalding soup right into their laps every time. But, clinging to their egos obstinately, they expect a more positive outcome each time. Generally, if a person does that, others will never serve soup if that person comes over for dinner. However, when the United States Government does that, people will bring the entire pot of boiling soup to the table and hand the ladle to the government to serve everyone. Thus, inviting disaster and painful burns for all seated who don't appear to be any wiser than the government.

How many wars, interventions, military operations and regime changes engineered by U.S. covert ops forces have we been through now? And how many of those were success stories, worth every American life lost in it? How many stable, violence-free governments were created in the Middle East by American military or covert operations since 2002?

Not one.

All of the so-called "success stories" fell into horror stories of violence not seen on such a scale for decades. But what's remarkable about it is the U.S. government expects a different outcome each time, even after getting burned on the previous catastrophe it created. These completely avoidable mistakes are unparalleled in the history of stupidity. And they might be hilarious if there weren't millions of people dying in or as a result of them.

Serious mistakes such as imagining it can win a guerilla war the French had just lost. Imagining it could create secular democracies in Islamic nations that had never, ever been secular democracies in their history. Imagining that trying to topple a leader who prevents sectarian violence in his country will not result in sectarian violence. The United States Government has burned itself on all of these hot bowls of soup, leaving the rest of the world and the American people to clean up the mess and pay for it.

To fully understand the dynamic in play, at least where the United States is concerned, we need to go back to World War One. To begin with, World War One was a fight between European colonial and imperial powers. This war did not concern the United States. A U.S. President was elected—promising to keep us out to that war. Yet, later on, we entered that war promising to "make the world safe for democracy." Actually, what it did was make the world safe for the rise of Adolf Hitler and the revolution that lead to the creation of the Soviet Union. These two events which came out of World War One, led to a chain of wars, including the Second World War, for the next ninety years.

By entering World War One, the United States tipped the scales and ensured victory for Britain and France. Germany's defeat led to the birth of the Nazi Party and, thus, World War Two. The Soviet juggernaut that came to be in order to fight Germany in World War Two then became our enemy in the Cold

War. The Cold War presented communism as the mortal enemy of the West, so the Korean War came to be. So did the Vietnam War, first for the French, then for the United States. And backing Islamic radicals fighting the Soviets in Afghanistan led to the rise of Islamic non-state armies capable of doing damage to the United States via terrorist attacks.

That is a highly summarized chain of events but it demonstrates that the United States is unable or unwilling to understand it is caught in a chain of wars all linked together. They all date back to World War One. Each war spawns the enemy for the next war, and each war insures the next one will happen.

The only way to break this chain is to stop the action causing links to be added. That is, the United States must stop getting involved in wars because they are literally perpetuating themselves. The wars in the Middle East are but the newest links in the chain and they will continue. The foolhardy policy of the United States to engage in "regime change" only accelerates this. In effect, it is pouring gasoline on to a bonfire.

The United States government founders in a miasma of ignorance, being coached by "experts" and "think tanks" that are book-smart but have no common sense whatsoever. Nor do they understand the very Buddhist concept of nothing originating of itself, for causes and conditions lead up to it. This thing occurs because that thing happened. That thing, in turn, happened because another thing preceded it. And all things are linked as such. The causes and conditions for the wars we see going on today lead back to World War One and are all linked to it. These events happening today are far beyond the ability of the United States Government to contain and control, change, prevent, or stop unless they do the one thing that can work.

Stop fighting.

These events are far beyond the ability of the government to fully understand. The government cannot and will not admit that what is in motion is far older than the politicians are. Therefore, they obstinately refuse to see the causes and conditions leading up to past and current wars.

The government cannot solve this perpetual chain of wars with war. War is what perpetuates it and sets the stage for the next one. Amazingly, the government prefers to remain ignorant and, clinging to their egos, cannot admit that the wars in the Middle East are but links in a chain that began with World War One.

One thing that happened after World War One was the victorious European powers gained control of the Middle East. It had been mostly under the control of the defeated Ottoman Empire, an ally of Germany in World War One. Britain and France then took a map of the Middle East and a pencil and literally drew the boarders of what are the Middle Eastern countries today.

They basically created these countries out of thin air with the intention of making it easy for Europe to control the region by fostering and encouraging sectarian differences. That is but one cause for the current violence. Again, World War One is the origin point. Had the U.S. not entered that war, it would not have been won by Britain and France. It would probably have ended as a cease-fire and the Middle East would have remained under the control of the Ottoman Empire, more than likely. The United States entering World War One was a colossal blunder that resulted in the United States entering the wars spawned by it ever since. To fully understand the nature of the mistake we need to discuss World War One briefly.

Many Americans labor under the illusion that our involvement in World War One was necessary. But ask them what the reasons were for that war, and they can't tell you.

They simply don't know.

The war was literally a hundred years ago. Some will think the German government of World War One was the same German government of World War Two and so that's how we got involved. In truth, there was no reason whatsoever for the United States to enter this war. This war was a fight between

European colonial empires mostly over territory and power. There was significant opposition to getting involved in this war. The anti-war movement in the United States was brutally suppressed by the government once the U.S. entered the war.

Now, again, the U.S. entering the war is what tipped the scales in favor of Britain and France. Everyone involved in the war had already collectively lost millions of men in futile human wave assaults against entrenched machine gun and artillery positions. And this was before America entered the war. So they were already running on fumes by the time we got there.

Had the U.S. not entered the war, a cease-fire would have become pretty much necessary once they lost enough fighting age men, which was about where they were when we got there. See, the thing is, had a cease-fire been signed, there would have been no humiliating Treaty of Versailles forced on the Germans. That single treaty alone is directly responsible for the rise of Adolf Hitler.

What's more, the winner of World War One forced Germany to pay for the war, which led to an economic depression in Germany. That alone led to the rise of the Nazi Party itself. Without World War One being a total victory for Britain and France thanks to U.S. involvement, World War Two would not have happened. Yes, no World War Two, no Holocaust, most likely no invention of nuclear weapons—or, at least, no actual use of them. The Manhattan Project that developed the atomic bomb was one of the most expensive projects in American history. They almost couldn't justify the cost even in the middle of World War Two. So how would they justify it to an America that hadn't even entered World War One, some twenty-odd years later? These things are all linked, and if we think they're not, we are condemned to repeating the same mistake endlessly.

As I said, Britain and France gained control of the Middle East and arranged the region so that they would keep them fighting one another and not Britain or France. This World War One legacy is still in play today and will be for quite some time going into the future. Modern "nation-building" efforts over there are doomed to fail, because these people are, quite frankly, sick and tired of being manipulated and lied to by the West. This area needs to be left alone and left to settle their own affairs.

World War One led up to the Russian Revolution and the creation of the Soviet Union. This might have happened whether the United States entered the war or not. However, the rise of the Soviet Union as a major superpower would not have happened if World War Two had not occurred. World War Two was the direct result of Germany's humiliation after losing World War One.

Again, that was only made possible by the United States entering the war and tilting the balances against Germany. It was because of World War Two that the Soviets became a superpower. It was because of World War Two that their military not only mushroomed in size, but became a highly proficient fighting force. Previous to World War Two, they couldn't win a war against Finland to the extent that they could capture Finland. But immediately after World War Two, the United States had a falling out with the Soviets and, within a year, they were the enemy.

The Cold War began under the premise that the Soviets represented communist tyranny and dictatorship, and were out to take over the world. The United States and Western Europe represented capitalism, democracy, and freedom. And allegedly wanted to spread those ideas. Therefore, competition between the United States and the Soviet Union led to an "arms race," each side arming itself to the teeth with vast arsenals of weapons. Each side possessed (and both Russia and the United States still have) enough nuclear weapons to destroy the planet.

The United States embarked on a policy of "containment," that is, to "contain" communism and keep it from expanding into other countries. That single reason, "containment," is the reason that the United States supported brutal dictators all over the world—provided they were anti-communist. That's why the

United States backed the Shah of Iran in a coup against the democratically elected government of Iran in 1953. That led up to the Iranian Revolution, the Shah fled, and then we had the 1979 Iranian Hostage Crisis. Be that as it may, the United States Government still cannot keep from burning itself with hot soup.

But it was this policy of "containing" the communist threat that led to the Korean War and the Vietnam War. There was no victory in the Korean War since a cease-fire was signed. In other words, 34,000 American dead for a cease-fire. So there's that. Then, not long after that, the French took a drubbing in Vietnam to the tune of 75,581 casualties KIA. The United States said, yeah, well that's the French. They couldn't build the Panama Canal but we did. So therefore, we can win this war in Vietnam that they lost.

American Exceptionalism and all that jazz.

One would think that after the Korean War the United States would have looked at another "police action" type of war with major reluctance. After all, both of these wars happened to be civil wars. In the world of fighting wars, civil wars are the worst to try and pick a side in. These are not people united fighting a foreign aggressor. These are the same people fighting amongst themselves. That such wars are often unwinnable is obvious.

The United States government thinks because it won the American Civil War, it can win civil wars it picks a side in elsewhere. It forgets our Civil War cost as high as 750,000 dead. And we accomplished that with single shot, muzzle-loading muskets and cannon. In a modern civil war, the casualties can go up to 250,000 dead a year. The Vietnam War cost the lives of three million Vietnamese. In the end, The United States couldn't achieve victory in the Vietnam War. Thus, in 1973, it signed another cease-fire as it did in Korea. This cease-fire cost the lives of 58,307 American to achieve.

But in 1975, Saigon and all of South Vietnam fell to communist North Vietnam. The impact on the United States was zero. Communism did not take over all of Asia as the U.S. government predicted would happen if the communists won, which they did in 1975. We'll come back to this later.

The United States did suffer a big defeat in Vietnam in that it could no longer project military power overseas without public outcry. Everyone knew someone who'd lost a son in Vietnam, or they themselves had lost a son, or a husband, a father, brother or friend. Massive anti-war protests and riots helped end the war. So the U.S. government was not able to involve itself in any wars from about 1975 until 1983 when Reagan invaded Grenada, a tiny Caribbean nation.

That was the "dabbling the toes in the water" that got America over the fear of another Vietnam. Because they had victory in Grenada, which is a foregone conclusion if you look at the size of the force that the U. S. Military was fighting there. That, though, was the watershed event that convinced the American people they could accept another war if need be. Americans had already been calling for war with Iran in 1979, but there were still a lot of people very skittish about another war considering what happened in Vietnam. Grenada got America over that. The government actually won a war, finally, even though calling it a "war" is really stretching it. We'll come back to the later, also.

The Soviets invaded Afghanistan in 1979. In the 1980s, the CIA was covertly arming and funding Islamic fundamentalists over there called the Mujahedeen. Some of these guys became Al-Qaeda. Now, the United States government started backing Islamic fundamentalists all over the Middle East during this time because they were strongly anti-communist. Most of the semi-secular countries in the Middle East, such as Syria, were in the Soviet sphere of influence.

Therefore, the United States opposed the actual secular governments in the Middle East that it later wanted to create. The United States supported the Islamic theocratic regimes that later sponsored Muslim fundamentalist terrorism.

Why?

To "contain" communism. The secular regimes of the Middle East were mostly friends of the Soviets. And enemies of Israel, by the way. The fundamentalist Islamic regimes were friends of the United States. They didn't like Israel, either, but the United States bought them off to leave Israel alone.

Now, all of this is going on because of the competition between the Soviet Union and the United States to garner countries into their folds. But it was the United States that warmed up to the fundamentalist Muslims that have plagued the United States government since the 1990s. They were all close friends of the United States government because they were so anti-communist.

In turn, the United States protected them from the Soviets. But when the Soviet Union collapsed in 1991 and the Cold War ended, the Islamic fundamentalists didn't need the United States government anymore. To be sure, they never liked the U.S. government at all. However, they needed American firepower to make sure they didn't end up like the Afghans. With the Soviet Union gone, though, at last, the American infidels could be gotten rid of. Muslim fundamentalists had been looking forward to that day for quite some time.

But, before too many plans could be made, Iraq invaded and seized Kuwait. Getting rid of the American infidels would need to wait until the American infidels got rid of semi-infidel Saddam. The United States couldn't sell this war as keeping communists out of our playground, as had been done with Grenada. And they didn't want to look like the hired guns of an Islamic king. So they had to go into the toy box and find the puppet, which hadn't been used since 1945: Adolf Hitler.

The United States government needed to protect its oil supply. It feared another Vietnam-esque "domino theory" (the "domino theory" was that if communists took over Vietnam, all Asian countries would then fall in a chain to communism like dominos stacked on a table) with Iraq then taking Saudi Arabia. In fact, Iraq had no intention of taking Saudi Arabia. That didn't stop the United States government from peeing down their leg, though, in fear of it.

The U.S. government is, rather like Stalin was, always far more paranoid of scenarios unlikely to happen in reality. However, it's also highly skilled in manipulating the American people and convincing other countries that its paranoia is based upon actual threats. For the Gulf War, the government could not just go tell the American people they need to get into a major war so Saudi fat cats aren't freaking out.

Therefore, they hired a high-profile American marketing agency to send out press releases telling lurid tales of Iraqi "atrocities" in Kuwait. Like Iraqi soldiers throwing babies out of incubators in Kuwaiti hospitals, for example. This type of "atrocity" propaganda worked for the United States government to get us into World War One, when it was said German soldiers where bayoneting Belgian babies. Well over a decade later, it was revealed the Iraqi "atrocities" in Kuwait never happened.

The United States also said that Saddam Hussein was another Hitler. That's what started the "Hitler-of-the-Month Club" that the U.S. government has used ever since to discredit world leaders it dislikes and wants gone. Recently, Russian president Vladimir Putin and Syrian leader Bashar al-Assad have each won a Golden Hitler at the United States Hitler-of-the-Month Awards. Saddam Hussein went on to win his Golden Hitler Award in 2003, so far the only world leader to win the award twice.

The fundamentalist Muslims in the region did want Saddam out of Kuwait. They half-way believed the United States and feared that he might go on to take Saudi Arabia. But it wasn't the oil they cared about, like the United States. It was about who controlled Mecca, the seat of the Islamic faith. This is the Islamic Holy Land and it was feared by the fundamentalists that if Saddam got a hold of it he'd place it off limits to them.

This is very important to understand.

Mecca is far beyond what the concept of Jerusalem is to

Christian and Jew. Making the Hajj, the pilgrimage to Mecca, is one of the Five Pillars of Islam. It's a key precept of the faith and Muslims are supposed to make a pilgrimage there if able to do so. Just as important as keeping Saddam out is keeping American infidels out of Saudi Arabia altogether. America acts like it doesn't understand this, yet claims that the Crusades are taught in high school history class.

The motivation behind the Crusades was Christian Europe wanted to evict the Muslims from Jerusalem and the Holy Land. This went on for 500 years! Yet, the same motivation by Muslims to keep non-Muslims out of their Holy Land goes misunderstood by the United States that descends from Christian European ancestors in large part. America thinks if it doesn't do something anymore no one else does, either. The Crusades happened before America was discovered, of course, but if the United States doesn't understand the concept of religious fundamentalism, it hasn't ever understood its own politics since 1980.

The "Holy Land" concept is one key reason the United States government supports Israel, but won't admit it. Fundamentalist Christians within the government lobby for Israel. So having said that, when Mecca is of vital importance to all Muslims and especially so to hardliners, it's easy to see why they were caught between a rock and a hard place over Kuwait. They couldn't accept Saddam threatening Saudi Arabia. But they also hated the idea of American troops in Saudi Arabia by the tens of thousands, which is what it'd take to defend Saudi Arabia and evict Saddam from Kuwait.

In the end, the wanted the United States to get rid of Saddam—then go home. What they failed to understand is that the United States never does that, not unless it's evacuating its embassy by helicopter as in Saigon in 1975. Otherwise, where the U.S. puts its foot, it stands there for good. That right there was one of the most serious mistakes the United States government ever made. That led right up to 9/11. But, again, let's not get ahead of ourselves.

Iraq was a client state of the Soviet Union. As I said, the Soviets tended to support the more secular and socialistic régimes in the Middle East. Therefore, when Iraq invaded Kuwait in 1990, Muslim fundamentalists were not at all thrilled by Saddam being just a hop, skip, and a road march away from Saudi Arabia. Because Saudi Arabia is where Mecca is, as I pointed out.

Muslim fundamentalists had just come home from a ten year war against the Soviets in Afghanistan, so they weren't happy about a Soviet client state threatening Mecca. However, that doesn't mean all of them agreed with the Saudi government pleading for American troops to sit there on Muslim holy ground and defend it. But there was nowhere else the American armored divisions necessary to defend Saudi Arabia and push Saddam out of Kuwait could go.

Now, a certain Saudi named Osama bin Laden told the Saudi government he and the men of his fledgling Al-Qaeda guerilla army could push the Iraqis out and there was no need to bring in the infidel Americans. The Saudi Government wasn't buying this. They didn't have the time or patience for an Afghan-Soviet War on their border and a ten-year wait for the Iraqis to depart. The Americans were willing to fight the Iraqis and the Saudi government surely saw it to be the most rapid and cost-effective solution. Because now, not just the United States, but an international coalition was coming together against Iraq. To say Osama bin Laden was disappointed by this would be a huge understatement.

To fully understand the factors in play, we need to step back a little to the Afghan-Soviet war that went on from the time the Soviets invaded Afghanistan in 1979 to the time they withdrew in 1989. Now, during the Vietnam War, the United States military was plagued by the problem that the North Vietnamese military was supplied with weapons by the Soviet Union, among others. There was nothing that could be done about it and they never forgot about it.

So, resentment simmered over that and revenge was hoped

for in a proxy war. That opportunity manifested with the Afghan-Soviet war and the perfect president who'd sign off on it came in 1980 with Reagan. Covert CIA operators began funding, training, and arming the guerillas, called Mujahedeen. But they never really vetted these people. All they cared about or knew was: here was the long-awaited chance to get some payback on the Soviets for what they did to us in Vietnam.

In fact, it was stated out loud that the intention was to turn Afghanistan into the Soviet's Vietnam War. However there's a problem with that. The North Vietnamese were a stridently secular communist government. The Mujahedeen were deeply-religious (and rabidly fundamentalist) tribal groups with whom a blood feud or clan war could be carried on for generations. The United States government failed to notice the difference. America had armed guerillas before, some that even became terrorists such as the Nicaraguan Contras in the 1980s. But with the Mujahedeen, they had made a serious mistake that would carry serious consequences all the way from the early 1980s into today. The Contras are now long gone. The terrorist groups the United States initially supported in Afghanistan are still with us, and thriving, today.

During the Afghan-Soviet war, there arose a Mujahedeen cell called Maktab al-Khidamat, or MAK. They set up shop in 1984 and in 1986 were recruiting fighters from a mosque in Brooklyn. All of this with U.S. Government approval and funding. The U.S. government ponied up around $600 million dollars, perhaps more, to fund MAK and other groups like it. In 1988, MAK re-organized as a group called Al-Qaeda and a charismatic Saudi leader of it, Osama bin Laden, emerged. The Soviets pulled out of Afghanistan in 1989 and, thus, Al-Qaeda lost its original reason to exist. Had the Gulf War never happened, Al-Qaeda might have faded away in time. Because by 1990, as we have seen and know, Iraq invaded Kuwait.

Getting back to the war-cheering antics of the United States government, they needed to make a case to the American people as to why this was even any of our business at all. The American people were looking forward to peace after the Cold War was obviously drawing to an end. The problem with Kuwait was there was a mechanized army occupying it. The government would not be able to sell a police action style war like Vietnam in this case. But the other thing the government could not afford was to wait so long that the emerging "domino theory" (that Iraq would take Saudi Arabia next) would be proven false. Therefore, the government used a lesson it had learned during the invasion of Grenada to sell the Gulf War.

The way that Reagan explained the Grenada invasion to the American people was that Cuban military forces there were threatening American students in the tiny nation. Reagan basically said he acted to stop another Iranian Hostage Crisis type of situation from happening. Since the Iranian Hostage Crisis was still fresh in the minds of Americans, not to mention still humiliating, this gambit worked so well, the government had learned the best doctrine it ever came up with to justify actually starting a war. Or invading a country that had not actually attacked the United States. And that is the doctrine of pre-emption, or, pre-emptive strikes.

Contrary to popular belief, President George W. Bush did not invent the doctrine of pre-emption. President Ronald Reagan did, and he also first used the doctrine in order to justify the invasion of Grenada.

Even better, Grenada also demonstrated that as long as the government said it acted in order to avoid an even greater tragedy, the American people would accept military action. But would they accept a war? Yes, if it was said that it needed to act to pre-empt the emergence of another Hitler and, thus, prevent an even bigger tragedy. Therefore, Saddam Hussein was cast in the role of Adolf Hitler. And to "prove" this, forged "intelligence reports" and bogus "eyewitness accounts" that originated in American public relations firms and marketing agencies were palmed off to the press as originating in Kuwait. This provided the "atrocities" that Nazi Germany was known for and, ergo, gave credibility to the United States government's claim that Saddam was another Adolf Hitler. And unless he was stopped now, he'd go on to take Saudi Arabia and all the other Arab Gulf states in one gigantic Jihad al-Blitzkrieg.

Easily manipulated, the American people fell for the scam hook, line and sinker. To sell even better, an international coalition had been formed first, so the American people wouldn't think we were going it alone, as they wrongly believed about the Vietnam War. Americans forget that Australia and South Vietnam were our allies in that war, and France had lost that war a decade before we jumped into it. Americans also forgot there was a United Nations international coalition along with the United States during the Korean War also, and that war ended in a cease-fire with North Korea intact. Eerily, the very same thing would happen in the Gulf War.

One other innovation of the United States government was to never call a war a "War" or even a police action, which is the phrase they used to refer to the Korean War and Vietnam War. From this time forward, the government would refer to its wars as "operations."

It's a nice piece of word-camouflage like calling genocide "ethnic cleansing" and so forth. Word camouflage works on toning down the alarm bells the mind hears when it hears the word "war." It thinks instead, "Ah, this is just a military operation. The kids will be home by Christmas!"

The United States government has far surpassed the linguistic acrobatics of Orwell's book *1984* and created its very own language. Therefore, having sold the American people on this war, oops, operation by use of preventing another Hitler, another world war, and stopping atrocities, Operation Desert Shield began in August of 1990. This was the mass movement of troops, armor, artillery, and air assets to Saudi Arabia. To say that Osama bin Laden was pissed would, again, be an understatement.

Here is where the rubber meets the road, so to speak. And

you'll need to pay close attention to what I'm saying. This is key to understanding the whole situation with Islamic terrorism that does not relate to the Israeli-Palestinian conflict, because a lot of it doesn't. Operation Desert Shield was the arming phase preparing for actual hostilities. This lasted from August 1990 to January 1991.

During this time, belligerent threats were made and Saddam was ordered to get out of Kuwait or face military action. Well, obviously, he can't back down and lose face when America is calling him out like that. He was probably rather shocked America even cared he'd taken Kuwait, because America had backed him in the previous Iran-Iraq War that dragged on for about eight years. He must have forgotten that President Ronald Reagan also sold weapons to Iran during that war. That's what the Iran-Contra Scandal was all about. Well, anyway, old Saddam was now stuck with the Kuwait hot potato and no good way to get it off his plate.

Saddam's major problem with retreating before American threats was his fear it would be read as weakness by opposition within Iraq and he'd be overthrown in a *coup d'état*. And he was not far wrong in thinking that. During Desert Shield, covert American entities spirited themselves into Iraq and encouraged Kurdish and Shiite rebel factions within the nation to rise up in rebellion against Saddam. They were told by these covert U.S. forces to wait until the actual war to push Saddam out of Kuwait began, and then rise up to fight him in his rear area, within his own country.

That way, with the American and international coalition hitting the Iraqi army in front, and Kurdish and Shiite rebels hitting them from behind, they would have victory. They never knew they were being used as pawns to cause Saddam to divert military resources from the war in order to restore order at home, thus ensuring a quicker victory for the United States. Not the Kurds or the Shiite. They never knew that the United States never planned on removing Saddam from power.

Meanwhile, Osama bin Laden had pretty much adopted a

"wait and see" attitude in regards to the hordes of infidel troops in his country. He couldn't say that out loud, but it is rather obvious. Otherwise the U.S. forces in Saudi Arabia during Desert Shield would have come under constant attacks and truck bombings. It wouldn't have been difficult to pull off.

In 1983, a U.S. Marines barracks, as part of a so-called "peace keeping mission" in Beirut, Lebanon, was hit by a massive truck bomb driven into it. This was supposedly the work of Hezbollah who wanted America out of the region. With 241 Marines killed in the bombing, President Reagan was badgered relentlessly until he pulled the Marines out of Lebanon. Had he not done so, the press alone would have eaten him alive and he'd have been hectored by them at every press conference.

As it was, American politicians were the ones that went after him and nipped at his ankles until he had no choice but to pull the Marines out. So, had Osama bin Laden wanted to attack Americans sooner rather than later, he'd have remembered the 1983 Marine barracks bombing that forced the U.S. evacuation of Lebanon. And he would have seized the opportunity to do hit and run attacks on arriving troops, supply convoys, and airports where the troops were arriving.

The arming phase of Desert Shield was hectic and frantic, trying to quickly get military forces in country and deployed before Saddam could make another move. An airlift like Desert Shield had not been done before, in the exact way that it was done. So you had the typical military ball-dropping and carelessness involved in moving large numbers of men as fast as possible. Had bin Laden wanted to force a Marine Barracks Bombing withdrawal, he had a target-rich environment to do it in. He could have truck-bombed the incoming troops repeatedly, had he wished to do so. But he didn't, and that is a crucial point to remember because he was in Saudi Arabia at the time.

I would say bin Laden probably wanted to wait and see what happened after America did what it said was its sole reason for being there. Would America then go home, happy that its oil supply was secure and having pocketed a much-needed military victory? No one doubted America and the international coalition would win. The only question that bothered everyone was, "How many lives would it cost?"

The war itself began in January 1991 and ended in February 1991. Of course, Iraq lost. There was no way they could've won, not in a conventional battle with the U.S. military. And, sure enough, when the war began, the Kurds and Shiite rose up and began plaguing Saddam inside Iraq itself. That such sectarian hostilities could even be fostered within Iraq is the result of borders drawn up by the winners of World War One. They basically used a pencil to create what we call "Iraq" today. They drew it up to encompass three distinct and rival groups. Groups that could be pitted against one another, as U.S. covert forces did in the Gulf war.

Again, World War One impacted that present. And Iraq itself had been armed by the Soviets whose military arms production capacity was created by World War Two. Which was, of course, spawned directly by World War One.

One thing the American people were certainly not expecting to come out of the glorious victories seen on television was yet another cease-fire. Americans were told this was another Hitler, so they were expecting the "Race to Berlin" not the Paris peace accords. If the Iraqi army was this easy to defeat, and with so few casualties so far, why not go ahead and take all of Iraq?

To the American people who could remember the 1978-1979 Energy Crisis and the 1973 Arab Oil embargo before that, it made sense to get hold of an oil supply it could truly control. Few remember this, but as troop convoys were moving to airports in the United States for Operation Desert Shield, American civilians lined the roads holding signs. The signs said: "Kick their ass and get the gas." Wow, the government could have sold this war to them saying it was about oil after all!

The war itself was not called the Gulf War then. That came much later. It was called Operation Desert Storm. It ended in a cease-fire that left Saddam in power and Iraq unoccupied. The American people were happy the war was over, but was this a victory or not? If this was another Hitler, why leave him in power? Did the allies leave Hitler in power in 1945?

The Kurds and Shiite in Iraq had an even bigger problem. They rose up being told that Iraq itself would be defeated with their help, and Saddam gotten rid of. That's what they wanted, so they could establish their own nation. Of course, that's not what the United States wanted. They had no idea they'd be betrayed by America who signed a cease-fire and left Saddam in power. Saddam then took his frustrations out on them and slaughtered them by the thousands. But they were useful to the United States during Desert Storm because Saddam had to divert military resources toward dealing with those uprisings.

So, here was a victory as quickly won as Grenada but with the cease-fire ending of the Vietnam War. At the time, no one understood what this decision was about or what it would mean for the future. Now, as Iraq lost the ground war, a mass evacuation and retreat of Iraqi military forces from Kuwait began. They were all crammed together in a crazy-quilt convoy of trucks, buses, tanks, armored personnel carriers and even cars. They were the proverbial sitting ducks for U.S. and coalition warplanes that had total air superiority. That convoy got caught flat-footed with their pants down, and were bombed repeatedly for quite some time. This event, and the place it happened, came to be called "The Highway of Death." Photos of the scene show carnage that many Americans were not accustomed to seeing so boldly displayed. Wrecked vehicles, charred bodies still seated at the steering wheels, and so on.

Americans were unaccustomed to seeing this so boldly photographed and published because, usually, the U.S. military would not permit those images to be shown to the American people. It would be seen as portraying the U.S. military in a very negative light. As having "shot those Iraqis in the back" while they were in full retreat. The scene would even have been cordoned off and guarded and no reporter allowed inside. Some anti-war folks think these reporters that took those photos somehow pulled one over on the government. They are only pulling one over on themselves. The government wanted the photos of "The Highway of Death" to be seen.

There is a very good reason the government wanted that to be seen. No, not to scare other countries. But, rather, to lend credibility to what it says were the reasons for the cease-fire.

It was said aloud that President George H.W. Bush was "sickened" by the gruesome photos of "The Highway of Death." And that there was little sense, from a "humanitarian" standpoint to continue doing such things to a defeated, retreating army. They were beaten fair and square and the United States is such a fair-player that it doesn't kick people when they're down. We're not that brutal.

So we had to sign a cease-fire, you see? America is merciful. Oh, really now? If Iraq was really beaten, they'd have signed an unconditional surrender. Yes, it smells fishy, doesn't it? About 1,000 Iraqi soldiers were killed at The Highway of Death and the United States was repulsed by that? How so? The United States incinerated tens of thousands of Vietnamese people with napalm during the Vietnam War just a couple decades prior to the Gulf War. And the men that ordered up and carried out those napalm strikes were now in the upper echelons of the military and the Pentagon.

When did the United States get such a weak stomach for incinerating human beings?

The United States reduced tens of thousands of human beings to ashes during the firebombing of Japanese cities in World War Two. The U.S. learned how to incinerate human beings quicker and efficiently by inventing the atomic bomb. So it used a nuclear weapon to vaporize tens of thousands of people at Hiroshima. Without bothering to wait for surrender, it dropped a second nuclear weapon on Nagasaki, and incinerated tens of thousands more. And both nuclear weapons dropped at a time the Japanese military was losing the war the same as Iraq was in 1991. But suddenly the Unites States gets a conscience? Come on! The United States government has even incinerated its own citizens when it wanted to, as it did during the Waco Siege in 1993, although it claims that was an accident.

I seriously doubt the United States government was somehow appalled at having incinerated a mere 1,000 or so Iraqi soldiers when it has killed hundreds of times over that number without blinking an eye.

What they needed was Kuwait back, yes.

But they needed Saddam still in power in Iraq to be the perpetual boogeyman for a while, scaring the Saudis. Leaving Saddam in power provided a pretext to keep a permanent force of American troops in Saudi Arabia and a pretext that the Saudis would pragmatically accept. Not to mention being able to keep troops in Kuwait, too. At the time, the U.S. was seeking a foothold in the region where it could park troops and play keep-away from the rest of the world. No more would another Soviet Union, if one arose, challenge America for the region.

The United State military is like that guy at a dinner party who just won't take the hint that the party's over and go home. Once the U.S. military gets into a country, it stays there. Osama bin Laden probably suspected that all along, but waited to see if it actually happened. Papa Bush had also rightly concluded that an occupation of Iraq would be very expensive and he knew bills were coming due for Reagan's military build-up. Worse, American occupation forces in Iraq would be targeted in a guerilla war sooner or later. Then he'd have another Vietnam War on his hands instead of what looked like a Grenada-style victory.

People said the cease-fire with Iraq in 1991 was "snatching defeat out of the jaws of victory." However, they are wrong. The government accomplished precisely what it set out to do and needed to do. First, to push Iraq out of Kuwait. And, second, establish a permanent military presence in the region. Keeping a garrison in Saudi Arabia and Kuwait would not incur any cost in military casualties to maintain, unlike an occupation of Iraq. Or so they incorrectly assumed.

At that point, Osama bin Laden knew damned well the United States couldn't be trusted. They just pulled one over on the Saudi King. They planned to keep troops in Saudi Arabia and Kuwait all along. And the plan never was to topple Saddam. The U.S. had just betrayed and backstabbed the Muslims in Iraq that had risen up having been promised a future without Saddam.

Worse still was the possibility the U.S. had not snookered the Saudi King, but that he was in on the scam too. American troops could save him a few bucks on his defense budget. Not to mention make him pretty much invulnerable to attack. Well, not long after the Gulf War ended and bin Laden noticed that not all of the U.S. military forces were packing to go home, he detected the swindle. So he started calling out publicly for these infidels to depart the holy land of his faith. For this, the Saudi government exiled him and he departed Saudi Arabia. But now it had become not personal, but jihad.

Americans wrongly think this all started on 9/11. What they fail to understand is that it was but one of a series of attacks by Al-Qaeda that dated back to 1992. Al-Qaeda had hit the World Trade Center once before in 1993.

Al-Qaeda did not just wake up one day and say, "We hate freedom, so let's attack America!" That's about as childish a reason for their attacks as can be imagined. Yet, this is what President George W. Bush told us was the reason.

In fact, these attacks had been going on for almost nine years. They were warnings specifically addressed to the United States to stay out of Saudi Arabia and to depart from the Middle Eastern and Muslim countries and, furthermore, to stop meddling in their governments. Those demands were written down and sent to the United States government in 1992. Of course, the government refused to recognize the fact that were these demands not met, attacks would begin. They knew that would happen, but they refused to understand the scope of them. They thought there'd probably be a few small-scale bombings as had happened before with various terrorist groups. What they truly failed to understand was that this was not the left-wing terrorists they were used to dealing with, like the Red Brigade and Bader-Meinhoff. Therefore, over the period from late 1992 to September 11, 2001 Al-Qaeda had been launching attacks specifically targeting the United States.

It all began with a December 1992 bombing in Yemen that tried targeting U.S. military forces on their way to another American adventure, this time in Somalia.

Another fiasco, by the way, the United States got into. In February 1993, a truck bomb in the parking garage below the world Trade Center in New York City exploded, killing a handful of people, but failing to topple the towers as hoped. In June 1996, the Khobar Towers in Saudi Arabia, which housed American military personnel stationed there, was targeted by a truck bomb. That killed 19 Americans and the U.S. tried pinning that bombing on Hezbollah. Probably to shield the Saudi government and conceal the fact that this was all about the Americans being in Saudi Arabia in the first place.

Hezbollah is an Iranian entity, so they made a convenient fall guy since they'd deny it and no one would believe them, taking the denial as proof they'd done it. No one asked what Hezbollah's motive was in such an attack. They didn't have a boxer in that fight. That was Al-Qaeda's deal. But the U.S. government couldn't admit that, because it'd tip off the American people they weren't wanted there. Plus, Americans would want our troops out of there if they knew that. But fingering Hezbollah made it look like they were targeted for being American, not targeted because they were in Saudi Arabia where Al-Qaeda said they didn't belong.

In August 1998, Al-Qaeda pulled off twin bombing attacks against the United States embassies in Tanzania and Kenya. About 224 people died in the bombings. Again, an unmistakable warning with the attacks growing in size, casualties, avidity, and target selection. The U.S. government sat there like Little Miss Muffett and acted like it didn't know what the reason were for these attacks or that it had been warned some six years prior this would happen.

The last warning before 9/11 came in October 2000 with the bombing of the USS Cole, a United States Navy vessel. Again, the United States acted like it didn't know the real reason these attacks were happening, nor ever would it admit it had been warned to depart the Middle East before they began. They weren't carrying out these attacks just to bloody the nose of the United States for kicks. There was a genuine motive and a mission behind these attacks

The United States government will defend itself by saying it can't back down to the demands of terrorists. But why does that give them the right to put all of our lives at risk over their ridiculous geo-political ambitions in the Middle East?

Did we all sign up to die in some shadow war to maintain a military base in Saudi Arabia? Were we asked if we minded risking our lives so the Saudi King could save a couple bucks on his defense budget? How does keeping a military base in Saudi Arabia benefit the American people? To defend the oil? Isn't that why we've got trillions of dollars invested in aircraft carrier battle groups? The cost to maintain a foothold in the Middle East and meddling in their internal affairs has been staggering in the number of lives and hundreds of billions of dollars spent. And it will continue costing that until the American people themselves stand up and demand that we depart from that region.

Finally, on September 11, 2001, Al-Qaeda successfully brought down the World Trade Center, having failed to do so in 1993. They also did major damage to the Pentagon. This avoidable tragedy was the beginning of a war that has been going on ever since. There is no method to obtain victory in this war, because there is no nation to sign a cease-fire, America's usually preferred route to ending quagmire wars. There truly isn't a nation that can be blamed by itself. So they can't very well expect surrender. The opponents are state-less, autonomous, mobile, and unwilling to surrender or give up.

Despite the crowing of George W. Bush in the aftermath of 9/11, there is no way to have victory in this war. Because getting into the war itself was the mistake. It's a cycle perpetuating itself all the way back to World War One. Each war has spawned the enemies of the next. Except the enemies now do not have a state. Some wish to create one. But the reality is, this "War on Terror" could actually continue for several decades. It's already entering the second half of its third decade, because it didn't start on 9/11, as I showed—it began in 1992 when Al-Qaeda effectively declared war on the United States if it refused to mind its own business.

Many of the causes and conditions for these wars date back to World War One, which began over a hundred years ago! Therefore, how can the United States possibly begin to bring all of this to an end, once and for all, when every war creates the next one? No one seems able to see we are stuck in a causal loop, if you will. There is no way by which another war can bring this to a final conclusion or stop the beginnings for the next war from manifesting in current wars. What we see going on today is not new. It has been going on for a hundred years. It can easily go on for another hundred years. If our natural resources last long enough.

The American people are often at a loss to understand the motivations of Islamic terrorism and what created it. In the case of Al-Qaeda, the motivations were quite clear and easily understood if one took the time to listen to what they were saying. Americans think, wrongly, the terrorists attack the West because they have deep seated anger towards the West. While that is partially true, it's because the West has meddled in the region for so long. The United States is the latest face of that, preceded by France and Britain who have long since abandoned ambitions in the region, for the most part, as far as a colonial presence.

The United States engages in imperialism and colonialism

over there and plays a childish make-believe of calling it something else. Like it calls wars "operations," it calls its colonialism and imperialism "defending American interests."

When someone calls out the United States on this and accuses it of imperialism, the United States fires back with allegations of "anti-Americanism" and "terrorism." One could very easily say British troops in the American Revolutionary War were "defending British interests" and be absolutely accurate in the assessment. Yet, the American colonial militias we glorify today are never called "insurgents" or even "terrorists" even though some certainly were.

If the shoe was magically on the other foot in 2003, and an Iraqi army invaded the United States and occupied it to liberate us from President Bush, it would not have taken but days for an American resistance movement to appear. They, too, would have used roadside bombs, truck bombs, snipers and hit-and-run motor attacks to inflict casualties on Iraqi forces. However, they would be seen as heroes by the American people—heroes defending their country from an invading army. Not "terrorists" or "insurgents." Not to mention the motivating factor of revenge-seeking for the actions of the Iraqi army. And we have an actual example of that, too.

Before 9/11, the deadliest terrorist attack on American soil was not pulled off by Al-Qaeda. It was perpetrated by an American who came from the "right wing militia" movement that began as a backlash against perceived tyrannical actions by President Bill Clinton. Basically, what began the whole thing was the federal assault of a compound being held by a religious group call the Branch Dravidians. This was in 1993, about the same time Al-Qaeda started kicking up their heels. During the 1993 Waco Standoff, federal forces ended up trying to breach the Dravidian compound using armored vehicles.

They ended up causing or starting a fire that left 76 dead, including many women and children. The right wing was furious and quickly accused the government of massacring the Davidians because they opposed the government. From this, and another botched Federal standoff at a place called Ruby Ridge, right-wing militants swelled in number.

In April of 1995, the Alfred P. Murray Federal Building in Oklahoma City, Oklahoma, was destroyed by a massive truck bomb parked in front of it. Of course, regardless of what the government says, it would have immediately suspected Al-Qaeda since they tried a truck bomb over at the World Trade Center just a couple years earlier. Except in this case, it proved to be a domestic terrorist who pulled the trigger on this one. Timothy McVeigh, ironically a Gulf War Veteran, carried out the attack as retaliation for the Waco Siege.

The Gulf War kept on generating echoes of affected players as it still does today. The Oklahoma City Bombing cost the lives of 168 Americans; it was carried out by an American, in retaliation for the American government killing Americans at Waco. Now if this happened, why is anyone at all unable to understand the desire for revenge against America for actions in the Middle East? It is perfectly clear. The government has been repeatedly warned to stay out of the region going on into three decades now. Yet it acts as if these are not legitimate warnings, nor should it acknowledge them. But it should, as I shall demonstrate next.

Since Waco and the Oklahoma City bombing, the federal government has been extremely careful any time it deals with the "right wing militias." It is terrified of another standoff falling into a shootout of another Waco. And then having another truck bomb delivered to a federal building somewhere in retaliation. The right-wing militias made a resurgence during the terms of President Obama, perhaps even gathering more followers and popular support.

There was another standoff against the federal government in Nevada in 2015 that the government went out of it way to resolve peacefully. At the time of writing this chapter, there is yet another in Oregon. Again, the government now handles these standoffs with the greatest care possible to avoid another Waco and another bombing in retaliation. Why, then is it unable to consider this same course of action in the Middle East, where a near parallel series of revenge bombings occurred against Americans? Obviously, it does all it can to avoid a domestic terrorist movement, but thinks it can deal with an Islamic one. Or, it thought it could. Then the 9/11 attacks dethroned the Oklahoma City bombing as the deadliest terrorist attack in American history on American soil.

The government seriously underestimated Al-Qaeda's ability to carry out such an attack. But what they actually failed to realize was that they were willing to go to these great lengths to accomplish their mission. The government failed to understand the importance that Mecca and Medina has to fundamentalist Muslims. This is their Holy Land and infidels do not belong there. Now, here's the West as a whole having fought the Crusades off and on for 500 years to kick the Muslims out of that Holy Land and Jerusalem specifically.

But the West cannot seem to grasp the fact those same taboos might still exist for others. Had the United States truly understood this, it would have never so much as left a footprint in Saudi Arabia. But thinking it could set up a military base there without any serious consequences later was pure foolishness. Not to mention other Middle Eastern entities who were looking to repay the United States for other insults and injuries.

However, the 9/11 attacks gave the government a textbook-perfect pretext for any war it wanted. The consent of the American people was pretty much a given, with the state of fear after 9/11. So there went the United States into Afghanistan, the very place the government had boasted it would turn into a "Vietnam War" for the Soviets just a little over twenty years earlier. Gee, did Afghanistan change that much in twenty years?

No, in fact, it has changed little in hundreds of years. But here goes America in there, thinking it can create a secular democracy out of thin air and call it the United States of Afghanistan or something else as equally stupid. And there the

United States still sits today, in the longest war in American history, without any solution or exits in sight. I'm surprised the government hasn't tried to get a cease-fire signed with the Taliban so it can hightail out of there and let the Afghan government fall to the Taliban two years later, as it did with South Vietnam.

Probably the Taliban, or its upper cadre, feel a cease-fire would be dishonorable or just figure they can outwait the United States. There are people in the U.S. military fighting in Afghanistan that were just school kids when it began. Another no-win quagmire but the U.S. government seems reluctant to let go of this one for some reason. Must be some type of valuable natural resource there we don't know about. No, it isn't opium. That's had easier elsewhere.

Where the U.S. government has truly won the "Golden Swamp Rat for Best Quagmire" is Iraq. That's the gift that has kept on giving. Now, it was easy for the government to make the case to go into Afghanistan. They said they needed to get bin Laden and Al-Qaeda and the Taliban, too. While we were there, people asked why they couldn't just send in a team in there to bump bin Laden off.

The government said they needed to make sure no more terrorists sprung up there. Right, like the scores that have sprung up with the U.S. military there, attacking them with seeming impunity even in their own headquarters. Bravo! Real good cultural assessment there, Bush Administration. They have to conduct staff meetings with hands on pistol grips in U.S. military operations centers in Afghanistan, if their Afghan "allies" are present.

Talk about a captive audience or a hostile crowd.

Again, the U.S. government's inability to understand revenge is spectacular, despite the fact their arming the Mujahedeen in Afghanistan was partially about revenge in and of itself. And there they are in Afghanistan, eyes wide open, not understanding that the Afghan colonel whose son you killed might want to take a shot at you. Brilliant.

Anyway, when the cease-fire was signed with Iraq in the Gulf War in 1991, there were elements in the Papa Bush administration that didn't like it. They were of the opinion that they should go ahead and take Iraq, since it was obvious U.S. troops would be in Baghdad in a week.

Those voices went on and on, throughout the 1990s particularly in a group known as "Project for a New American Century." They figured the Middle East would be better off with strip malls, amusement parks, big box stores, fast food chains, a huge American corporate structure sucking the lifeblood like a massive tick, oh, and democracy, too—voting for candidates the U.S. government selects, of course.

Opposition members could always have mysterious car accidents. Or exploding seat cushions, as the U.S. has also done.

But how can they sell this to the American people? "Oops. We guess we should have taken Iraq in 1991. We need to go back before they close." No one would have gone along with that. But after 9/11, now it was possible. Rather conveniently right after 9/11, mysterious anthrax-laced letters were being mailed to American politicians. Innocent people died as a result, both those who handled the letters, and those who died in the Iraq War those letters helped start.

Anthrax is not a bio-weapon easy to make.

It takes a government with the right technology. And, gosh, it just has to be Iraq, right? Of course! Never mind that the anthrax came from a U.S. Army bio-weapons facility, allegedly smuggled out past supposedly impregnable security measures and fail-safes by a top-level employee with a top security clearance. Who, by the way, very helpfully committed suicide before much could be learned. The anthrax "special delivery" in the mail gave the Bush Administration a much-needed boost in making the case to invade Iraq. The Bush Administration said Saddam not just tried to build, but actually had biological and chemical weapons and was well on his way towards building a nuclear weapon.

We knew that Saddam did have VX nerve gas at one time

because we shared the recipe with him. That's what the photo of Reagan Administration official Donald Rumsfeld (Dubya's Sec Def) shaking Saddam's hand in 1983 is allegedly about. We gave chemical weapons technology to Iraq during the Iran-Iraq War so they could gas the Iranians with it.

Again, the United States government always seeks revenge, that time seeking revenge for the humiliation of the Iranian Hostage crisis of 1979. Yet it consistently fails to understand that others want revenge against them. However, after the Gulf War, Saddam was ordered to destroy those weapons and UN Weapons inspectors certified that. Iraq had no way to manufacture a nuclear weapon in the first place.

An Israeli air force raid on the Osirak nuclear power plant in Iraq had destroyed that capability way back in the 1980s. Everyone knew that! Osirak had never been rebuilt, or the United States would have destroyed it again during the Gulf War or in the 1990s even afterwards.

But here it was after 9/11 and the Bush Administration is going into hysterics that Saddam could have a nuclear weapon in just a hop, skip and a mushroom cloud and already had chemical and biological weapons. No one said, well, then why did you clowns say he wasn't enough of a threat to go all the way after in 1991? How come you signed a cease-fire then, instead of going all the way to Baghdad? No one asked exactly why Saddam was now such a huge threat all of the sudden. Because of 9/11? That wasn't Iraq. That was Al-Qaeda. The same Al-Qaeda composed of men that proposed to eject Saddam from Kuwait in 1990. So, no, they were not, nor were they ever, Saddam's allies.

Bush dusted off Reagan's idea about a pre-emptive strike that Reagan had successfully used in the wholly unprovoked invasion of Grenada. But instead of acting to prevent another hostage crisis, as Reagan had lied about, Bush said he needed to prevent Iraq from nuking America, or gassing us, or infecting us with some terrifying disease. And, look! There had been letters mailed out with anthrax in them and no one knew where they came from or who mailed them! It must have been some Iraqi government sleeper cell in America! We must act! Who knew where that anthrax was coming from?! From the United States Government, of course, But no one knew that at the time.

The anthrax-laced letters were absolutely critical to selling the invasion of Iraq. And the government played it beautifully by not leading the American people into thinking it was Iraq that mailed them. But, rather, letting the American people lead themselves into believing that so they'd not just accept an invasion of Iraq, but literally demand it. This was simply brilliant and on that alone, people underestimated the ability of the government to pull off such a thing.

Not just get people to accept a war, no, but get them to pound the table and demand one.

This government is a master in the art of manipulation. A famous American industrialist once said he could pay half the American people to shoot the other half. He said this in order to disprove claims of American solidarity in the workplace. However, the United States government can do him one better than that. The Unites States government can convince the American people to demand the government shoot half the world!

Nothing terrifies people more than the specter of a biological weapons attack. Well, maybe a nuclear war frightens them more. But, hey, the Bush Administration served up a double-header on that! After all, there sat Colin Powell up in the UN, holding a vial of laundry soap or talcum powder, saying it was enough to kill thousands of people, or maybe do a load of laundry, blah, blah, blah.

Then the Bush Administration came right out and lied, saying Iraq was trying to obtain enriched uranium ore from Africa to build a nuclear weapon. You have to understand that Bush needed to make a compelling case as to why he needed to invade Iraq as soon as possible. To avoid an even greater tragedy, you see? But more so before UN weapons inspectors who were in Iraq looking for these nuclear, biological and chemical weapons Bush said

115

existed discovered that they didn't and told the world so.

Bush could not afford to wait because every day that the UN inspectors found no such evidence of those weapons cast more doubt on the Bush Administration's case for invading Iraq. If Bush administration people hadn't even been in Iraq and said they had evidence of those weapons, why couldn't the UN inspectors who were actually in Iraq find them?

The only reason Bush waited to invade Iraq was not to give time to the UN inspectors. The UN weapons inspectors were just theatrics designed to entertain and distract the world as Bush readied his invasion force. Bush had already decided to invade Iraq, regardless of what the UN found there. However, he couldn't allow the UN inspectors enough time to tell the world there was nothing there and blow his cover.

Therefore, without waiting for UN inspectors to spoil a good plan, the United States invaded Iraq in 2003. The United States knew Iraq had no illegal weapons. Again, that was a cover story used as a pretext to justify the pre-emptive invasion. Just as President Reagan cooked up a half-baked story that Cuban military forces were preparing to take American citizens hostage in Grenada. Therefore, he invaded Grenada to "pre-empt" another hostage crisis as had happened in Iran. The American people fell for this story and fell for Iraq along the same doctrine.

Now, cooking up a pretext to justify an invasion had been done before in history. In fact, that is what launched World War Two in Europe, when Germany invaded Poland in 1939. What many Americans don't know is that Germany didn't just roll over the border into Poland one day and that was that. Germany actually faked an "attack" on Germany by Polish army soldiers. Those Polish "soldiers" were actually concentration camp inmates dressed in Polish uniforms and left dead at the scene of the "attack" to "prove" that it happened.

Germany then claimed it had been attacked by Poland and so was justified in invading the country. Except the world didn't fall for the scam, because they knew Germany had created a false-flag attack to manufacture an invasion pretext. Germany had been making claims to Polish territory before this "attack," so everyone knew what it was really about. Just like American claims about Iraq pre-dated 9/11. But the difference was a lot of the world that didn't fall for Germany's scam in 1939 fell for the American scam in 2003. You've got to hand it to the United States government. They can steal a page from the other guy's book when they need to.

As would have happened if the U.S. had pushed on into Iraq in 1991, the Iraqi army was quickly defeated. But, once again, the United States decided to stay. That was the whole reason for the invasion of Iraq: To Keep Iraq. The Bush Administration said Iraq needed "regime change," thus coining a new phase to describe a new doctrine, which is tragically flawed and ignorant.

That one American idea—"regime change"—has caused the deaths of more human beings due to war than any other idea in the 21st century. The current maelstrom of terrorist activity manifested in the aftermath of U.S. government "regime change" activities in Iraq, Syria, and elsewhere.

We don't need to analyze what went wrong in Iraq. We already know from the 1991 Gulf War that the decision of the U.S. government to stay in a Middle Eastern country results in terrorist activity. And we know that the action of the U.S. government in the region motivates them to resist, especially when the U.S. government meddles in their affairs. Iraq turned into a quagmire, and a bloody civil war erupted, because the U.S. decided to stay there and keep the oil resources, among other things. Now, the U.S. had in mind to topple other countries in the Middle East after Iraq. However, the civil war in Iraq became a bloodbath with urban warfare not seen since Stalingrad, so the U.S. had to abandon its plans for the region. Or, rather, postpone them. Right then, though, it was all they could do just to hold on to Iraq.

If anything, the Iraq War should have taught the United States that "regime change" was as much of a flawed doctrine as the equally catastrophic "domino theory" of the Vietnam War. And like Vietnam, thousands of Americans died in the Iraq War for a cause, the reasons for which were changed by the U.S. government like sheets on the bed. But all boiled down to the "regime change" thing.

Who invented this idea?

Was it "Project for a New American Century"? Or did it originally come from Ronald Reagan himself, handed down as quasi-legacy from him and carried by former Reagan Administration officials into the Bush Administration? Men like Dick Cheney and Donald Rumsfeld, for example. We may never know for certain. The U.S. had covertly toppled governments before, but the use of military force to do so going into the 21st century was a new phase. Be that as it may, those who believe in the regime changed idea are still within the government and the Pentagon.

The Iraq War—in its civil war phase—trained a core cadre of guerilla fighters how to fight a war against a conventional army. This was highly valuable training because they couldn't just learn it from books. They needed to learn in actual practice what a conventional army does when under attack.

How it responds when hit by a roadside bomb.

Where its vulnerabilities are as well as its strengths.

How it moves, how it supplies itself, how to best sap their will to fight.

The Iraq War was the perfect classroom to teach thousands of guerilla fighters how to fight a professional army with a guerilla army and succeed. In turn, those that survived could teach others how to fight such a war. There was no other place to learn this. Not even Afghanistan could teach it as well as the Iraq War.

Eventually, the American people began to become angry over the mounting casualties of the Iraq War and the government incompetence that was perpetuating the grim death toll. People wanted it over. As a result, in 2008, Barrack Obama was elected President promising to end it and stop fooling around over there.

The Iraq War did end, in a way. The troops were mostly pulled out, leaving behind a small token force. But America forgot something. It had inadvertently trained thousands of Islamic radicals as highly skilled guerilla fighters. This went totally unnoticed. It was assumed they would just go back to their jobs as shoe salesmen and taxi drivers. Wrong, many had come up with a new idea that maybe the key to keeping the United States out of the region was to first take over the government of the Middle Eastern nations they were in. This is sound logic because you can't keep the United States out if your government welcomes them in. Osama bin Laden had fought the United States for some almost twenty years and couldn't kick the United States out even after the 9/11 attacks.

Around 2010 began what are called the Arab Spring Revolts. All across the Middle East, protest erupted wanting change in their governments. People won't like this comparison, but I'll make it anyway. In the United States, the "Tea Party" movement began, wanting change in the way things are done and being fueled by anger at both political parties.

But not long after, because most of the Tea Party were right-wing conservatives, their movement was quickly infiltrated and co-opted by elements ultimately loyal to an emerging hardliner Republican base. That moved the Republican Party so far to the right, Ronald Reagan is damn near liberal by their standards. What happened with Arab Spring was that it originally was a group of people disenchanted with their governments. But it was infiltrated and co-opted by groups of fundamentalist Muslim radicals whose solution was to push for Islamic Sharia-based governments.

The Obama Administration blundered right into a quagmire deserving of a Golden Swamp Rat for Best Failure To Learn From Past Mistakes. And Obama had just helped clean up the one Bush made in Iraq! I'm talking about Syria. But what gave him the idea he could pull of a "regime change" in Syria was the success in Libya and Egypt. The United States had been looking for revenge against Libyan dictator Muammar Qaddafi for decades since the 1980s when he funded all the "alphabet soup" terrorist groups from the IRA to the PLO. So Obama committed U.S. warplanes, along with European help, to toppling him. This worked, but Libya is nowhere near the "secular democracy" that American regime change schemes are allegedly aiming at.

Obama gave support, though not military, to an Arab Spring inspired revolt that toppled Egyptian strongman Hosni Mubarak. Obama made a serious mistake there and Egypt almost ended up as an Islamic theocracy that would have certainly exported terrorism, probably after liquidating the minority Coptic Christians in Egypt. Over Obama's objections, current Egyptian leader Abdel al-Sisi took power and jailed the Muslim Brotherhood folks that Obama likes. Right, the ones who would have plunged Egypt into a theocratic regime ruled by Sharia law.

The grand prize of sheer stupidity, however, was awarded for Obama's performance in Syria. On the heels of the Arab Spring protest, which were co-opted by Muslim fundamentalists, began the Syrian Civil War in 2011. There are not many utter foreign policy disasters the United States has involved itself in that have resulted in such gargantuan death tolls and widespread destruction as the Syrian Civil War, as far as covert operation go.

For some asinine reason that makes no logical sense (nor indeed, is based on any common sense), President Obama decided that Syrian leader Bashar al-Assad needed to be deposed. Now, this was also an aim of the previous Bush Administration, but the quagmire in Iraq obviously postponed it until the Obama Administration took over. This demonstrates how little true difference there is between Democrats and Republicans.

At the present, the Syrian War already carries within it not one, but the seeds of several future wars. The United States is now recklessly involved to the point where American lives have been lost and terrorist attacks have been carried out on American soil.

And for what?

What, exactly, do the American people stand to gain from this insanely foolish enterprise? Instead of safety, the government has actually increased, by at least a hundred-fold, the risk from terrorist attacks on Americans. To fully understand how the government played with fire, we must understand that they actually created much of the problem.

The United States saw Arab Spring as a great way to co-opt what it hoped were new emerging governments in the region. That is, a new dawn for the horrifyingly flawed "regime change" ideology. Therefore, covert American forces began funding, arming, and training various Syrian irregular forces and guerilla armies that were battling Assad's government. What the government did was the same thing it did in the Afghan-Soviet War: back the side against the secular regime, which will always be the fundamentalist Muslim side, which will later morph into a terrorist organization. Because the Arab Spring had already been co-opted by Islamic radicals.

What's more, in the case of Syria, these were seasoned, battle-hardened vets almost fresh back from the insurgency against the U.S. military in the Iraq War. Now, they didn't really need the training from the U.S., except to brush-up on tactics.

But, what they did need was money and weapons, which the U.S. gladly supplied from its usual covert arms pipeline originating in Eastern Europe. These guerilla armies began scoring battlefield victories against Assad's professional army, which tells us these certainly were not college students that found their dad's old hunting rifle in the closet and went out to start a revolution. And, no, it wasn't the somewhat simple training the U.S. usually gives to guerillas they don't mind losing in battle.

It is absolutely clear that these men battling Assad had great knowledge of how to fight and win against a modern army. They could have only gained that knowledge through experience— which they gained while fighting against U.S. forces in Iraq. The United States government certainly knew who these people were, but foolishly thought it could control them and use them to topple

Assad. This is as crazy as a guy who catches a rattlesnake, then takes it home and keeps it in a rickety cage inside his bedroom. He assumes the cage will contain the reptile, even though a rodent he kept in the cage prior escaped from it. Worse, he thinks the snake will not bite him should it escape because it "knows" he feeds it. This is exactly what led up to the creation of ISIS. The United States caught this snake and fed it. It then escaped and began biting everyone that entered the house.

The U.S. government tries to disavow knowledge that it helped create ISIS. Are we to then believe this group just appeared out of thin air, highly proficient at winning battles against a modern army? That we all just awoke one morning and, overnight, ISIS had not only manifested as a highly skilled irregular army, but now this Syrian conflict had spilled over into Iraq? And now ISIS was scoring battlefield victories against the Iraqi Army as it had against that of Syria?

A person would have to be a fool to believe the United States government's "aw, shucks" story about this. They obviously created this entity and sat by idly while this went on, thinking Assad would throw in the towel. They probably had some "analysis" that said Assad would flee, his army would take over, and then the U.S. could cut a back-door deal with them. ISIS would then be their problem to deal with, and the U.S. could actually keep ISIS on a covert payroll and play both sides against each other if necessary.

They foolishly thought this would remain in Syria. When it blew up out of a proportion that covert U.S. forces could manage and spilled into Iraq, now the U.S. was in the mud up to the wheel wells. The U.S. was stuck. It needed Assad to go, because it had openly boasted it would see to that. Plus, the U.S. had hundreds of billions of dollars and dirty covert ops invested in that outcome. But on the other hand, the United States needed to look like it was "doing something" about ISIS. However, ISIS was the most effective fighting force against Assad. Therefore, the U.S. began a silly "air war" to "stop" ISIS that never even dented any battlefield victories that ISIS continued scoring. This "air war" was probably a military fiction, dropping bombs on empty desert. How else could ISIS get stronger while under attack, unless there really was no attack? Black market oil was flowing freely out of Syria and some country was buying it. Who knows what covert entities are and were involved in that? And if some nation was not supplying ISIS, they would have run out of ammunition a long time ago.

Further, during this U.S. "air war," ISIS was able to launch a coordinated, multi-pronged attack against Paris, France. Proving, once again, U.S. covert aid to another Islamic "resistance" movement had resulted in yet another worldwide terrorist organization capable of carrying out attacks anywhere.

As I said, one war leads to another. The United States war in Iraq led directly to another war. Because had those men that became ISIS not gained battlefield experience against a modern army during the Iraq War, Assad's forces would have wiped them out quite some time ago.

I think the world tends to want to close its eyes and pretend what's happening isn't what's happening. Obviously, some nation is supplying ISIS. It can only be a nation with the military capability to get in and out of the region using plausible reasons to be there in the first place. It can only be a nation with unlimited access to vast stores of virtually untraceable weapons. It can only be a nation that also has the ability to launder vast amounts of black market oil onto the world oil market. Some nation that has recently seen a "boom" in its own domestic oil production to account for all this oil it now has.

It has to be a nation that wants Assad toppled at all costs and has quite a bit invested in that goal. A nation with experience in this sort of thing, that's done this before, and knows how to do it. And that can leave as little evidence behind as possible. I would have to say that sounds like the United States government.

The theatrics of it all were award-winning to say the least. The United States government said it wanted to build a coalition to fight ISIS. The U.S. had been spending hundreds of billions of dollars to train and arm these Syrian "moderate" guerillas to fight ISIS and Assad at the same time.

No one can fight and win a war like that!

They can't fight a modern army and highly effective guerilla army at the same time, being a guerilla army themselves. The United States couldn't win a war like that, either. The United States couldn't win the Vietnam War fighting the North Vietnamese Army and the Viet Cong guerillas at the same time, and they had more resources than they were giving these Syrian "moderates." Those "moderates" did the only logical thing they could do. They defected and joined ISIS, taking the weapons the U.S. gave them along with them. In reality, the whole "Syrian moderates" thing was probably a cover story to provide plausible deniability for the U.S. government supplying weapons to a group they knew damn well were ISIS. Because ISIS was the only group over there capable of defeating Assad's army in open battle and holding on to captured territory.

When the U.S. said it wanted to build a "coalition" to fight ISIS, it wanted to do so on its own terms that included Assad being deposed in the process. This is, historically, literal insanity. If a country is fighting an enemy and you say you want to defeat that enemy by toppling the country fighting that enemy, you need a reality check, not to mention a mental health assessment. But this is pretty much what President Obama said!

The key to defeating ISIS, in his mind, was to topple Assad. Excuse me, but does anyone notice how similar that is to Bush thinking the key to defeating Al-Qaeda and terrorism was to invade Iraq and topple Saddam? I suspect the same people that put forth that idea to Bush are still in the government and put forth nearly the same idea to Obama.

Here was Assad who'd been fighting ISIS from the very beginning, and had scored some victories against them, and the U.S. refused to work with him. Nor would it allow him into the "coalition" to fight ISIS. No, instead, the U.S. said Assad needed to go. Think about that clearly. The guy in charge of the army fighting ISIS, and he steps down, what's going to happen with a leaderless army? They'll crumble when ISIS pushes to take advantage of Assad's exile and capture the capital. Thus, they'll declare themselves the new government of Syria. Who knows? Maybe that's really what Obama wanted but couldn't say so openly for obvious reasons. But I wouldn't pin that on Obama alone. I think he got coached by entities within the government who have vested interests in these regime changes.

Then there was Iran, whose military and paramilitary forces were operating in both Syria and Iraq and scoring some impressive battlefield victories against ISIS. And Iran pulled off a hugely successful air attack against an ISIS convoy and used fifty year old F-4 Phantoms to do it. There's the U.S. using the latest warplanes and can't even make a dent in ISIS for a year!

Of course, the United States refused to work with Iran, too, and would not invite Iran into its "coalition." The Unites States started whining about Iran's nuclear weapons program as a propaganda device to keep public opinion in the United States firmly against Iran. Nobody stopped and said, "Hey, hold on a second! The government also told us Iraq had a nuclear weapons program, too, and lied us into a war that cost thousands of American lives!"

No, instead many Americans fell for the exact same scam that scammed us into a war with Iraq. If some president succeeds in getting a war started with Iran over its alleged "nuclear weapons program," Americans will again be clueless as to how they fell for this scam twice in a row. But only after thousands of lives are lost and then it comes out Iran didn't have a "nuclear weapons program" and the government knew that all along. In the meantime, the charade provides a semi-plausible reason the U.S. can refuse to work with Iran to defeat ISIS.

Russia then entered the war in Syria and, as everyone can guess, the United States refused to cooperate with them too. The United States complained that Russia backed Assad, therefore the

U.S. could not cooperate with Russia. Well, of course Russia backs Assad! They both have the goal of defeating ISIS firmly in mind and they're not taking their eye off of that ball to play silly United States foreign policy games. Those games are what created ISIS to begin with! And if the U.S. really had defeating ISIS as its top priority, the U.S. would have worked with Assad the same as it has worked with other dictators in the past to defeat insurgencies in other countries. Again, the United States suddenly gets a conscience? After backing the Shah of Iran and right-wing dictators throughout Latin America?

Assad was only half the reason the United States didn't want to cooperate with Russia. The other half was simmering resentment towards Russia over events in Ukraine about a year prior. The United States government is very good at holding on to grudges. The grudge against Iran dates back to 1979. But the grudge it held against Cuba went back to 1962! It's just that the United States government doesn't understand there are lots of other people out in the world that have even more recent and valid grudges against them.

But because the United States felt slighted and thwarted over Ukraine, it was still (and will remain) very angry with Russia. Now, Russia had done nothing unusual. Ukraine is Russian's backyard. You can't criticize Russia for backing Russian separatists in Ukraine and then give President Reagan a free pass for the exact same thing in Nicaragua and El Salvador back in the 1980s. Not to mention Nicaragua and El Salvador are further away from the United States than Ukraine is from Russia. If the United States can claim "backyard privileges" to meddle in Latin America, Russia can do so with Ukraine.

Not that it kept the United States from smearing Russian President Vladimir Putin as, you guessed it, "another Hitler." They even did that old tactic one better and also labeled Putin as "another Stalin." Now, if Putin really was another Hitler or Stalin, we wouldn't be alive to be having this conversation. Because the moment U.S. troops appeared close to Russia, which was done repeatedly to provoke the Russians, Putin would have nuked the United States into the Stone Age.

People forget that Hitler and Stalin both had no qualms about using military force. Many countries hadn't even provoked Hitler and he invaded them. If Hitler had the nuclear weapons Putin has, Europe today would still be a collection of radioactive craters. This whole "another Hitler" crap needs to come to an end and be put to bed once and for all. To call people "another Hitler" just because you don't like the way they run their countries insults the memories of the tens of millions of people that died because of the real Adolf Hitler. It trivializes the whole thing and reduces their very real suffering to cheap political grandstanding and a ridiculous grade-school gambit for attention.

Therefore, because the United States got their feelings hurt in Ukraine, the government was willing to let an epic slaughter continue to avoid mending fences and moving on. Refusing to let bygones be bygones and cooperate for the greater good is something usually seen in bratty toddlers with discipline problems. And also the United States government, which is the same thing. The United States would rather let thousands die than put its grudge with Russia to rest.

By the time the Unites States government had half-heartedly and grumblingly decided to accept that Assad might just stay in power, and the armies fighting ISIS on the ground, like them or not, was who were available to do it, tens of thousands of people had died. Had the United States government said ISIS was a greater threat than the legitimate government of Syria, tens of thousands of lives could have been saved. Had the United States government cooperated early on with Iran, Syria and Russia, tens of thousands of lives could have been saved.

It needs to be pointed out that tens of thousands of people died in vain to salvage the ego of the United States government. If the United States government fails to realize that that fact is not going to be forgotten any time soon, then they are even bigger fools that they appear to be. Those chickens will come home to roost one day. Just like they did in Iran in 1979, Al-Qaeda throughout the 1990s and 2000s, and other entities we surely have yet to see.

When the United States government meddles in the Middle East, there is always an oppositional force created by it. The United States government is unable to recognize the simple science that for every action there is a positive and negative reaction. For every action (regime change), there is a positive reaction (a foothold in the region), and a negative reaction (a terrorist movement is birthed). Therefore, since the positive reactions do not bear fruits that make the negative reactions worth the cost, the logical conclusion is to stop acting there altogether.

Was a U.S. military base in Saudi Arabia worth Al-Qaeda coming to be? No. Was the removal of Assad from Syria worth ISIS coming into existence? No. What we need to see is any more action over there will create yet more terrorist entities.

After all, it was the United States that had, once again, created a terrorist organization it failed to see was an oppositional force, not an ally. Now it is a worldwide threat, not a regional one. If anyone thinks that should the war in Syria end, that will be the end of it all, it is a serious mistake.

Just as the Afghan-Soviet war led up to the creation of Al-Qaeda and the Gulf War set them into motion, so, too, is the dynamic with ISIS. The Iraq War led up to their creation and the Syrian Civil War set them into motion.

The aftermath of the Afghan-Soviet War continues on today, because Al-Qaeda remains a potent threat capable of inflicting serious damage worldwide. Now, Al-Qaeda dates back to 1980s, as I have shown. Therefore, that threat has been continuous since then, some almost four decades now. The reader can, thus, see that the threat from ISIS has only just begun. Furthermore, the United States never achieved victory against Al-Qaeda and is still at war with them some fifteen years after 9/11.

How, then will anyone think some type of victory shall be achieved against ISIS? The only way this cycle of wars can be broken is by refusing to engage in them. There is no other alternative. That supporting any side in any war will only lead to them being a future enemy is also quite clear. Even should they not become an enemy, the seeds of future wars are planted when the United States picks a side in any war.

I could go on and on about Syria. However, we must focus on the questions that truly need to be asked. Were the American people asked by the government if they were willing to become the target of terrorism in order to topple Assad? How would deposing Assad benefit the American people whose actual hardship and struggles are economic and not caused by a foreign government?

Why is it acceptable to divert taxpayer money to this cause? What benefit and what return-on-investment will it show? When did the government give a true threat assessment to the American people as to the risks involved in this attempt to overthrow Assad? Why is the government allegedly concerned about the political voice of the Syrian people under Assad, but does not care about the voice of the American people in regards to Syria?

No, not the Congress and the Senate, who are often under the influence of vocal lunatics within who support these fools' gambits. The supports these Senators and Congress people overtly and covertly give to non-state terrorist organizations now and over the years is and has been treasonous to say the least. That several thousands of American lives have been lost as a direct result of these Senators and Congress people is obvious to all who look truthfully into history. At no time were the American people made aware of the risks involved in pursuing foreign policy objectives that, themselves, are not truthfully told to the people.

I accuse the United State government of treason in so much as the lives of the people it allegedly protects are jeopardized and sacrificed for causes and reasons that are opposite of the true interest of the people. The American people will not benefit from someone other than Assad running Syria. That much is clear, as we are no better off now that someone besides Saddam runs Iraq.

The government must answer these questions but it will refuse to do so, instead preferring to act in a "we know best" rule consistently proven as false and ignorant of history. It isn't enough to vote anymore. The American people must demand an end to the wars, military operations and covert operations of the United States government.

If we do not demand an end to this senseless risk to American lives and the actual loss of them, we will soon come to regret not having done so.

Sooner or later, the government may pick a fight it cannot win. It may underestimate the resolve of a nation such as Russia, for example. It may underestimate the ability of a guerilla arm to morph into a terrorist organization capable of attacks within America that will dwarf 9/11. Indeed, it may have already done so.

There is no sane reason for the United States to get involved in a war that does not concern it. That's how we got involved in the Vietnam War, which also did not concern us. And it was the imagined humiliation of that war that led up to us getting involved in the Afghan-Soviet War. The benefits of minding our own business become quite clear when you look at those facts.

I said earlier in this chapter that we'd come back to the Vietnam War. This point I shall make will make it abundantly clear that our government is literally throwing away American lives and slaughtering others on this planet for no tangible reasons anyone beside itself can justify and still claim to be a moral government. In the end, the United States government threw away the lives of over 58,000 Americans and 3 million Vietnamese who died in this war.

The U.S. signed a cease-fire in 1973 and then, in 1975, South Vietnam fell to communist North Vietnam anyway. People that defend the Vietnam War say, "Yeah, well, look at Cambodia and Laos!" Right, but where are those two nations at today, North Vietnam having won the war? And for that matter, look at communist Vietnam as a whole today. American corporations do business with them and goods are imported from there to the United States.

Therefore, if the United States had just allowed events to take their natural course in Vietnam, we can see that eventually the American corporations whining about communism then would be more than happy to do business with them to get lower labor cost. And higher profit margins. Therefore, over 58,000 Americans died in the Vietnam War for a theory proven as a failure and to fight a country the U.S. would later do business with.

People say, "yes, but we fought the Japanese and Germans and we do business with them!" Not the same thing. The Vietnamese Government of today is the exact same government we fought in the Vietnam War. The government of Germany and Japan are not the governments they had in World War Two. Seriously, can anyone imagine the uproar if the government of Nazi Germany was intact today and American corporations wanted to do business with them? Not that they wouldn't attempt to do so were it the case that Nazi Germany was still around today. Some American corporations did business with them prior to the United States entering World War Two, after all. Again, the pretext as to why outcome victory was said to be so necessary as to be worth tens of thousands of American lives was proven to be wrong.

Let me digress for a moment here. Victory in World War One was said to be absolutely necessary to guarantee democracy. Victory was achieved in World War One. But rather than worldwide democracy, what manifested were dictatorships and another world war. So, again, the pretext as to why outcome victory was absolutely necessary was proven to be wrong.

Therefore, we have proven that it is not whether or not a victory is achieved can it be said a war is worthwhile for the United States. The actual question is: "Why get involved in any foreign war at all?" The reasons the government tells us victory is of vital importance to the long-term survival of the country are proven to be wrong time after time.

Let's continue on this.

The government did not get victory in the Vietnam War. Nothing of serious damage resulted to the United States. The United States got victory by meddling in the Afghan-Soviet War. As a result, Al-Qaeda came to be and this led to a war still going on today. There is no logical way to ascertain the long-term effects victory or defeat hold in foreign wars.

The only positive outcome the United States can obtain is by staying out of them. And, indeed, there have been wars we've been told we absolutely needed to get into for our national survival but did not. And, not having gotten into them, we're all still alive and the United States exists. Recently we've been told we needed to go to war with Russia over Ukraine. We didn't and, as a result Russia had military resources to fight ISIS instead. But the United States government doesn't see it that way. Nor does it see that ISIS itself and the war in Syria became the conflagration it is due to the U.S. meddling in a foreign conflict.

People may say, "But we can't just ignore world events!" We can't? We pretty much ignored world events for most of the period of American history where American folktales and Americana resides, and we came through that just fine. In fact, an America strong enough industrially to have participated in a world war was only possible due to the fact we had not depleted national resources in drawn-out foreign wars of large magnitude. That Britain and France and others could was due to the fact they had extensive colonies in other countries to exploit. Be that as it may, the United States managed to stay out of foreign wars for quite a long time with no detrimental effects on the nation.

Others will say, "Okay, what about Pearl Harbor?"

But is anyone aware that was a pre-emptive strike against a nation increasingly hostile to Japan through embargoes? When the United States justifies "pre-emptive strikes," keep in mind it is using the same logic that Japan used in attacking Pearl Harbor. Japan feared the naval fleet at Pearl Harbor would soon be used against it.

Therefore, they acted.

At any time, the United States government could have acted to prevent Pearl Harbor but chose not to. There was no other way to bring a reluctant America into World War Two than to ignore the credible intelligence that Japan saw American activities as a threat. Again, even when attacked, one cannot dismiss the fact that the United States government has in some way provoked the attack or has knowingly allowed causes and conditions to manifest that lead up to it. In some cases, the government has actually lied and claimed to have been attacked or threatened when no such thing occurred. The gulf of Tonkin Incident that was a prelude to the Vietnam War is but one example!

When you find yourself in a hole getting deeper, it is time to stop digging. The chain of events set into motion by World War One cannot be stopped by wars. Only by refusal to be provoked into wars, and refusing to participate in them regardless of who is already fighting, can an endless continuation of this one hundred year cycle be stopped.

All alliances such as NATO must be withdrawn from and those countries can keep it if they so desire. But the United State cannot continue to perpetuate this cycle. It is American military power that is in large part, responsible. Few other nations can afford to engage in this ultimately self-destructive waste of life and resources. Nor do they have the desire to do so when they are not being provoked. It is a wrong conclusion that the Middle East is warlike by nature. When not attacked nor provoked, much of the region is at peace when geographic area is considered. To assume the Israeli-Palestinian conflict is responsible for the entire Middle East being at war is mistaken.

This is like saying since American inner-city areas are crime ridden, the entire United States is lawless and anarchic. In truth, if the United States would leave the Middle East alone, the region would return to a somewhat peaceful state given time and patience. Middle Eastern terrorists are not seeking to conquer the

United States. Anyone who thinks that is living in a delusion. What they want is the United States to stop meddling in their affairs and trying to ham-handedly chart their destinies knowing little to nothing of the region or their wants and needs.

Finally, we need to understand that we simply cannot afford to go on like this. If we continue perpetuating the cycle begun by World War One, it must, by necessity, result in a third world war. The pattern is clear to see. The First World War led directly to the Second World War. Had it not been for the invention of nuclear weapons, the Cold War would have certainly erupted into the Third World War. That's what the Cold War was all about: preparing to fight the Third World War even with nuclear weapons.

Over time, the Cold War has become a distant memory. The fallout shelters are gone and the air raid sirens have been taken down. As a result, a Third World War is now possible. The United States government provoked Russia in Ukraine and the American people for the most part never even saw the peril of such foolish behavior. Many American politicians were calling for a military confrontation with the Russian at the time. The American people seem to have forgotten that just because the Soviet Union collapsed does not mean Russia doesn't still have those nuclear weapons. In fact, Russia has been adding more to the arsenal, thanks to the belligerent behavior of the United States.

The cause and conditions for a Third World War to manifest already exist. It will only require those causes and conditions to come together at the right time and place for it to begin. The United States government arrogantly refuses to see that it no longer has the industrial capability to wage and win another world war without the use of nuclear weapons. The industrial power of the United States is truly what helped it win World War Two.

Today, that industrial capacity no longer exists.

China will not be America's de facto industrial capacity in a world war against Russia. Not to mention a naval campaign will make importation of overseas war materiel and equipment costly or impossible. It only takes submarines to inflict severe losses, and Russia has plenty of them. The United States military would soon find itself where Germany did in late 1944. All kinds of great weapons, but no way to replace them when lost in combat. The United States government not only repeats its own mistakes, but repeats the mistakes of countries it fought wars with. And mistakes the United State exploited at the time.

What's more, it is unlikely the United States government will be able to cease-fire its way out of a Third World War. Even if it could negotiate a cease-fire, there would certainly be severe consequences that could include having to pay reparations. That's what caused Germany to go broke after World War One. A major depression in the United States after a cease-fire exit from the Third World War is a foregone conclusion.

Heaven help the United States if it actually lost the Third World War. That could result in a foreign occupation, disarmament of its military, or the loss of territories altogether. People think a resistance movement would make a foreign occupation costly. And it would. But don't forget an invading army can bomb a U.S. city in retaliation for what it'll call "terrorism." The point being, the cost in lives will make U.S. losses in previous war seem trivial.

The worst case scenario is if the United States begins to lose the Third World War, it then resorts to the use of nuclear weapons in a last-ditch effort to win it. This was the actual fear of how a nuclear war with the old Soviet Union would begin. The Soviets would invade Western Europe and quickly overwhelm conventional NATO forces.

The United States' plan, at that point, was to use tactical nuclear weapons on Soviet troops and armor and pray it remained a theater nuclear war when the Soviets retaliated in kind. Of course, everyone knew sooner or later a major city in the Soviet Union would get hit with a U.S. tactical nuke and the Soviets would retaliate with their strategic nukes against American cities.

Then: Doomsday. There is no deviation or difference today, with the exception of where it will take place. The United States will absolutely panic and resort to the use of nuclear weapons once it begins to lose a Third World War and cannot cease-fire its way out of it.

People wrongly assume none of this can happen. The Russians have been warning the United States government that it's playing with fire for some years now. The Russians have come right out and said this can lead to the Third World War. The United States Government ignores those warnings and continues to provoke the Russians.

How can the American people, thus, assume another world war cannot or will not happen? Because the United State government would defuse a crisis leading up to one? They're the fools creating crises in hopes they will lead up to one! How can this not eventually lead up to the United States government starting a world war it thinks it can win but, in truth, cannot? Let's not forget the United States government cannot even win a war against people without an air force or a navy. The government imagines it will be able to win a war using the same "shock and awe" tactics it used in the 2003 invasion of Iraq. They think that will win the war quickly, as it did in Iraq, and so it won't turn into a long slog needing a huge industrial capacity to re-supply.

Two things are wrong with that. First, Russia can visit the same "Shock and Awe" upon the U.S. military. Second, the war in Iraq did turn into a long slog. Just because Saddam's army threw in the towel didn't mean that war was won or over. The United States has not faced a power like that of Russia in any war since 1945. The United States government is marching headlong into the Third World War, foolishly thinking it can win it. And foolish Americans think that they can. They'd better ask themselves what'll happen if they don't. Because losing it is a much more likely outcome.

Furthermore, the United States government has already

made targets of the American people for terrorist entities such as Al-Qaeda and ISIS. The government itself, since 9/11, is more or less invulnerable to attack by these terrorists. They are all heavily guarded and their buildings protected by surface-to-air missile batteries. Thus, terrorists attack, and will continue to attack, the common American citizen whom they can hit. The government knows this, but refuses to value the lives of its own citizens who are obviously expendable in the war effort, be it an actual war or a covert one. And it might be the covert ones we should worry about, because we won't even be aware of revenge-seekers coming out of those.

At some point in the future, terrorist attacks within the United States will come with horrifying regularity. If the United States government continues provoking these people, not only will attacks continue, but new terrorist groups will emerge, seeking retaliation. Just because the government thinks it is not provoking these people does not make it true. It is enough that they are feeling provoked by United States government action in the Middle East. The United States government likes to say it won't give in to the demands of terrorists. They can say that because it isn't them that have to pay for it. It's us. How many of our lives is it worth to continue foolish policies in the Middle East? We're the ones killed in terrorist attacks, not them. Not since 9/11 have we truly been safe. Nor will we ever be safe again.

We cannot afford any more "regime change." The "regime change" needs to happen right here. This warlike regime we have needs to have the control of the military taken away from them because they are jeopardizing all of our lives with senseless wars and operations in the Middle East.

The CIA needs to be disbanded and all of their documents handed over to the American people so we can see what's been going on. The Pentagon needs to answer to the American People, not the president. We have pretty much granted dictatorial power to the office of the presidency to start and wage wars. Look where that's gotten us. We've sat and watched the government start and wage wars against nations that have not attacked us and for reasons the government refuses to fully explain.

How long will we continue to accept this?

Until your son or daughter dies in a war over what guy runs some country in the Middle East? No, we need to demand an end to this insanity once and for all.

No, not by voting for another liar who'll get us out of the war of his predecessor but then start a couple of his own under the table. We need to speak up loudly and clearly and resist enlisting in the military. Refuse to support any war. Speak out, demand answers, march in anti-war demonstrations.

We've got to start somewhere in creating peace.

All of our lives depend on it.

CHAPTER SIX—THE ECONOMY

WHAT WOULD YOU say if I told you that our economy is one of the greatest scams ever perpetuated? That the economy itself is merely a mirage of prosperity? An illusion that people believe to be an actual physical thing of reality?

In actual truth, the economy does not exist as some kind of genuine entity the way the government and Wall Street speak of it. To hear them talk about it, you'd almost believe the economy is some kind of sentient being, although one helpless to control its own fate. They speak of the economy as if it is a newborn infant which needs round-the-clock care and feeding. This is patently absurd, but people go right along with the illusion, thinking their own actions are either "good" or "bad" for the economy.

This is a fine example of mass hypnosis by Wall Street and the government, but if you carefully investigate the facts, you will discover the economy to be nothing more than a false idea of what is or is not prosperity. Wealth is not prosperity and the economy does not create either. Humans assign the value to things they call "prosperity" and "wealth" even in cases where the things they assign that value to are neither—this is what the entire American economy is built upon.

If you think the wars of the United States are a series of catastrophic disasters, the so-called economy is no better. But to examine the economy, we need to go back a little bit in history to fully understand the current economy. There will, of course, be lots of economic "experts" that think I am too simple to comprehend the obvious.

But the fact is, these economic "experts" are as clueless as the military and political "experts" behind recent American wars. You see, they're all professional college students with little to no experience in the real world. All of their economic theories sound good on paper but not one has ever created long-term prosperity or economic stability for all.

The government has been listening to the advice of these experts for several decades now, and not one of the ideas put into practice has ever truly worked. In fact, the result is usually the opposite from what is intended. Economic theories that will "create jobs" actually cause more job losses than job creation, for example. The reason for this is because the financial sector from whence these experts come is staffed by highly skilled liars being paid by Wall Street to sell these flawed ideas to the government.

The financial sector—as a whole—makes its living by getting people to pay far more for an object than it is really worth, which requires exemplary skill in lying and deception. They call this "salesmanship" by which con men and flim-flam artists engage in deception and then call the unwholesome fruits of it "the economy." Therefore, they will say and do whatever is necessary to keep people from detecting the swindle. Thus, they must continue "advising" the government to do this or that thing in order to "help" or "grow" the economy and are nothing more than paid shills for Wall Street.

Let us now proceed to history. Prior to the First World War, the United States manufactured its own goods and grew its own food, for the most part. The thought of importing, for example, a railroad locomotive from France would have been unthinkable. Yet, this is not just unthinkable today, but might be considered good business. Back then, there wasn't a military large enough to justify gigantic defense contractors whose sole reason for existence was based on there being a perpetual and present enemy of the United States. Many Americans owned farms and small shops, there being a handful of chain stores.

The economy, to call it that, was based on the manufacture and sales of goods within the nation itself. There were a lot of exports and it needs to be said the United States exported railroad locomotives back then. It did not import them. There is nothing wrong with trade, however, provided it does not result in the loss of jobs instead of the creation of them. That is important to remember. Trade is only beneficial when it improves a nation, not when it results in widespread unemployment and urban decay.

I am not trying to romanticize this era or claim it to be the perfect model to go back to. For one thing, it is very difficult to truly go back—various attempts have been made in communes and so on and they have failed. Nor should it be overlooked that there were no labor laws or workplace safety laws in this era.

What's more, large corporations existed then, too, many of whom are still around today. But what was different was that the economy was based on the buying and selling of tangible goods that had intrinsic value. That is, food, household items, clothing, textiles, building materials and so on. There was no entertainment sector worth billions of dollars, trading in things that have no genuine worth as does, say, a bed or a chair or a bushel of apples. No one will perish if they cannot get some singer's latest CD.

The thing that illustrates this perfectly is how Wall Street today banks on good Christmas shopping for many retailers to show a profit for the year. If someone said a retailer in 1890 needed to rely on Christmas shopping to stay in business, they would have called that person crazy. Yet, here we are today with a so-called economy of which the retailer sector is sitting atop a house of cards in the guise of Christmas shopping.

Can anyone detect the foolishness in that?

One must spend beyond their means to help the economy— it's nearly put forth as a patriotic duty. People are also expecting massive amounts of expensive Christmas gifts as well, which is tantamount to putting forth the human failing of greed as a social virtue. If people binge on drugs, it is seen as a bad thing even if they are only hurting themselves. If people binge on spending money, it is seen as good for the economy even if it plunges them into debt and it affects everyone in the end. In a true, healthy economy, Christmas shopping purchases would simply be a ladle of gravy over the meat and potatoes of selling goods people needed that were manufactured here.

The manufacture of those goods here means jobs and, therefore, money in the hands of people to buy the goods being manufactured. It does not take an economist and fifteen hours of tedious lecture to understand this. If you send jobs overseas, then build your economy on people spending money they really haven't got to spare, sooner or later this shack comes crashing down. It isn't hard to understand, really. Unless your economy perpetuates itself by manufacture of goods people buy with money earned in the manufacture of those goods, your economy will fail at some point. Then the "experts" come out and blame a downturn in consumer spending. Hey, genius, they can't spend money they don't have.

They talk about creating jobs by lowering corporate taxes. That doesn't create jobs. It rewards greed. They've lowered taxes since Reagan and more American jobs are lost than new ones created. And most of the "created" jobs the government crows about are low-wage service-sector jobs never intended as actual careers. Many are part-time jobs. I'd like to see Senators try and live on the wages those jobs pay. Then they'd be the first ones whining about not getting paid enough.

It really isn't about increasing the minimum wage. Prices will just go up and everyone will be back at the beginning again. The only way to solve this is to return to a self-sufficient manufacturing economy where the American people are manufacturer, buyer, seller, and customer. But what I am about to say next will probably shock many people.

We keep hearing about "economic growth." We don't need that. We need to shrink the economy. Yes, we need to start being realistic about living on a planet with an increasing population and diminishing resources. This is not some bubble-headed "green" theory about having our cake and eating it, too. It is simply a fact that if you have a planet that is finite, but more people are put upon it every day, you need to start using those resources wisely. It takes about nine months for a human being to manifest upon this planet. It doesn't require anything other than two other human beings, a male and female.

We know that and we also know making children is very fun for humanity. However, it takes billions of years to create a barrel of oil. Therefore, if every day, the number of people who will lay claim to that barrel of oil increases, what will eventually happen when that resource is gone? What, is humanity going to collectively go into suspended animation for a few billions years until more oil manifests? The causes and conditions that created oil might not be present at this time. It might be, and probably is, a one-time resource that lasts a few hundred years.

But it isn't just oil we've talking about. The problem is the American economy is built upon the premise of constant growth being necessary for it to be healthy. Therefore, the idea is not just that more people are born to buy oil, but that the economy tells people to buy more of it.

The economy itself is what drives the increasing depletion of resources. Each year, corporations want to make more profits, at a higher rate, and faster. Technology has given them the tools to make this possible. For example—in the past, you might have ordered a book via a mail catalog and it took two weeks to arrive and you spent two weeks reading it, but now you can have it overnight. After two weeks, you've read it and are ready for another. Thus, two weeks have been eliminated from the time a corporation needed to wait for consumer demand. This is just an example of how technology has rapidly sped up consumption of resources.

People might think, what's the harm? Well, for one thing, all the overnight shipping uses aircraft, which use a lot of fossil fuel. Then the delivery trucks use more, you've increased the amount of fuel being used every step of the way. At every step and every facet, every corporation wants to increase its profits as quickly as possible. And the only way to do so is by increasing consumption and telling people this is what creates the economy. People think this can go on and on as if we live in a universe of unlimited resources. But the truth is, the choices we make today, imagining this to be "freedom," are consigning future generations to a world with little or no choices.

And has this myriad of "choices" we have today increased our happiness? The United States probably has the highest amount of consumer choices and level of consumerism. Yet, the United States leads the world in the use of anti-anxiety and anti-depressant medications. Profits are increasing for the pharmaceutical industry too, I guess. Americans don't realize they're caught in a false paradigm of what they're told is prosperity.

Seriously, if one truly has prosperity, one would not be depressed or anxious over it. One would rejoice at the good fortune. What happens is, the mind knows that buying happiness is not possible and rejects this notion as false. But another part of the mind related to input from society and authority thinks that buying more will satisfy this longing for happiness because society says so. The mind is caught between two opposing forces and this conflict leads to depression and anxiety.

In other words, society says thus-and-so is true and cannot be questioned. But experience and reality do not bear this out as fact. However, Wall Street cannot afford to have people start figuring it all out. Therefore, enter the entertainment industry to take their minds off of it through mindless escapism. Once there, they can be sold more stuff because the entertainment industry is heavily marketed and rife with advertisements. Americans complain they can't afford to buy nice shoes for their kids. And what are nice shoes? The $300 pair of sneakers the celebrities wear. But look in the car of the mom that said that and you'll find about $300 worth of CDs from various singers. Thus, those singers can afford to pay $300 for a pair of shoes that mom's kid thinks are necessary.

We did not arrive at this point by accident, but this behemoth we call the economy is actually fairly young. You see, it was during World War Two that American corporations learned that profits could be made which would put the old robber barons of the late 1800s to shame. Companies with a modest profit margin making jukeboxes and postal meters discovered they could make huge amounts of money manufacturing rifles for the military. That's just rifles. Imagine what the aircraft manufacturers found out when the demand for hundreds of aircraft was present, rather than the usual peacetime demand for a handful of airliners. Do you think they just wanted to give up on that in 1945 and go back to jukeboxes and crop dusters? We didn't help win World War Two because we were smarter tactically than the Germans and the Japanese. It was because we had a huge industrial capacity that we were able to quickly convert from manufacturing consumer goods to weapons.

We learned a lot of things during World War Two. One thing we already knew was it wasn't efficient, for example, to build things like a tank from the ground up, every piece of it made right there on the premises. It was far better to assemble the tank, making what you needed to make there but bringing together other components from other manufacturers. Like ball bearings and bolts, for example. Let the manufacturers of ball bearings and bolts concentrate on what they do best and just have it delivered to the tank factory.

In this way, one tank factory might have a hundred small businesses associated with it that supply it with parts like bolts and ball bearings. In some cases, there were satellite factories around the tank factory that were independent businesses, but mostly manufactured parts just for the tank factory. That's why we were able to go into a war industry footing so fast. We already had huge plants manufacturing bulldozers. The suppliers and satellite factories for them already existed, too. It wasn't that difficult to go from manufacturing bulldozers to tanks since many of the parts used are the same. And the same is true going from building passenger planes to military transport planes and bombers. During the war, one of the best military transport planes was also a passenger plane.

Therefore, one thing we knew about this was if a critical component to a war industry was lost, weapons productions could be crippled. This is why the United States did casualty-heavy daylight bombing raids over Germany. The British preferred to bomb German cities at night, just aiming at the industrial areas in general, hoping for the best. Drop the bombs and run. The United States knew that to bomb with precision at that time meant bombing in the daylight. This would cause substantial increases in the losses of American planes and crewmen. But it was seen to be worth the loss to cripple German weapons production and sap the German military's ability to fight.

The most popular target of these daylight raids was often a ball bearing factory. Again, remove one critical component, and it all comes to a halt. No matter where the Germans hid the tank factory, they couldn't hide all the factories supplying critical components. I will demonstrate later why this is important to understanding our economic problems. American industrial know-how made bombing German ball bearing factories possible as a tactic. American industrial know-how is what created the idea that bombing the ball bearing factory would be a war winning tactic. But later, we shall see how this tactic was forgotten when applied in a different direction.

After World War Two ended, American corporations made good profits rebuilding a Europe and Japan whose industries were all bombed into rubble. People seem to forget that the highly successful manufacturing of Germany and Japan are in large parts the fruits of 1940s American corporate know-how long since forgotten by the United States. But in the aftermath of World War Two arose a new enemy whose industrial and military power could match the United States: The Soviet Union.

What we call the Cold War truly began right after World War Two. But it wasn't until the 1950s that we saw the rise of what we call today the defense industry. This entity didn't exist in the scope it does today until the Cold War. And it does not exist today in the scope it did during the Cold War.

By the 1950s, entire sections of major U.S. cities were wholly dedicated to the manufacture of weapons. Contractors and construction companies became fabulously rich building underground missile silo complexes for intercontinental ballistic missile systems. Defense industries and all businesses associated with them became extremely wealthy manufacturing the missiles and the parts that went into them. There might be, for example, an aircraft factory in Los Angeles that assembled fighter planes. There might be nearly a hundred independently owned satellite factories around it, feeding them parts. And beyond that, even more small businesses manufacturing parts for them.

All of these businesses employed thousands of people all-told when the numbers are collected for the entire effort to build one model of fighter. All of these jobs paid high wages to attract and keep skilled workers. There needed to be a good reason people went to work at Acme aircraft and not Smith Garden tool company.

That reason was high wages and benefits.

The defense industry could not afford to fall behind schedule on a military contract because of a labor shortage. A military contract was awarded to deliver a specific weapon within a limited amount of time. You'd better be able to deliver on time or the next contract will go to someone else. It was called an "arms race" with the Soviet Union, not an "arms leisurely stroll." We needed to get our latest weapons out there before the Soviets beat us to it and had the advantage. About ten different models of fighter planes alone were built over about ten years under this philosophy. So imagine the jobs created just in building those fighter planes.

Now, with those higher wages emerged people with quite a

bit of money left over to spend after the necessities were paid for, this is how Americans could afford to buy a new car every couple of years. And that's why Detroit automakers started making a few different models of cars and each year often a new model on top of that.

Not everyone worked in the defense industry, but even other manufactures paid good wages. All those defense workers had money to buy refrigerators of the newest model, televisions, new furniture, and American corporations made all of those things and people were buying them. They needed to pay their workers a good wage or they might quit and go to work for a defense industry. Then where would they be, with demand out there for televisions but no one to build them? All the industries were competing for labor and so wages were good. But that was fine, because the employers got some of that money back when the workforce bought their products.

However, one major problem with the Cold War was that it carried within it the very real possibility of doomsday. The money today was great but there might not be a tomorrow to spend it in. The reasons the defense industry existed was to produce weapons necessary for a war with the Soviets. Some of the most expensive were nuclear weapons and their delivery vehicles. But the culture of the era glorified this period of weapons-wage prosperity through television shows depicting allegedly "Average American Families" living in suburban bliss.

People watched this and figured that this image they saw on television was not only worth risking a nuclear war to defend and maintain, but the near-perfect ideal to attain and aspire to attain. Therefore, the defense budget became a pork barrel of bottomless depths as Congressmen and Senators all wrangled to deliver defense contracts and those jobs to their constituents.

The government could afford this at the time because taxes on the corporations and the wealthy were several times higher than they are today. But because these corporations were making gigantic profits in the whole deal, even higher taxes were just as affordable as paying higher wages to workers. Therefore, the possibility of a nuclear war was downplayed because everyone was seeing on television that the American way of life was worth the risk.

The entire culture of the 1950s and early 1960s was a product of the Cold War and the defense industry. People romanticize this era and have no idea it was all built upon the arms race with the Soviet Union. Take the suburbs, for example. Those were built because people wanted the defense industry jobs in the city, but they didn't want to live in the city. But for the suburbs to be built, something else had to be built first. That was the interstate highway system that, going through cities such as Los Angeles, became known as the "freeway." The freeways made the commute from the defense industry jobs in the city to homes in the suburbs possible. What's more the wages paid by defense industry jobs made the buying of those homes possible.

What Americans don't realize is those interstate highways were not built for them to use originally. They were built for the military as part of national defense so the army could move men and materials quickly in case of attack. When he was General Eisenhower, old Dwight D. saw the autobahns of the Third Reich during the war and knew America needed those. Since the American people would be graciously allowed to use them, too, everyone applauded this massive expenditure. Those are what made the suburbs possible that were later glorified in television as the "American Dream" every good American ought to embody and aspire to.

A slight detour here is that some Americans like to point out that the "Space Race" occurred in this time and up into the 1980s. They even think it was a good thing, and not what it really was, which was just a manifestation of the arms race with the Soviets. It was a contest to see who had the best and most accurate missiles. This all began in earnest when the Soviets sent up the Sputnik Satellite and the United States government crapped their collective britches over it. They feared the Soviets had better missiles.

Even worse, what if the Soviets thought they had better missiles? So NASA was created to prove to the Soviets that American missiles were bigger and could go further for longer. Look, I know it sounds like international penis-envy, but that's what the Space Race was. It was called a "race," not exploration for peaceful purpose. The astronauts were coming out of the military, not from the Quakers.

But, again, here is another aspect that was glorified as "American Exceptionalism" when in fact the mission to the moon solved no human problem besides needing to show the Soviets we could do it. Liberals today act like pulling the plug on the Space Shuttle was a tragedy. The Space Shuttle was created to launch military satellites under cover of a "Hey kids, isn't this swell?!" song-and-dance of looking like science. Americans forgot it was science that gave us nuclear weapons that made the arms race of the Cold War happen in the first place. Liberals tend to think of sciences as the "savior." It most certainly is not. American liberals that yearn for the days of a NASA budget that could feed Africa for a decade don't see what I just said when they whine about world hunger.

Space exploration is useless and unnecessary. It was invented and put into practice by the government to justify spending obscene amounts of money on perfecting ballistic missile technology. And also military satellite launch and retrieval.

If there *is* extraterrestrial life, they obviously do not wish to hear from us. They would have long ago seen television broadcasts which echo endlessly into outer space. Knowing that, it is easy to see why they have no desire to contact us. The Unites States government couldn't find Osama bin Laden for years on end, but they're going to find extraterrestrial life in an infinite universe? Sure they will.

However, the Space Race and NASA created another high-wage segment of industry. It was directly connected to the Cold War, as I said. With the building of various space vehicles, lunar landers, and other Rube Goldberg contraptions with no use other than outer space, came lots of jobs. Satellites were being manufactured, too, and the Space Shuttles were being built.

No one stopped to think that if it wasn't for the Cold War, none of it would even exist. No one except science fiction writers ever cared about or desired to land on the moon. Telescopes had proven that it wasn't even as fertile as the Sahara Desert and there was nothing there to see that couldn't be seen inside a vacuum cleaner bag. That the United States government thought it worth vast sums of money to land on this rock was telling the Soviets, "We can't win the Vietnam War but, hey we can land men on the moon! That means we can drop a warhead dead on to Red Square, so don't forget that." But Americans thought these high paying jobs would go on for decades because they thought space was the "future."

These jobs did go on for quite some time—enough that generations were born that had come to expect the American lifestyle created by the Cold War economy. The Cold War was the actual birth of what we are calling today "the economy." People think that, right after the American Revolution, the Founding Fathers sat down and created "the economy." This is quite simply ridiculous. What we call "the economy" today is nowhere near the economy of even 1938. Today's economy is the child of the Cold War. This is exactly why it is so failure-prone and, in fact, cannot continue much longer without massive changes. It has long passed its viable lifespan and is sitting here comatose on life support from the government. It is time to pull the plug on the economy. It's been brain-dead since 1991.

When the Cold War ended in 1991, there was no need to keep buying massive amounts of weapons every couple of years that kept factories going constantly. Defense plants began to downscale or shut down. Now, remember how I said the United State targeted ball bearing factories in Germany during the war to shut down arms factories? What, then, happens when that is reversed? You shut down an arms factory, and all those little satellite factories around it that have been supplying bolts and ball bearings shut down, too.

If one major aircraft factory shuts down, so, too, do a hundred smaller businesses that were supplying bolts and ball bearings shut down. This is what Americans have failed to understand. The entire economy was built on the massive "boom" of the Cold War. You can't just think Acme Aircraft shuts down and it affected their workers alone. Acme Aircraft was sourcing parts from a hundred independent smaller factories that also shut down and those workers lost their jobs, too.

Where is the massive civilian sector "boom" that would take the place of the Cold War? Space? That was going to soon go the way of the defense industry. Almost overnight, an untold number of high-wage jobs literally disappeared and all those workers would need to compete for jobs that paid less. Because of this, there was less money to spend for consumer goods overall.

Corporations were in a bind. How could they protect profit margins they had grown accustomed to during the Cold War when their goods were not affordable to people earning lower wages now?

Costs needed to be cut some place to drop the price of consumer goods. The answer was amazingly simple. The consumer goods would need to be sourced from a nation where workers were paid far lower than American workers. That lowered the cost of the finished good to a price American workers could afford. This, however, became a race to the bottom. In a healthy economy, prices and wages co-exist together in a fairly harmonious relationship. In the American economy prices and wages are like two deadly snakes in a barrel battling each other.

In the short-term, outsourcing worked to plug the gap between income and expenses. Consumer goods dropped in price to a point that Americans now earning a lower wage could once again afford them. Unfortunately, two things happened that made this short-term solution very short-sighted.

First off, sourcing consumer goods from overseas meant

American factories producing them would have to be closed. This increased unemployment and, again demand for consumer goods fell because there were fewer people with available income.

Second, once many other American corporations saw the profits that could be maximized by outsourcing, they all jumped on the bandwagon to move their manufacturing operations overseas. Even corporations that weren't struggling with lower demand moved manufacturing overseas simply out of greed for more money. This of course, increased unemployment and lowered demand for consumer goods.

The major problem here was that American corporations failed to realize the Cold War was a one-time boom economy that was now over. They could not expect those huge profits anymore, but they had become so attached to them, they felt entitled to them. When people refer to social programs as entitlements, they also fail to understand that corporations demanding the same profits as during the Cold War is an "entitlement." But instead of accepting a lower profit margin and moving manufacturing into new directions, they instead began searching for the next big boom.

Anyone familiar with the ghost towns left over from the 1800s gold and silver strikes of the American West can instantly detect the fatal flaw in "boom" business models. In the American West, a major silver strike would be discovered. A town would be built, such as Tombstone, Arizona, for example. People in these towns often lived as if the silver in the mines there would not run out someday and the town would therefore die. The town's sole reason to exist was the silver mine. There was nothing else to keep the town alive. Sure enough, the silver ran out and the town died on the vine. Everyone moved to the next big silver strike, another town sprang up, and the cycle was repeated. You can go throughout the American West and find towns like this. So it's not like American corporations were unaware or unfamiliar with this dynamic.

Therefore, after the boom of the Cold War, corporations

began looking for the next big strike to hit pay dirt so they could build another town (an economy) around it and based totally upon it.

And, once again, when that boom went dry, the town (the economy) died and they had to go looking for the next big boom. We saw this with the Dot Com Bubble and the Housing Boom. Then we saw a little blip with the "carbon trading" scam, and another with the "Green Energy" scam, neither of which made it past the beginning before they fell apart.

No one would come to see that the money of the Cold War was as much a part of the past as the Gold Rush. In fact, there really was no difference between the two. The gold and silver mining heyday was mimicked by the weapons manufacturing heyday. Americans still refuse to accept the fact that eventually, when no more "booms" can be found, which is upon us now, the economy must return to a pre-Cold War size. Not even two wars, one still ongoing, and another possibly on the way, have resurrected the Cold War military spending that created the Cold War economy. It does not require sophisticated and large numbers of weapons to fight terrorists since they do not have an air force or a navy.

Nowhere is the fatal flaw of the boomtown economic model more obvious than in Housing Boom of the 2000s. Now, buying a house really requires an income fueled by Cold War era wages. In the past, before World War Two, this wasn't necessarily the case. But the demand for houses was steady and prices stable.

More importantly, because nearly all American manufacturing was done here, jobs were steady and stable. In 1910, if Bob worked at Acme Boiler Works, Bob could count on that job carrying him into retirement. Acme Boiler works was stable because no one even thought about closing the factory and buying boilers from China. So if Bob crunched the numbers and found he could afford house payments on his salary, he could easily sign a twenty or even thirty year mortgage. Acme would certainly be there that long. But also, because everyone in

America wasn't going to run out and want a house tomorrow, housing prices remained steady and stable.

House builders wanted to sell houses, not sit on a bunch of new but empty houses no one could afford. However, the demand for houses increased during the Cold War and the suburbs were built. Not just to provide houses which were in greater demand, but houses away from the cities. With higher demand came higher prices. But this was no big deal because the Cold War wages were higher. They also thought those jobs were steady and stable. And they were for a few decades, so this worked.

Obviously, after the Cold War ended, prices on several things needed to return to realistic levels. Wages had, for the most part. People mistakenly believe wages need to be steadily increased to keep up with prices.

This is incorrect.

What needs to happen is prices need to match the available pool of cash people have that can be spent. Not what they can put on to a credit card, but cash they have that can be spent after living expenses are deducted. And the living expenses themselves must have realistic prices that match the wage level being paid. If you increase wages to cover higher prices, prices will go up again to cover the increase in labor costs and because the corporations see an opportunity to capture more available money.

People should refuse to buy expensive products they don't need. If living expenses go up, they need to stop buying all but the necessities. Now, yes, this can lead to outsourcing. But most outsourced products are often things not truly needed like CD players and so forth. If you can't do without a new CD player every year or a new TV every year, don't complain about prices.

You're the one driving them with demand.

The only way prices can be kept stable is by "voting with your wallet" and only buying reasonably-priced items. This absolutely includes housing. There is no sane reason to own a house you obviously cannot afford. Or do not have a stable and steady job that warrants buying a house and justifies it. When houses cost the same or higher in a lower-wage era than they did in the higher-wage era, houses are obviously not a good purchase. It is far better to not buy them until the house builders realize their error and reduce the prices to realistic levels.

Sadly, Americans don't have this kind of discipline or patience. In the 2000s, thanks to a cultural fad being perpetuated by magazines and television, the American people arrived at the wrong conclusion that they needed to buy a house right now. No matter what job they had, or whether or not the house was realistically priced, they needed to buy a house without waiting.

Having said that, I doubt the American people collectively woke up one day and decided to buy houses. Quite obviously, the Housing Boom was a scam engineered by banks, mortgage companies, homebuilders and investment firms under pressure to increase profit margins. They didn't have time to wait for the next boom so they created one. By the use of craft and guile, they used press releases authored by public relations firms they hired to write articles pumping up demand for houses.

Magazines and television shows were all tailored around owning a house. Then a mysterious myth went around into general circulation that if you were paying rent, you were "throwing your money away." Now, renting has been around since Biblical times but, suddenly, it took America to reveal to the world that the world has been wrong for thousands of years. This is typical American arrogance, but many Americans fall for this every time. In fact, most of the rest of the world has grown quite skilled at detecting American poppycock, even though many Americans have not.

In the 2000s vast areas were being turned into suburban housing tracts. But where were the jobs to justify this? There had not been a huge influx of new, good-paying jobs. The wages that could realistically afford these houses simply did not exist. But what did happen was the Housing Boom created its own jobs. Thus, the "good jobs" created by it relied on the Housing Boom to continue in order to exist. These were not steady and stable jobs in the first place! Constructions jobs are often seasonal and travel from place to place.

But, what's more, there are only so many houses you can build. The government read lower unemployment numbers as success, when what they were seeing was not anything steady or stable even for a decade. They mistook that alone for a strong economy. They failed to see this was the same phenomenon as a silver strike. Silver is discovered and a mineshaft is sunk. The mine hires more miners and an entire town is built. But when the silver runs out, the miners are out of work, the town is abandoned and whoever is left with the titles on the property is stuck with it, as worthless as it now is.

There went the government, also reading all this house-buying as economic success when they should have known the jobs and wages did not exist to sustain it. It was even dumber than a Gold Rush. In a gold mine, gold is being mined or the mine has no reason to exist. In the Housing Boom, money was being created out of thin air when a house worth $100,000 before the boom jumped in value to $200,000 overnight. If it wasn't worth $200,000 prior, why is it now worth that? Because of demand? So what? Is it the last house on the planet? No, but Americans acted that way.

It took the creation of a dangerous home loan and mortgage structure to enable people to buy homes—people who could not, in truth, afford them. Things such as sub-prime mortgages were created. We all know what happened later. What people are not seeing is that this wasn't just the banks that ran a scam here. Now, yes they did. Yes, it was engineered by making home-buying a fad with built-in peer pressure. But the American people walked right into it, eyes wide open. People knew damn well they couldn't afford those houses on their salaries. They knew damn well they didn't have steady and stable jobs.

Who did in the post-Cold War era, what with outsourcing, and all?

Not only that, but here is some house that took about

$50,000 to build and you're paying $250,000 for it? Or here's a suburban house built in 1954 that sold for $15,000 then and it's selling for $250,000 now even though nothing whatsoever has changed in or around it? People say, "Well, that's why a home is an investment!"

Wrong!

A home is a dwelling place you live in because human beings require shelter! There is no fundamental difference in that purpose between a house and an apartment. Gold is a way to protect wealth from the inevitable demise of worthless paper currency. But a house is to live in. Thinking you deserve or should make a profit because you live in some dwelling is ridiculous.

People were whining about this when the Housing Boom fell on its face. "I paid $250,000 for this house and now it's only worth $100,000!" So? Whose fault is that? Yours! You obviously paid too much for it, but you were thinking down the road it will be worth $350,000.

Am I right?

If you had just been concerned with an affordable and realistically priced place to live without its value increasing over time, this would not be an issue. It wouldn't matter to you if it was worth $250,000 or $2.50, you bought it to live in and you're staying there, so what difference does it make? "Because I needed to move and couldn't get back what I owe on it!" And you needed to move because your job ended. See, there again, the steady and stable jobs necessary to buy homes were simply not there.

Also, had the houses been realistically priced in the first place, they couldn't have lost so much value so quickly. What happened in actuality is values dropped to what they were actually worth. So, no, they did not lose value. They returned to the correct price, which was still too high.

Why was this demand for houses so high as to jack these prices up so high in the first place? As I said, a coordinated campaign of television and magazine exposure made home buying the "big" thing everyone needed to do in order to measure their own success. In other words, so they weren't losing money by renting. This was a stupid reason to begin with. First of all, paying rent is paying for a service. Like buying medical services. Does a person need to buy a doctor or a hospital to avoid losing money because they did not own those services? Of course not. People, liberal Democrats included, fell for the President George W. Bush "Ownership Society" myth hook, line, and sinker.

People were told by Bush they needed to "own" stuff because that's what being an American meant. Ironically, if you said that's a good idea, and therefore workers need to own the factories they work in, the same "Ownership Society" cheerleaders would criticize that as communism. The reality is, you don't "own" a house until you pay it off. The bank owns it until the mortgage is paid off, which could take twenty years. Your state government charges you a yearly rent of the point in time and space your home occupies and they call that "property tax." So, technically, you're still paying a type of rent, except to your state government. If it was the Medieval Period, it would be called rent that you paid to your feudal lord.

Everyone was in a dither in the early 2000s! In every workplace, the conversation would be, "Are you going to buy a house?" And if you said no, you were met with incredulous stares and exclaims of "Why not? Renting is paying for nothing! You're throwing away your money!" In the end, it was the ones who said that who threw away their money when houses they owed $250,000 on were only worth $100,000 when their job was terminated and they couldn't keep the house.

As I said, renting is payment for the services of having a dwelling to live in. That's all it is. There's no mystery there and it has not been thought of as a "waste of money" for thousands of years before America was discovered. That said, the peer pressure to "keep up with the Joneses" was immense, thanks to a constant barrage of television shows, magazine articles, and even entire magazines devoted to owning a house.

The financial establishment had created the "boom" they had

been dreaming of. Where the financial establishment is to be blamed is because they knew damn well these people couldn't afford these houses. And they knew damn well this would all collapse and when it did, it'd be enormous.

We all know what happened next. I don't think we need to go into detail about that as many books have already been written about the great Recession. The purpose of this was to demonstrate why these booms desperately trying to renew the days of the Cold War are doomed to fail.

What was the government's response to it all, after bailing out the banks?

Right, their response was how to get home-buying happening again. In other words, here's a silver mine that just ran out of silver. The geologist examines the rock and tells you the silver is simply not there. But here comes the government saying let's sink the shaft a thousand feet deeper and wish hard that we hit a new vein of silver. The government's "plan" on the economy was to try and resurrect the decaying corpse of the Housing Boom! Why? Because they don't have any other ideas!

There is another idea that we all will need to wrap our heads around. We need to shrink the economy. We can't spend our way into prosperity. That created debt. We can't keep buying crap we don't need. We're literally consigning future generations to a bleak future, if any at all, just so the corporations can desperately try to maintain the profit margins they had during the Cold War. We are literally converting hundreds of square miles of forests into dollar bills. That's not a correct trade-off, where you cut down a forest to build a strip mall in a city where ten strip malls are unoccupied. So that you can amass a few billion pieces of paper the government says is worth that forest in value. This is slow motion global suicide.

We need to return to the understanding that no one is entitled to some standard of living we call the American way of life. No one is entitled to own a home. No one is entitled to a new car every two years or enough income to buy a bunch of electronic gadgets each month. No one is entitled to a house full of stuff. And there's a flip side to that coin. No one is entitled to be rich. No one is entitled to have a billion dollars or even a million dollars. No one is entitled to harming society and calling it "business." No one is entitled to economic growth or increased profits. These are not things to which a human being is entitled. But neither is "the market." No, the economy is not going to get better or grow into a steady and stable thing.

We need to return to a community-based economy where money spent stays predominantly in the community or nearby communities that earned it. Not put into a corporate bank account a thousand miles away where it is hoarded and not spent. You want to see what it needs to look like?

Go into a predominantly immigrant neighborhood in an American city. What do you see? Mostly small, independently owned businesses. Small family restaurants. Very few chain stores and restaurants. They're just trying to make a living, not necessarily get rich. They also have to answer to their neighborhood, so they can't sit there and screw their community. Their community is loyal to them, which is why the chain stores and restaurants can't make it there.

Everyone there can open his or her own business. Rents are affordable. Housing is affordable. They don't answer to some corporate CEO a thousand miles away who thinks a 10% profit is too little. They're not spending billions of dollars on marketing and advertising. The community knows who they are and word of mouth travels fast. They're not under a demand to grow 20% per year or else. They don't need to convince their community to buy crap they don't need. They sell what the community wants or they don't carry it anymore.

This could be a Hispanic, Somali, Middle Eastern, or Indian community. It makes no difference. What you're seeing is the way American communities all used to be, before World War Two and the Cold War consigned us all to big box stores, malls, and samey-same chain restaurants. When you could own a small grocery or clothing store and make a living. You could own a bookstore and not go broke. The immigrant communities in America are not showing us just the way things are done in the countries they came from; they're showing us a way of life that is steady and stable. The way things need to be all over once again.

The economy needs to shrink down to reality.

The Cold War has been over for decades. We've had a few booms that created their own disaster legacies. But the time has come for us to realize we are truly living in a ghost town and indeed, the Gold Rush is over.

Come the next economic disaster, the Wall Street corporations need to be let go.

If they fail, so be it.

This is as must be. All things come into being and then pass away as causes and conditions change. Propping them up with government aid is only postponing the inevitable fact that Wall Street itself is but a Cold War legacy. They are not "too big to fail." In fact, we cannot move into the future until this corpse tethering us to a long-gone past is finally laid to rest. Then we can truly move on.

No, it won't be easy. But for every major corporation to finally go the way the corporate dinosaurs need to go, hundreds of smaller, community-based businesses will come to take their place.

The dinosaurs were gigantic, but they went extinct. Smaller animals appeared. Nature itself teaches us bigger is not better. American corporations and Wall Street are lumbering dinosaurs that need to go extinct. They are blocking the way for hundreds of small business to rebuild the communities that have fallen into ruin thanks to the voracious appetites of these dinosaurs.

There is no alternative.

There is no boom on the horizon. No one has a plan. Not Wall Street, not the government. And not the experts.

They're all sitting there on the deck of the sinking Titanic discussing the possible temperature of the ocean water. It was not immediately clear that the damage to the Titanic was fatal after it stuck the iceberg. Right now, we're at the point that the crew knows the ship is sinking, but no one else does yet. There's nothing that can be done to save the ship. The only thing that can be done is to get into smaller boats.

Many wealthy people went down with the Titanic. Many wealthy people will go down with the economy.

How much time we have is unknown.

But the ship is sinking.

Jack Perry

CHAPTER SEVEN—HEALTH CARE

YOU'D THINK THAT with all of our great "American Exceptionalism," the United States government would have been able to create a national health care system that smaller European nations created over fifty years ago without computers. What's more, they are all NATO allies of the United States, so it's not like the government couldn't have approached them for help.

You might think that, but you would be wrong.

No one can deny that Barrack Obama, in 2008, campaigned on a promise of creating a national health care system. The point here is not whether or not you agree with such a thing. Everyone has an opinion on that, pro and con. What cannot be denied is that health care far exceeded affordability for a great number of Americans. The prices far surpassed the wages able to purchase it. What's more, the prices were in all actuality not realistic. I'm sorry, but a doctor spending less than five minutes with a patient to write a prescription he's written before is not worth several hundreds of dollars.

If you, as a health care insurance company, want to avoid socialized medicine, you need to make your product affordable. Or on the other hand, maybe you buy a few politicians to co-opt on the upcoming national health care plan.

Look, people want to pull the wool over their own eyes and pretend what's going on is not what's going on. And what's going on? Obviously, the government got huge bribes to turn a national health care system into a health insurance plan everyone was forced by law to buy.

When Barrack Obama was campaigning for president in 2008, he said that the current system of private health insurance was "broken." And this was and still is true. However, Obama promised to fix this and create a national health care system. This is one of a few reasons that he was elected. But what he (and the Democrats) ended up delivering was the very same private health insurance system he said was broken!

Except now you were required by law to buy into the broken system! This is as if a certain model of car is a lemon. And saying the solution is to make everybody buy that model of car and then once everyone has it, maybe the manufacturer will make the needed improvements. Why should they? You just forced everyone to buy it!

Here is the big problem with the whole thing: the federal government passed a law forcing citizens to buy a product from a private corporation whether they want it or not. The bigger picture: if the government can force citizens to patronize private corporations against their will, why should we think this will end with health insurance?

You can't say car insurance is the same thing because it isn't. Not everyone drives, so not everyone is forced to buy it. You only buy it if you own or drive a car. And it isn't a federal law that says everyone must do it, whether they have a car or not, just in case they drive a car at some point. Had the government created a health insurance plan buy-in program they wanted to partially subsidize without forcing everyone to buy it, that would be one thing. But what the government said was that unless everyone participated, it wouldn't work. What?!

Excuse me, but what?! At a place of employment that offers health insurance, not everyone working there opts to take the plan. The company doesn't then say, "Well, everyone but Tim and Susie took the health insurance, but we can't provide it unless they take it, too."

Even more hilarious, are we then to assume if one senator didn't take the federal health insurance prior to Obamacare, the government said the health insurance plan would not work as a result? Better still, why didn't the government just give all Americans the chance to buy the health insurance the Senate and Congress get at the rates *they* pay and subsidize the balance on a sliding scale by income?

Because that would make sense.

Plus, that wouldn't have enriched the gigantic private health insurance corporations while forcing their competitors out of business, that's why.

The usual con artists up there in the Congress didn't even read the Obamacare bill they were voting on! And admitted it! Famously, Nancy Pelosi said, "…we have to pass the bill so that you can find out what is in it, away from the fog of the controversy." Oh, come on, now! What if there was a proviso in the bill that said everyone over the age of 70 would need to be shot to keep health care costs down? What, are they just going to pass the bill and say, "Oops, I guess we didn't know that because we couldn't see what was in the law until we made it a law. Sorry but it's too late now to do anything about it. But we'll attach a rider to the bill to cover the costs of the firing squads." Are we to believe they just pass laws up there without even reading them? Yes! Because they do!

Well, why not?

They start wars without plans on how to win them. They went about trying to topple the leader of Syria without a plan as to who was going to take his place. "You have to start the war to see if we can win it!" Pathetic. With good paying jobs as scarce as they are, the American people do not need one more expense. What's more, it's an expense many can't afford. The government might think a person could afford a $150 a month payment, but how long has it been since one of those jokers actually worked a real job?

Forcing people to buy something they may or may not be

able to afford is not a "solution." You can give them the opportunity to do so if they want to, and make it voluntary. But making it mandatory is morally wrong no matter how they want to justify it.

Don't hand me this legalistic crap about what the "commerce clause" and "tax law" says they can do. That doesn't make it right. Was the Vietnam War right because they could do that? How about the Iraq War? How about assassinating American citizens with drones, is that right, too, because they say it is? At this point it has become painfully obvious that the government is abusing its power and authority. They can sit there and say Obamacare is a "tax" all they want, or whatever other bogus shibboleth they conjure up. Forcing people to buy the product of a private corporation is not a "tax." What it happens to be called is "extortion."

In organized crime, they would go around neighborhoods back in the 1920s and force the storeowners to buy "insurance." This was known as a "protection racket" and it was, and still is, illegal. Well, except for the government and corporations anyway. Anyone else goes to jail for it. Basically, the store owner was told that paying a monthly fee to the organized crime boss protected the business from arson, vandalism, and theft. Which the organized crime gang would perpetrate against the business if they refused to pay. But the way the gang sold it was that it "protected" the business against everyone else besides the gang, too. Even if the business had no problems before the gang showed up, obviously they'd better buy the "insurance" or they certainly would have problems if they didn't.

Now, I ask you, how is Obamacare different from a protection racket? You are not allowed to decline participation. The law says you must buy insurance. And if you don't, they'll take a whopping chunk of money out of your tax return to punish you. Plus, that penalty goes up each year you refuse to participate. Just like if a business refused to buy "protection" from a gang.

First, they'd break the windows. If the business still refused, then they'd rob the store. Then if they still refused, they'd torch the store. So how is the increasing penalty for not buying into the Obamacare protection racket different from that? Loss is loss, whether a gang steals the money or the government does. But I repeated myself there.

It nearly goes without saying that if people could not afford to buy health insurance prior to Obamacare, neither would they be able to after Obamacare. Even with the government subsidies, it still remains unaffordable to millions of Americans. Except now, they must buy it by law or suffer a financial penalty on their tax return. For millions of people, that financial penalty is cheaper by far than health insurance.

Thus they opt to not enroll in Obamacare and instead just pay the penalty. However, paying the penalty means that the government quite literally steals from its poorest citizens who fall into the niche between Medicare eligibility and being able to afford Obamacare. In many cases, this demographic group is, in many ways, poorer than people that qualify for government assistance. This is the working poor, people with jobs that barely even provide for the basics. This group regularly goes to food banks because they cannot afford groceries after paying the rent.

This group gets no food stamps from the government despite the fact their paychecks often create a deficit because expenses are more that income. Therefore, they sometime must seek payday loans that take a year or more to pay off. Or they pawn things, if they have anything valuable to pawn. These are folks that desperately look forward to that tax return check so they can buy new shoes, clothing or new tires for the car. They simply did not have the available income to buy those things on their income. So they postpone it until they get their tax return check.

And here goes Obama, taking that money away from them because they can't afford his scam of a "health insurance plan." Well, it's a "plan" all right. A plan to steal the shoes off the feet of working people. A plan to rob the working people coming and going. It isn't affordable because even with the tax return penalty most people still save more money taking the penalty than buying Obama's "Affordable" heath care! It's cheaper to do without and pay the penalty than to buy the Obamacare insurance and pay those premiums each month using money you obviously don't have. Or you'd have brought the insurance if it was cheaper than paying the penalty, right?

However, the penalty goes up each year to make everyone buy into it once they can no longer afford to pay the penalty. That is, once the penalty amount exceeds the amount of money that the IRS owes them on the return. Within the next two years is when we'll see the true economic injustice of Obamacare when people have to come up with the money for monthly premiums they can't afford in the first place.

On the other hand, people may figure out a way to arrange their withholdings for taxes to the point they won't be owed a rebate on their taxes. Then the penalty will be assessed against a tax return that the government owes no money on. How will they collect the penalty then? Probably by a court order and garnishing paychecks for the money owned. I don't think there's any way out of this nightmare for most people.

But we're not going to see the genuine, deeper problems with Obamacare for another two years when the penalty exceeds the cost of the insurance. And the insurance itself is unaffordable, which is why people aren't buying it. And that's why they had to make it a law forcing people to buy it.

The whole Obamacare system is very difficult to navigate. You go online to this pathetic marketplace that, if it was a brick-and-mortar store, would have long since gone out of business. Prices are too high and it's too difficult to truly understand. Not to mention, and I will say this repeatedly, why am I being forced to waste time with this?! Why is there not an option that says, "I can't afford it and I don't want it," is what I'd like to know.

The Democrat hogwash that they need everyone to participate to make it work is one of the most ridiculous things I've ever heard. What, is this a ball game? How is this "freedom" when I'm forced to buy something I don't want from a private corporation? Even the die-hard Democrats admit Obamacare is a disaster when you engage them in a private conversation, away from Republicans with whom they feel the need to save face.

From the beginning, Obamacare was one disaster after another. But the government kept trying to pound the square peg into the round hole. They trumpeted their "success" because a few million people signed up for it. Yeah, well, people tend to do that with a gun to their head. That's like a state crowing over how many people bought car insurance. It's mandatory, so you can't hail it as a success. Any product can be hailed as a success with statistics if you make it a law that people must buy it. But even the numbers the government reported still say millions of people have decided that they'd rather pay the penalty than pay twice to four times that amount for health insurance even with Obama's "free money" scam.

Hilariously, in Arizona, a bunch of people enrolled in Obamacare using one particular private insurance company. Evidently, the company couldn't afford it, or some damn thing, because the company went out of business and all roughly 60,000 people that enrolled were now back to square one.

All that headache and hassle for nothing.

I daresay this was planned. The big private health insurance corporations got more customers because those customers are forced by law to buy their insurance. But even better, due to the way Obamacare is set up, the smaller competitors are going out of business. Thus, the big corporations get even more customers! And who could forget Odumb-O's famous, "If you like your health care plan, you can keep it." Many people discovered that to be a complete lie as they could not keep their plan and had to buy one they didn't like.

I think we have yet to see the true damage Obamacare will do. Ask the average American to explain Obamacare to you. They can't. All they know is they had to enroll or face a penalty that goes up every year. So they did the bare bones thing they had to do to squeak by. Others just gave up and resigned themselves to the penalty.

We can argue the pros and cons of socialized medicine all day. But Obamacare is not socialized medicine. It's a scam by which you are forced to buy a product from a private corporation. You also pay taxes out of your paycheck that go, again, to those private corporations when the government pays subsidies. Oh, but that's a tax credit, right? It is still government subsidizing a private corporation any way you slice it. All Obamacare does is subsidize private corporations. You don't get Obamacare and then don't pay a penny after that. Even after paying your premiums each month, you still have deductibles, co-pays, the cost of prescription drugs, and other out of pocket expenses. Again, all Obamacare does is force the American people to subsidize private corporations.

People defend Obamacare saying, "Well, it's better than nothing!" Oh, is that so? A bowl of instant noodle soup is better than nothing too, but you can't live on it. Excuse me, but after all of Obama's glorious campaign promises the best they could come up with was, "Well, it's better than nothing..." Maybe instead of "change you can believe in," the campaign slogan should have been, "Well, it's better than nothing."

Really, this is the kind of crap parents tell their kids when all they got for Christmas was a pair of socks. A lot of things are "better than nothing," but, when you have to trot out that excuse to justify your "better than nothing," often it isn't truly better than nothing. In some ways, even worse.

Next up in the Democrat excuse hit parade is, "It was the best we could do!" Oh, is that so? All this "American Exceptionalism" of winning World War Two, building the Panama Canal, and sending a man to the moon, and then they use the phrase "it was the best we could do"? Man, if they had thought that way when sending a man to the moon, he'd still be there. Because they wouldn't have thought of a way to bring him back, but only realized that once he got there. "Well, it was the best we could do. Our condolences to his family…"

So, you can plan one of the biggest invasions in history, D-Day, without the use of computer, but you couldn't create a decent national health care system like our biggest ally in that invasion has? A much smaller nation, too. With a smaller budget, I may add. This is the type of pathetic excuse a kid makes when he brings home a "D" on his report card when everyone know he's damn well able to make an "A" if he really wanted to. If we'd trotted out the idea of "it was the best we could do" in World War Two, the Third Reich would be sitting on the UN Security Council today.

But the winner of the Golden Baloney Award goes to this excuse: "We had to work within the existing system!" Oh really now?! Is that a fact? And who told you all that?

Wait, let me guess: the private health insurance corporations told you that.

At least we now know who pulls the string in the government. Wall Street does. Now, I seem to recall Barrack Obama on the 2008 campaign trail telling us the existing system is "broken." But then they had to work within that existing system? So, then, the government couldn't have done what they do to get military contractors for a war? Put out a bid process for three private health insurance companies to win the contract to provide national health care based on prices the government stipulates? With monthly payment per person for health insurance based on real income, after taxes, rent and utilities as well as an average household food budget?

In other words, payments people can afford, not what the government says they can afford based off of gross income, which is before taxes and expenses. The government fails to understand that things like student loan payments can reduce what they think is a middle-class income to a working-poor income. If the corporations were told that in the event that no one bid, a true socialized medicine network would be created and directly compete with them on prices, watch how quickly they'd return bids with affordable health care plans.

Because they know damn well that government can buy prescription drugs at prices far below what private insurance plans sell them at. They know that because that's what goes on in Europe. If you want to sell your medication over there, you have to play by their rules, not yours.

Furthermore, since when has the United States "worked within the existing system" when it comes to things they wanted to do but the Constitution said they can't? Such as waging wars, for example. The law of the land requires a Congressional declaration of war to use military force. But not anymore. What happened to the tough guys that said you absolutely must work with the existing system? The Bill of Rights says the government can't just assassinate a U.S. citizen without arresting him, having a trial, and a conviction by a jury of his peers. But the United States government has already bypassed that law, stubbornly refusing to work within the existing system.

So they can't sit there and say they're bound to work within an existing system when the private health care industry is not even a United States law! The government does not work within the system of United States laws, but it steadfastly must work within the system of private corporation profit margins? At last, we have detected the swindle!

It is as obvious as the sun in the sky that Obama and, indeed, the entire Democratic Party never intended to create a universal health care system. To be sure, the Republicans furiously opposed such a thing, calling it communism.

However, many Republicans (and allied Tea Party followers) happen to be military veterans that are already using a socialized medical system. The Veterans Administration health care system is socialized medicine. What happened to the tough guys that were against socialism? "They served their countries! They earned it!" So? Everyone in the United States serves their country. Laborers died by the droves building the Transcontinental Railroad, without which the country could not expand. And most of them weren't even Americans by birth, but immigrants.

By the way, when Republicans whine about the immigrants, they should remember the Transcontinental Railroad. Miners died by the droves in the gold and silver mines of the American West to extract the gold the government used to back its currency and the silver they used to mint coins. It wasn't the United States' military prowess that helped win World War Two. It was industrial capacity. We weren't just supplying *our* military, but that of the British and the Soviets, too.

We could not have helped win World War Two without the men and women working in the arms factories, farmers growing food to feed the military, and miners to extract the metals needed for weapons. So now who earned what by serving their country? It is no different today. Who pays the military? The taxpayers, from taxes levied on the income they make working.

Everyone paying taxes or who has paid taxes is and has served their country. When the United States Government starts a war with fundamentalist Muslims and foolishly volunteers American civilians as combatants, those civilians are unknowingly serving their country in an undeclared, unannounced war. The government knows terrorists will target American civilians and still engages in actions that provoke it. Thus, all the American people are unwitting, unarmed solders in this "global war on terrorism." Where, then are the VA benefits for all?

When the Republicans oppose a universal health care system for all, but justify it for themselves if they're veterans, they're setting themselves up as an elite that deserves it. Whereas, the people that built the weapons they carried do not. This is absurd. Either you provide it for all or for none at all. Our system is supposed to be based on equality without one group of people having advantages not available to the rest. Don't give me that crap about who "earns" it. Everyone earns it. But not everyone gets it.

The Republicans also like to claim we "can't afford" a universal health care system. Gee, I don't hear the phase "we can't afford it" when it comes to a war that costs a billion dollars a day. I bet a billion dollars a day would have built a rather nice universal health care system. Maybe we should have asked our NATO allies what theirs costs.

How about the budgets for the Department of Homeland Security and TSA? What do those run per year? How much is the Pentagon spending on aircraft that can do everything but make a cocktail sandwich when we're fighting people without an air force? How much is all of that costing, and how come we can afford that without discussion? We can always afford to kill people, but we never have the money to save them.

Some Republicans say, "Government is not the solution to health care costs! We need market driven solutions!" Okay, you want some market solutions? I've got some for you.

First, the Food and Drug Administration and the Drug Enforcement Administration need their claws clipped and then told to stay out of the way of peoples' health care decisions. Those two agencies are responsible for some of the most ridiculous things ever to manifest in human history. My solutions are highly controversial. But a careful investigation of the true facts, as opposed to the lies packaged as "facts" by government agencies trying to justify their existence, will reveal why these solutions will work.

First up, marijuana legalization across the board. Not just the state-by-state medical-use legalization or even recreational legalization. But the total and complete federal legalization and the ability for it to be sold as any other over-the-counter medication or even culinary herb. You see, marijuana has been used as a medicine by human beings for thousands of years. But here came this upstart nation in humanity, and with a scant history of a couple hundred years, overrules thousands of years of human history.

Thus, making criminals out of people for growing or possessing a flowering herb they'd always had historical and legal access to. How can this make any logical sense whatsoever? More to the point, the government has wasted hundreds of billions of dollars to enforce a series of futile and oppressive laws forbidding the use and possession of a flower. Further along, were the government to truly believe in the "democracy" it claims to be exporting with its wars, it would see a majority of its citizens want to have free access to this plant. We would surely be appalled if we knew the true amount of money governments from city to federal have wasted enforcing laws against a flower. Especially as education in all states continues to suffer from budget cuts.

Hundreds of books have been written about marijuana, the laws against it, and the health benefits of it. But these books do not need to justify it. Human history justifies it. Nothing survives as a medicine for thousands of years unless it works. Just because the United States government refutes that does not make them right. That same government said it could win the Vietnam War.

People need free access to marijuana. The health care benefits are legitimate and many, from physiological to psychological. The government needs to step out of the way of peoples' health care decisions. They're not our mommy, as much as they wish it to be so.

The old stories about "drug abuse" are not told with truthfulness. Drug abuse is not caused by easy access to drugs. Drug abuse is a socio-economic problem related to the breakdown of community, family, and culture. But one more thing is the hypocrisy of a society that says a bunch of men drinking alcohol together is so wonderful that we even advertise it on television. However, if a bunch of men are smoking marijuana, then they're all "drug abusers" that need to be arrested and carted off to jail. Where is the freedom of choice, I ask?

Many things are imbibed for the psychoactive effects they have on human beings, and the sense of well-being they impart. Chocolate, coffee, tea, alcohol, and even chili peppers all have effects on the nervous system. Marijuana differs in the intensity, duration, and effects. However, unlike alcohol, it won't kill a person that over-imbibes. Yet, alcohol is legal despite a death toll that eclipsed that of the Vietnam War quite some time ago. This is another hypocrisy.

Be that as it may, marijuana laws must be abolished so market driven solutions to health care costs can be purchased and pursued by individual Americans. Marijuana can provide realistic alternatives to expensive prescription drugs and treatment regimens. People can grow their own medicine, and if that doesn't make health care affordable, people simply do not wish to see the facts. Governments never have made real health care affordable.

In a brilliant stroke of hypocrisy, it is federally illegal to cultivate marijuana, but perfectly legal to grow opium poppies in your front yard. In any nursery, garden shop or plant store, you can grow opium poppies from seed. Now, they're legal to grow, but you can't harvest the latex from them and consume it. As if the average cop would recognize an opium poppy flower if he saw one among a front yard garden. Or one being milked for latex by a human being. As opposed to one under attack by a grasshopper. As you can see, the hypocrisy is self-evident. A person could milk a legally grown poppy, and put it a container marked "Milk Thistle Extract" and a cop would never know the difference. Am I saying we should ban opium poppies?

No, far from it.

I am saying that the opium poppy is proof the government is full of nonsense in the whole "drug war" philosophy. Anyone can buy the opium poppy seeds and grow them. Even harvest the latex undetected and use it. Has this spiraled out of control into a social disaster? No. Were marijuana laws federally repealed tomorrow, you'd have about five years of a "fad" where everyone was growing it and so on.

After that, people would become accustomed to it and it'd occupy the same niche as any other herb-gardening or self-help activity. I say the solution is to, across the board, give people the freedom to grow their own medicines, be that marijuana or the opium poppy.

Let's not forget that United States law also justified slavery in the past. Therefore, once a law becomes obvious as to being an unjust law, or at least an unenlightened one, it must be repealed and abolished immediately. Otherwise, injustices are heaped upon the injustice of the law itself when it is enforced. People are then jailed and the injustice creates even more human suffering just so the government can save face and refuse to admit it was wrong.

When the government would rather jail people than admit it was wrong, this government has become exceedingly dangerous to the people it allegedly serves. It "serves" them, all right. It serves them bologna sandwiches in prison.

Therefore, any and all medicinal plants and herbs must be wholly legal for a citizen to cultivate. The FDA must not be permitted to regulate it, or license it. The DEA must be disbanded and its duties handled on a local basis by state, county and city jurisdictions. But no local government should be allowed to attempt to enforce its own laws against free public access to medicinal plants.

I'm going to go even further.

Drug testing by employers needs to be banned as a violation of an American's rights against unreasonable search and seizure. This is not an action that ought to be within the rights of an employer to perform. What people put into their bodies is not for an employer to judge. Only in professions, such as pilots, where a direct link to impairment would be a severe problem, should drug testing exist.

But there is no sane reason as to why drug-testing employees of a retail store that sells cheese should be performed, or is even an intelligent action to perform. The hysteria over drugs comes from the government, seeking to justify its failed "War on Drugs" that continues to cost hundreds of billions of dollars. Drug-testing employees needs to end, because it's simply none of the employer's business. If a person can do their job well, what difference does it make what he does at home as long as he comes to work alert? People need to be free to make their own health care decisions without fear of losing their jobs over them. Because if the government abolishes marijuana laws, but employers say they'll still drug test and deny employment or fire employees for marijuana use, nothing has been achieved. People must be allowed to have control over their own bodies.

Next is an even more controversial issue. The current prescription drug system needs to be scrapped and the FDA and DEA stranglehold on it removed. The DEA has no right or authority to tell a doctor what he can or cannot prescribe, or how much. The DEA are cops, not doctors.

As I said, the DEA needs to be disbanded as a government redundancy of police. That the DEA thinks it should tell people who are in pain what they may or may not have to relieve pain is, though, like the decision of a certain doctor: Doctor Mengele. Cops need to be kept out of the medical decision between doctors and patients. That the DEA has also involved itself in governing medications used to treat anxiety disorders and panic attacks speaks volumes about the tyrants and wanna-be Gestapo that run and staff this agency. Again, this agency needs to be disbanded because it has proved itself to be an agency of repression, tyranny, and injustice dangerous to the well-being of the American people.

The FDA will fast-track prescription medicines with a little payola from the pharmaceutical corporation while road-blocking medicines that could save lives. Often, the medicines they fast-track end up to be the dangerous ones and the ones they road-block have been successfully used for years by other countries. The FDA has pretty much become an arm of the Big Pharma corporations while disempowering the American people from making their own health care decisions. The FDA has far outlived its usefulness. It needs to get out of the way so the American people can come to realize huge cost-savings in health care.

Take for example the whole paradox between what is and what is not an "over-the-counter" medicine. Does anyone realize that many of them began as prescription medicines? If prescription medications needed a doctor's supervision, why then did some of them suddenly become available over the counter? Because they realized there was a better profit margin to be had selling them over the counter because those medicines have long since become available as lower cost generics.

Plus, the DEA had no control over them because they were for allergies and nausea. Basically, once prescription medicine becomes available as a generic is when we finally see what the real cost of that medicine is. Does anyone really believe that a $4,000 per month diabetes medication suddenly drops down to $20 with the private health insurance plan paying the remaining $3,980 balances?

They couldn't do that and justify that to their shareholders.

They'd simply refuse to cover it and mandate some other, less effective medication be prescribed. What happens is that the private health corporation can get the medication from the pharmaceutical corporation at its true cost. Just like the governments who have socialized medicine can when they say, "This is what the actual cost is, we know that, and that's what we will pay or we'll kick your company out of our system." The pharmaceutical company wants the sales to the governments and private health insurers, so they offer the medicines at the actual price. Not the highly inflated price they'll sell it to uninsured people who have been effectively locked out of access to many prescription drugs.

Now, the United States government sits there and thinks the solution is some asinine government prescription drug plan. No, it isn't. Again, all that does is subsidize the existing system which we know to be the problem. The biggest problem is the system of prescriptions themselves. Prescriptions have gone from what they once were, which were doctor's recommendations, into being a de facto permit to buy a medicine you are not otherwise allowed to obtain.

You can buy a gun easier in most states than you can an anti-anxiety medication or even an antibiotic. Think about that for a moment. You can run out in many states and buy an AR-15 rifle and 1,000 rounds of ammunition with less hassle and time involved than getting an antibiotic for strep throat. Which, by the way, could be self-diagnosed just like pregnancy if test kits were available over the counter. Imagine the cost savings in that alone. And were the test kits and the antibiotic available over the counter, you just cut a doctor's visit out of the equation, or an emergency room visit in many cases.

"But a doctor needs to prescribe those medications!" Why? And says who? For thousands of years in human history, it did not take a piece of paper from a doctor to permit you to buy medicines you need. In American history up until around the 1930s, you just went to the drug store.

That why it was called a drug store and not a prescription refill center. It was a store that sold drugs. It really was that simple, once upon the time, before the government got involved and made our lives better.

The word "pharmacy" comes to us from the Greek word *pharmakon*, that being a person who compounded and sold medicines. In ancient history, you went to this person to buy medicines, cooking herbs, and incenses. This was the guy who knew all about it, not necessarily the doctors. These evolved into apothecaries that performed the same duties. The apothecaries evolved into what we call drug stores and pharmacies today. And up until about the 1930s if a doctor told you to take thus-and-so, you just went down to the drug store and bought it.

In many cases, what the prescription note actually did was to give a "recipe," so to speak, of a compounded medicine the pharmacist would assemble from the ingredients he stocked. That's why you see old style mortar and pestles used in the signs of modern drugstores and pharmacies today. Because that was a tool the pharmacist used to compound the medicine the prescription called out for.

The prescription was not a permit to buy the medicine, which is what it's turned into today. If you possess or use a prescription drug without a prescription (or with an expired prescription) you are in violation of the law and can be arrested or prosecuted. That's thanks to the DEA meddling in the prescription drug process, as well as the FDA.

Say you had five hydrocodone tablets left after your prescription expired. If you use the tablets, you're breaking the law. If your spouse was in severe pain and used the tablets you'd both be breaking the law. And even further, if you or your spouse's employer did a random drug test, they'd find the hydrocodone in the urine. And then, because there was no valid prescription for it, you or your spouse would be fired for "illegal drug use," despite the fact that this was a legal drug that became illegal because of the calendar. Even more ridiculous is if the hydrocodone had a current prescription date, but your spouse was in terrible pain and took one, your spouse just broke the law and so did you if you knowingly allowed it.

On what planet does this make any sense?

Where providing humanitarian aid to your own spouse is illegal because of a change of date on a slip of paper? Only the government could conjure up such a fiendish scenario by which the law orders a husband not to give medicine to his suffering wife that he knows will help her. Where is the rule of compassion? Obviously, if someone in a household has a prescription for medication, it is the private property of that household just the same as food. No one should be penalized for using private property they bought and paid for. Nor should they be required to throw away valuable medicine just because the calendar changed. Especially since the prescription is a hassle and expensive to obtain again.

Now, I know that people will say, "But we have to make sure people don't abuse it!" You mean like they already abuse it, despite the fact this prescription process allegedly stops that from happening? Where, then, are these abusers obtaining this hydrocodone, seeing as how you supposedly cannot get it without a prescription?

And, also likely, it is possible drug distribution companies are moving some of it illegally. Be that as it may, no amount of restriction or bans have ever successfully kept things out of the hands of people determined to get them. As I said, drug abuse is not created by access to the drugs. It's a socioeconomic problem. If a vast number of Americans feels the need to abuse drugs, then we certainly aren't living in the "greatest nation on earth" now, are we? Obviously, the reality doesn't measure up to the image depicted by the government. Therefore, people seek to escape from that reality. Fix that problem, and the drug abuse problem will correct itself.

Am I saying we should abolish the system of requiring a prescription to obtain medicines? Before I answer that, let me continue. Now, people with anxiety and panic disorders must take anti-anxiety medications for which a prescription is required. Anxiety and panic disorders cannot be cured, therefore, taking medication for it will be lifelong. However, people taking this medicine must return to a doctor each year to obtain the prescription. Why? That person will not have been cured or no longer need the medicine. This is not like taking an antibiotic until an infection is healed and, so, the prescription obviously does not need to be renewed. If you have noticed I use the words "obvious" and "obviously" a lot, it's because these things should be obviously obvious!

People with anxiety disorders know what they need—when a medicine works, you don't want to fool around with it or change it. Because going back to having panic attacks is not an option.

But, going back to the doctor for renewal of the prescription sometime results in the doctor insisting on using or trying a new medication. If you start having panic attacks again, or severe side effects, well, oops. Now you've paid for medicine you can't use. You can't take it back for a refund. (Maybe that's what they should have done to get back hydrocodone still out there on expired prescriptions—offer refunds for unused medications.)

But, no, they'd rather you got stuck with the often more expensive "new" drug that didn't work and then have to buy the cheaper one that does when the doctor makes a wrong call.

Another thing about anxiety medication is you can't just stop taking it. Or go off it a couple weeks until a doctor can see you to renew the prescription. Or until you can afford a doctor visit, or get into a low-income clinic. All of those scenarios are real and happen daily. These folks are part of the crowd in emergency rooms. It's not their fault they end up having to go to the emergency room to get their needs met.

This is directly the fault of the prescription drug system. When a person will have to take a medication for the rest of his or her life, there is no logical reason why that drug cannot be prescribed for ten years at a time. "What if the medicine stops working?" Trust me, the patient will be the first to make a doctor's appointment if that happens. This crap about needing a doctor to yearly renew what is truly a lifelong medication is a waste of medical resources and patients' money! Let the patient decide for him or herself! We don't need or want doctors, and certainly not the government, acting as the gatekeepers for the medicines we already know we need for the rest of our lives.

Our lives are difficult enough without those hassles and hoops to jump through every year. Get out of the way! We know what we need! We're adults here, and we don't need to be treated like children unable to understand our own health care needs.

There are doctors that, when you call to have a prescription renewed, refuse to do so even when you are nearly out of a medicine you just can't stop taking. They say, "Well, I haven't seen you for a year!" Okay, doc, check this out. Have I called you saying my medication isn't working? No. Have I called you to report any weird side effects or problems? No. What did I call for? To get my prescription renewed, because it works for me and I want it and it's the one I want to stay on. So what is so difficult to understand about that!? Why do you need to physically see me so I can tell you that again? Oh, so you can collect more money! No, just renew the damn prescription, how about that?

This game goes on and on and almost everyone on a lifelong medication can tell you a horror story of being out of medication with a doctor refusing to renew the prescription. This is one reason why people end up in the emergency rooms! And they wouldn't need to be there if the prescription drug system actually worked! The reason it doesn't is because it treats the prescription as a permit or a license to own medicine rather than an actual medical document.

A true medical document would say, "Hey, this person cannot stop taking this medication for any reason and, come hell or high water, it must be sold to them. And we'll sort through the red tape later." Instead, everyone out there is covering his ass at the expense of suffering human beings. This is not right. It's like a person has to obtain permission to get medicine they know they need already because they've been taking it for years. How in the hell is that right?

People with lifelong health problem like anxiety disorder, diabetes, asthma and heart problems know what they need. In some cases, they would no longer be alive if they didn't. These people have a human right to unrestricted access to medication. The prescriptions are no longer true doctors' orders, but actual restrictions and roadblocks that deny medication to those who need it. The UN calls restricting medicines human rights violations. And that's what our prescription drug system is. It has become a threat to the well-being and safety of the American people. It is long past time to get rid of this failed system.

So, yes, I am going to say it. The prescription drug system must be abolished in favor of a free market. Yes, and I will say it again: abolish the concept of prescription drugs. A doctor's prescription should only say "Joe Smith needs to take this medicine" and give a dosage and a number of tablets he can buy, and no dates in regards to things where true supervision is ongoing and a doctor is using it as a therapy or treatment regimen.

But any and all medications for lifelong conditions need to be removed from prescription drug status and sold over the counter. A true doctor's prescription for those would say, "Go down and buy those pills and take one every night. See me if you have complications." Sell the antibiotic over the counter. Let the competition between manufacturers take place on the shelves, where we can see it, and not behind closed doors in Congress. Let us enjoy the cost savings when we can buy what we need from among several brands on the market.

Big Pharma will say, "How are we supposed to make money?"

Well, how did you clowns turn a buck back in the old days when a person could buy your medicines over the counter? No, in a free market, you'll have to compete to make that buck. Which means you guys will have to sharpen your pencils and discover new medicines that work better. Because those you could sell at a higher price.

One thing, though, we've all got to remember. Medicines do not exist to make corporation rich. That's not what they're there for. They exist to alleviate human suffering. The reason we act on abolishing the prescription drug system is not because we're trying to push Big Pharma out of business. It's because we need a true market where medicine is freely available and affordable to the American people. Medicine needs to be returned to its rightful place in humanity.

For thousands of years human beings could purchase medicine without bureaucracy forbidding them to. We need to return to what our ancestors knew before the government stepped in and created a medical bureaucracy as a result. Being able to freely buy medicine is no different than being able to freely buy food, clothing, water, and shelter. Medicines belong on the market, not kept behind locked doors only opened with some ridiculous slip of paper.

Further along with that, anything that can be diagnosed with a test kit, those kits should be made available over the counter along with the antibiotic. "What if someone has an allergic reaction to an antibiotic?" Did you know that even the doctor can't know the answer unless the patient knows the answer? So why would a person buy an antibiotic they know they're allergic to? Because a number of people are allergic to peanuts, do we require a prescription for everyone to buy peanuts?

Come on now, let's use common sense. But one thing we need to get on the market is more community clinics. Not more "urgent care centers" but actual community clinics where preventative and alternative medicine can be practiced. This is a theme I wish to explore in depth.

I propose a community clinic where people can "subscribe" to it as they would a gym or any other service. Or buy "shares" as they would with Community Supported Agriculture. Why not Community Supported Medicine? No, not health insurance. That's where we went wrong. People can't afford that and many people don't actually need it. Let's say you only need diabetes management, for example. Then you subscribe to the clinic for that service alone.

Or let's say that you have weight problems. Then you subscribe to the clinic for that service alone. Or if you want to be covered in case you have the flu, or an infection, or need a regular check-up, then you subscribe to a diagnostic service. But all of this money goes directly into the clinics, not some private insurance corporation a thousand miles away.

Make it possible for anyone that was in the medical services of the military, United States or foreign, to do at the clinic whatever he or she could do in the military. Say that someone cuts himself and isn't sure whether it needs stitches or not. Rather than go to the emergency room, if he is a subscriber to the first aid and suturing services at his local clinic, he goes there. It would cost less for community clinics to offer tailored-to-needs subscriptions than for private insurers to offer their "one size fits all" plans as a solution. If a person just needs a blood test every six months and a check-up when feeling ill, why should a person pay the same rate as a person in the doctor's office every week? But the person in the doctor's office every week could subscribe only to that service he or she uses.

Therefore, that person's cost will be lower, too.

We need to return control over our health care to the communities. The government and corporations try to control it and micromanage it some thousand miles away and this is why the costs are so damn high. You've got a hundred government employees and insurance corporation executives that all need to make a buck off of each medical transaction. This is truly absurd. Why should someone not actually in involved in a medical decision make medical decisions? The community knows what it needs. The federal government and the medical insurance providers do not. That's why when both of them together created Obamacare, it flopped worse than a fish out of water. Only the fact that the law forces people to participate in Obamacare keeps it alive.

It really isn't some arcane thing that requires a thousand bureaucrats and a hundred "experts" to figure out. Back in the 1800s you had the "country doctor" that often didn't earn a whole lot more than a blacksmith or the owner of the general store. "Well, they didn't have the technology we have today!" Is that a fact? Technology is supposed to make life easier and reduce costs. So, what happened?

We still must address why a doctor seeing a person for two minutes costs hundreds of dollars for an office visit. The old country doctor didn't screw people that way. Because he was the member of a community and he had society obligations and responsibilities to them. No one denies a skilled surgeon performing a very highly complicated five-hour surgery deserves to be paid well for it. However, you can't justify a doctor charging two hundred dollars for a two-minute office visit just to renew a prescription. Those two things are not equal. Therefore, we need Community Based Clinics and Community Supported Medicine to return control of basic medical care to the American people. That also allows fields such as traditional healing, herbal medicines, and alternative health care to be offered as subscriptions that can coexist peacefully alongside Western medicine. Imagine an on-call midwife subscription, for example. The possibilities are nearly endless, and genuine, fulfilling jobs will be created in the community. Money will stay in the community and not be siphoned off by health insurance companies hundreds of miles away.

You see, the Community Based Clinic would have opportunities for people in the community who have medical talents and skills but cannot afford medical school. Discharged veterans, for example, as I said earlier. The clinic could network with the community college to train medical personnel. The clinic would pay the tuition and the graduates could pay it off in payments to the clinic. Payment would be via installments deducted from paychecks.

Imagine the possibilities for low income communities that are desperately trying to find something for their youth to do that'll keep them out of trouble. There could be volunteer, programs and internships. Programs through the local high school for students to learn on the job through unpaid vocational training at the clinic. Think about traditional medicines they could learn from elders in their culture at the clinic. Then practice it when they graduate. Clergy at local churches and mosques could volunteer at the clinic, as could their congregations. They could sponsor aspects of the clinic; provide spiritual healing for patients who seek it. But the government cannot create this. In fact what they need to do is to get out of the way and stay out of the way.

The community clinic is a market-based idea that gives each person in a community a say and a share in his or her own medical decisions. People can get what they pay for and only what they pay for. There are probably a hundred federal laws that say why a community clinic as I described cannot legally exist. Not to mention the fact that the community clinic can recommend marijuana for medical use openly. This is why the government cannot create solutions. It's too busy writing laws telling you that you can't try new solutions unless you want to go to jail. The government has no solutions of its own, to begin with.

The solution is not Obamacare. The solution is also not universal health care.

The solution is the community, as it has been for thousands of years in human history before governments decided they needed to control every aspect of our lives, including our health care decisions. When Obama used the campaign slogan of "Yes, We Can" in 2008, what it turned into was, "No, I Won't." We cannot count on or expect the government to provide universal health care or even an affordable health care plan for all. The private corporations and the government are too closely tied together. Obamacare proved this beyond a shadow of doubt.

Therefore, health care needs to be wrested from the hands of government and corporations and returned where it belongs: the community. The American people can't afford to sit and wait for affordable health care to be created for them. That's not going to happen, not for everybody.

People have to create it for themselves just like their distant ancestors did. Sitting around and waiting for the corporations to give us health care is what got us the unaffordable private health insurance. Sitting around and waiting for the government to fix that and give us health care is what got us Obamacare.

The reason this all started is people stopped taking personal responsibility for their own health care and wanted it done for them.

Well, they got it done for them.

Look how that's turned out.

CHAPTER EIGHT—CORPORATIONS

ONE OF THE biggest lies ever told is that private corporations are run much more efficiently than the United States Government. With both of them so closely tied to one another, how can that possibly be true?

It's hard to know which encourages, rewards, instigates and provokes the inefficiency and incompetence of the other. It's a classic "which came first, the chicken or the egg?" argument.

Nowhere has this been so perfectly demonstrated than in the Iraq War. Out of that war are countless examples of corporate incompetence, both unknowingly done in ignorance, and willfully done, knowingly, simply for an increased profit margin.

By now, everyone should be familiar with the no-bid contracts awarded during the Iraq War to provide support functions to the U.S. military and to rebuild Iraq. We will never know how many hundreds of billions of dollars were literally wasted through corporate incompetence that nearly, and in some cases, did, dwarf that of the government.

They could not supply electricity, something that Saddam Hussein, evidently, had no problem accomplishing before the U.S. showed up to improve the lives of Iraqis. Buildings were built with faulty plumbing and electricity lines. Brand-new buildings with sewage backflow problems that rendered them uninhabitable. Private military contractors that perpetrated massacres of innocent civilians, including women and children.

191

Meals provided to military personnel with a per-meal price higher than most American restaurants. Showers set up for American military personnel that somehow had live electricity being conducted through the water pipes, turning the showers into a death trap.

Where, then, are the oh-so-superior corporate operating procedures? Where, then, is that superior corporate intellect? Obviously, this folktale that corporations run better than the government was being told by the corporations themselves. Over time, repeated often enough on silly television and radio talk shows hosted by right-wing marionettes, this came to be accepted as some kind of a truth. And people forgot where this folktale originated. Politicians that came into politics directly from executive positions in major corporations began parroting the folktale, thus cementing it into American politics as justification for privatization scams. Scams that, ultimately, robbed the American people and gave the proceeds to the corporations.

Let's call up a little history here.

First of all, the mythic figure of "Uncle Sam" was based on a real person. He was a defense contractor employee who inspected the shipments of salt pork that went to Americans troops. This is also the genesis of "pork barrel politics," by the way, to some extent. The government has always had to do business with contractors even when they provided rancid salt pork and hardtack bread full of weevils. That a defense contractor became the mythic personification of the U.S. government is rather sinister, to say the least, but the history between these two goes back some ways. But the contractors didn't have the power then that they have today. However, a line was drawn between what the corporation did and what the government did. In other words, government property remained government property.

Now, towards the end of the 1800s in the United States, it became obvious that unless something was done, corporations would cut down the last tree in America without hesitation.

Corporations were responsible for the extinction of the

Passenger Pigeon, for example. Unless some wilderness areas were set aside, lumber and mining companies would make sure to lay claim to all of it. There might be no wilderness area left otherwise. So, the federal government established national parks to preserve wilderness areas. This was mostly through encouragement by President Teddy Roosevelt, a Republican by the way. Republicans today would probably call this iconic American president a "flaming, tree hugging liberal" and an "environmentalist wacko." He'd lose a Republican presidential election primary today. "Roosevelt will cost us American jobs in the lumber and mining industries! He's anti-business! He sounds like a communist, trying to socialize wilderness areas that corporations have been running efficiently for almost a hundred years now!"

On and on it'd go.

But what this action did was create a legacy for future American generations as yet unborn. An inheritance of wilderness to enjoy, technically owned by the American people. The government held the lands as government property to protect it from corporations. This needs to be fully understood because we have forgotten that fact. The national parks were created in order to protect wilderness from corporations. Not in order to hand them over to corporations a hundred years down the road.

Now, most national parks have concessions in them run by major corporations that provide such services as food, lodging, boat rental, and so forth. Most people would agree it makes no sense for the United States Forest Services to run a hotdog stand in the Grand Canyon. No one is denying that. But when we have Republican politicians arguing to literally hand over or sell the national parks as a whole to major corporations, then we've crossed into violating the public trust. There are several reasons for this and I will go through them below.

First, the national parks are not truly the property of the government to sell like surplus military vehicles or obsolete office furniture at a government auction. Those are items that have been replaced with new ones, so the old ones are sold to the American people. You cannot sell the Grand Canyon this way. You can't replace that, especially seeing as it is one of a kind in the world. One could even argue the Grand Canyon doesn't even truly belong to the American people alone, but to all of humanity.

Here is where a lot of the free-market libertarians get it all wrong. They confuse government land ownership as a whole with the legacy concept of a national park system. There is a huge difference between the Grand Canyon and Dugway Proving Grounds of Nellis Air Force Base. If the government wants to sell Fort Irwin or a former federal office building, future generations as yet unborn will not be affected. They will not, one day, say, "Gee, it would have been nice to see the Old Podunk Federal Building before they tore it down and put up a hotel…"

But with a national treasure, and a world heritage site at that, you simply do not have the moral authority to even contemplate selling that into private hands.

The Grand Canyon, for example, is actually the private property of the American people as a whole. More importantly, it is the private property of Americans yet unborn. Even if a majority of Americans voted to sell the Grand Canyon, it would not be a moral act. It's not their property to sell, even though it is their property. Future generations have a claim on it and they cannot be asked if they want to sell it, obviously. Therefore, it cannot be sold into private hands because it is not the property of the government to sell.

The entire premise behind the creation of national parks was to preserve them in perpetuity for future generations. This is what's called a covenant established for future generations. You don't just scrap a covenant because of some far-fetched privatization scam. You can't get another Grand Canyon if privatizing it turns out to be a bad idea.

Second, it is not a true value to sell a national park. How do you arrive at a "price tag" for the Grand Canyon? Obviously, with what we know today, you can't truly put a price on it. Therefore, how can you sell it? Where is the Second Grand Canyon we can compare it to in order to establish a true market price? You have to compare apples to apples, not apples to the Grand Canyon.

We know the value of a thing like a used car because we can compare other used cars of like age and model to arrive at a current market price. That simply cannot be done with the Grand Canyon. Once sold, even if a price is arrived at via typical government and corporate sleight-of-hand tricks, the money would be quickly squandered by the government on such things as fighter aircraft that became obsolete in ten years. Money wasted on very short shelf-life items.

But the American people lost the Grand Canyon forever, as did their great-grandchildren, And, as I said, sell it to do what with the money? Pay off the national debt? They'll just spend their way into another one. Because what would they do with that money once they had it? Right. Spend that money, plus money they didn't have. Giving money to the government is the same as giving the keys to a liquor store to a chronic alcoholic. Republicans tell us to sell our national parks, but they never say exactly what it is that they want to do with the money. Knowing them, probably give it to the military.

Third, if corporations wholly own national parks, they can eventually do with them as they like in order to increase profit margins. They could build a "Grand Canyon Phantom Ranch Luxury Resort." They could even build an electric tram in order to take their customers down to their new Grand Canyon Phantom Ranch Luxury Resort.

Right now, of course, there is no such thing. You have to book for the very tiny Phantom Ranch something like two years in advance. But give a corporation complete ownership of the Grand Canyon and that'll change. They'll see there's a two-year waiting list for potential paying customers to stay at the bottom of the canyon. They'll fix that. They'll build a huge resort down there. And since the walk down is legendary for creating heat-stroke casualties, they'll build a tram to the bottom. Yes, then the canyon would be truly accessible to everyone.

But the Grand Canyon as we know it will die.

The Grand Canyon is already beyond maximum visitor capacity. Increase that a thousand-fold, and the canyon will literally die. An epic canyon full of people, shops, junk, trash, and devoid of wildlife. This is why the government stepped in to protect these places to begin with. To preserve them in some way close to the condition in which they were first found. The only benefit a corporation could see to owning a national park outright rather than just the concessions would be to develop them vastly beyond what the government would have allowed. That way, they would bring in far more paying visitors than the park could have accommodated under government ownership.

That's the only way corporations could justify the purchase to their shareholders and the only way they could increase their profit margins. That alone is the only reason they'd want to own something like the Grand Canyon. Their allegiance is to the profit margin, not the environment.

Fourth, there is a moral dimension to this that I have, so far, only briefly touched on. We in America tend to live this illusion that business and profits justify everything and all manner of immoral behavior. Corporations are regularly allowed to do things that, if it was a foreign government doing it to *their* people, would be called human rights violations.

America has a serious character flaw when it comes to morality in the sphere of making money. Money making and "business" justifies immoral behavior in the United States. At some point, it needs to be remembered that there are actions which no amount of money can justify. For example, if a person slipped deadly bacteria into food people ate, he would be arrested for terrorism and possibly even executed if people died due to his act. But if a corporation knowingly allowed food they knew was tainted with deadly bacteria to be shipped to markets, they would probably never even see jail time even if people died as a result.

Why?

Because the corporation didn't do it with the intention of killing people. Oh yes, they knew people probably would die. But the profit margin dictated that course of action because they didn't want the loss of not shipping product. If caught, at the most, they'd pay a fine. But the fine would be far less than the profits they made doing wrong.

Further, if the Soviet Union dumped radioactive rocks over Northern Arizona and Southern Utah and got caught, the government would have called that an attack and declared war. However, uranium mining companies did just that, leaving massive tailings piles of uranium mining exposed. Many people died of cancer as a result, but not one mining company was held accountable and no one went to jail.

Therefore, we see the consequences of excusing immoral acts just because a business commits them in the process of making money. A healthy society must maintain moral parameters that cannot be thwarted simply because money is to be made by doing so.

For all of the self-professed devout Christianity of many Republicans, they don't seem to recall that the Bible tells them this over and over and over again. It cannot be missed. Things that belong to future generations occupy a moral niche in the social contract. That being, it is not moral to even think of selling national parks into private hands. It is the property of future generations, ergo, it actually cannot be truly owned in the present moment insofar as transferability to a private owner.

If we cannot assign a moral value to something such as protecting the Grand Canyon for future generations, we are lost. It would be as if corporations genetically engineered a race of human beings with four arms to be more efficient in certain factories. But any children those genetically engineered humans had would be born with four arms.

Down the road, those four-armed children look at pictures of other non-engineered people and realize those people had only two arms. They rightfully ask, "Why was the decision made for us to have four arms? Why weren't we asked? What gave you that right? What made you think that was right?" The answer to them would be that increased profit margins justified that. It wasn't anything personal, it was just business.

The corporation never entered into any moral question before acting. The profit margin dictated their action. However, there is absolutely a moral dimension. Corporations do not wish for us to see it, because they're all guilty of immorality. You can't sell national parks because it is not a moral act to take away the rightful property of future generation that was bequeathed to them by the creators of it.

Fifth and last, there need to remain public commons that no corporations own and that citizens have free access to. The politicians need to get it through their heads that these are not their lands to sell. These belong to the public. There is no sound financial reason to cede lands over to corporations. Some of the corporations that run concessions in national parks have the same incompetency and inefficiency as any government agency. The same types of people derided as bureaucrats if they were a government agency staff some of them.

The reason: they have a captive customer base. They alone own the concessions and there's no competition. So they can run with even worse-than-government inefficiency and incompetence at times. Employees of these corporations can tell you some very interesting stories about their employers and the goings-on in the national parks. Oh, right, what great efficiency and skill! Getting back to the point, the end of the story is that these belong to the American people. Period. End of story, roll credits, cue theme song.

Now, privatization advocates all sit there and preach the Private Ownership Gospel (their version of the "prosperity gospel") as if this hasn't been done before in the past. They think every government agency sprung fully formed out the foreheads of the Founding Fathers or something.

No, often federal government agencies were created when a

major event demonstrated the need or the perceived need for such an agency to either regulate or prevent certain things from happening again.

Take the Federal Aviation Administration, for example. They came into existence after two airliners collided mid-air and crashed into the Grand Canyon in 1956. Gee, we were just talking about the Grand Canyon. Imagine that. Anyway, the reason for this mid-air collision that created one of the worst airliner tragedies in American history was multi-fold.

First, airliners regularly deviated slightly from flight plans or even did so as part of a flight plan to offer passengers a glimpse of the Grand Canyon from above.

Second, there was no standardized network of control towers all in communication with each other and all airliners and other airplanes. Nor even did each control tower know which aircraft were in their area for certain. Pilots also had some autonomy to deviate from flight plans, as I said. These events are the causes and conditions that led up to two airliners not knowing exactly where one another were and colliding over the Grand Canyon. It was a perfect storm of communication failure because a system to do so did not exist.

Therefore, the federal government stepped in and created such a system with the FAA. The public had no idea that this dangerous situation even existed until 1956. There are politicians to this day screaming to deregulate the airline industry, even to get rid of the FAA among some of them.

Excuse me, be we tried that.

There are pieces of two airliners and dead peoples' luggage still sitting in the bottom of the Grand Canyon to show you what happened. Now, prior to that tragedy in 1956, the airlines certainly could see the dangers of the current air traffic control system. They weren't stupid. The opportunity was there for them all to cooperate and build a standardized system together and avoid the government regulating it. But they didn't, probably because it would cost too much money. So if we privatized air traffic control, what will happen when Air Traffic Control, Inc. decides to cut costs by laying off half its controllers and forcing the rest to pick up the slack? Or decides to go to an unstandardized system? Or there are several private air traffic control corporations and not all of their software systems match, so communication is spotty?

Right back to 1955 all over again, waiting for the big mid-air collision of 1956.

Privatization is not progress. It is a return to a system that did not work or that became obsolete. As long as we have corporations willing to sacrifice public safety to make a profit margin go higher, they can't be relied upon to watch over themselves in something as on-the-spot critical as air traffic control.

Some privatization advocates take a local approach. Why must we have a public fire department? Why can't we privatize that? Well, for one thing, because we already tried that. It didn't work. In the 1800s, we had privately-owned fire departments. You had to basically subscribe to one and they affixed a brass plaque to your front door. If your house caught fire and you didn't have a subscription, well, too bad for you—they wouldn't put out the fire. The problem with this was the fact a house fire would spread and before you knew it, half the city was up in flames. The other problem was that private fire departments didn't have standardized fittings. Hoses and hydrants had different couplings, so one company couldn't use that of another. Prevents theft, and all that. That's another reason entire cities went up in flames in the 1800s.

It's like some people are in such a hurry to privatize everything, they don't check to see if it's been done before and what the results were. They don't stop and ask themselves if they want a crew coming to their house to save their lives on minimum wage. Or at what point the private fire company decides it isn't cost-effective to keep fighting your house fire and just lets it burn. Or a risk assessment decides attempting to rescue you would involve danger to company property so cannot be justified. Are those the decisions you want to be made when time is of the essence and your life is on the line? It all sounds good on paper until it's your ass being sacrificed to uphold the bottom line. So to speak.

Then there're the people that equate privatization with taking power away from the government. Very well, let's examine that, shall we? The government owns Star Spangled Wildlife Refuge and has a sign that says "Government Property. No Trespassing." People are deeply angered and a team of Republican geniuses call for privatization to "get government out of our wilderness areas." Some hunters support that, hoping to gain access to the area.

So the government capitulates and sells Star Spangled Wildlife Refuge to the Fuzzy Bear Wildlife Management Corporation. They take down the government sign and put up a sign that says "Private Property of Fuzzy Bear Wildlife Management Corporation. No Trespassing." What, then, has anyone truly won? Five years down the road, it is revealed that Fuzzy Bear was hired to manage the wildlife, but now it cost five times what the government could do it for. And Fuzzy Bear won the land on top of that. Wow, that's brilliant! I can hear the Liberty Bell ringing already! Oops, that's what made it crack. An omen, to say the least.

The worst idea was privatizing the military. How can a corporation provide meals while paying food service workers the same rate of pay as a soldier? They can't, because all things considered, a soldier earns below minimum wage in reality. So when private contractors said they could feed soldiers for less money than the army itself could, that anyone believed this speaks volumes about the so called intelligence in the Pentagon.

Gee, why didn't Napoleon, Hitler, and Stalin all think of that when their massive armies were on the march? They could've saved billions of francs, Reich marks, and rubles between them if they had just farmed out feeding their troops to some major corporation.

Leave it to the United States government to cast aside thousands of years of history in favor of what some corporation said last week. If the U.S. military had farmed out support functions to contractors during World War Two, we might be entering the Battle of the Bulge sometime in 2025 and the Japanese would still be sitting on every island in the Pacific. The prowess of the United States military to squander hundreds of billions of dollars and call that "cutting costs" is as legendary as Achilles' prowess in battle.

Think about it logically. A soldier that cooks earns below minimum wage when you take into consideration there is no eight-hour day or overtime pay in the army. You can tell him to cook for twelve hours a day and he's got to do it. Not so with a food services contractor. They've got to pay an attractive wage to convince people to go cook meals in some war zone or foreign country. I can state that it's pretty far above minimum wage. Therefore, how can it be said they'll save money? The military says because they only need to contract for services during a war! Oh, so, what then? The soldiers stop eating in peacetime? Absurd, to say the least.

Then the military says farming out the cooking to contractors frees up soldiers to fight. Gee, really? How'd we manage to win World War Two in that case, what with all the cooks and bakers in the army at that time? The army trains people to be cooks and bakers. It's not like some sergeant comes down the line to a bunch of men firing machine guns, fighting for their lives, and says, "Private Jones! Private Smith! Go back to the headquarters and cook dinner! Hopefully we won't get overrun before then." No, from the very beginning, the United States military cooked its own meals. But slowly it began privatization until one day, here we were farming out a war.

You had these private military contractors in Iraq that could perpetrate civilian massacres and claim immunity because their contract said they could not be prosecuted. What!? If this is true, here's a corporate contract that comes right out and says they can break the law and get away with it. I mean, we know they do, but when it's actually in writing, that's a bold step forward to saying they're above the law.

The State Department pretty much ran around guarded by these guys in Iraq as if they were the State Department's own private praetorians. Which is what they were, if you look at your Roman history. Here's the Pentagon claiming cost savings and these PMC's are paying a hundred grand a year, tax-free, to some of these guys. That's several times over what a soldier earns doing the same thing. The American people are duped into thinking these are patriots and not mercenaries, which is what they are. But they're called "private military contractors" to get around Constitutional legality problems.

In Middle Ages Genoa, mercenaries were called contractors, so the more the excuses change, the more they stay the same. But here's the American people not even understanding these PMC's could be used against them one day. The government could call in a private military contractor outfit to handle urban unrest in the event of such a thing. And if they got itchy trigger fingers and mowed down some old women and kids with machine gun fire, well, what are you going to do? Their contract says they can't be held liable for it. The government will say, "Gosh, what do you want us to do about it? That wasn't us that did that. Their contract simply says they can't be held liable for such things. We were under a mandate to cut costs, so we hired them to handle civil unrest issues on an as-needed, per-diem basis."

The government actually has no right to hire mercenaries. It was actually against United States law to do so, at one point. We didn't like it when, during the Revolutionary War, the British hired Hessian mercenaries to fight against us. Why, then, is it acceptable now to hire mercenaries? And pay them far above soldiers fighting and dying in the same war?

This whole privatization scam creates a private government with zero accountability to the American people. These mercenaries are not sworn to an oath to defend the Constitution as far as I know. Some of them are foreign citizens and, therefore, cannot swear such an oath and mean it even if they did.

Generally, as soon as a nation begins the hiring of mercenaries, it has become a tyranny run by avaricious despots many would not be willing to otherwise fight for. History shows this. Time and time again, a king would hire mercenaries because his own troops were not loyal enough to die for his government. In other words, people didn't see his government was worth dying for. Is this what our government is trying to tell us, albeit unknowingly? That they're not worth risking your life for unless you're getting paid a hundred grand a year?

In the end, a privatized government is still the government. Does it make one shred of difference whether tyranny is at the hands of a private corporations or the government? Often, there's even less recourse when a corporation screws you than when the government screws you. If a government municipal water district lets tainted water go into public use, heads might eventually roll over it. Notice I said "might." But let a private water supplier do that and what can people do about it? Fire the CEO? No one has that authority except the corporation itself. Besides, the government sold them the waterworks, so they'll just say it was like that when they bought it.

People forget ensuring clean drinking water was the reason city government got into providing it in the first place. Private water suppliers had failed time and time again to place public safety over their profit margin. As a result, epidemics of water-borne diseases swept through cities.

No, of course local government isn't perfect. Yes, mistakes are made. But we also need to draw a clear line between what the public as a whole owns and what the corporations can own. Water is a public ownership thing. No one should be allowed to own that resource completely. If corporations want to sell their own water, too, that's fine. Let's see if they can build the proverbial better mouse trap. But that in no way means they get to own and control the entire resource of water as a whole. That's as bad or worse as the government owning all of the resources of water up to the point they own the rain, too.

There is again, a moral dimension that tends to get ignored or even knowingly violated when it comes to ownership of a resource like water. Water, regardless of what anyone in business or government thinks, is the common property of every living being on this planet. Furthermore, because it is necessary for life, no one has the right to deny it, or access to it, to other living beings. While it can be sold as a product, no human being has any moral right to own water to the extent he can obstruct or deny it to other human beings.

Again, profits and business cannot override the moral boundaries of what is right, or society will soon decay and begin to crumble. And we are seeing this very phenomenon today as Wall Street justifies all manner of immoral and wrong behavior in the pursuit of profit in the name of business. There absolutely must be strict boundaries that private corporations and even government may not cross. One of those boundaries is that water is the common property of every living being on this planet. And while water can be sold, no one gets to own the entire resource of water, itself. Water does not even belong only to humanity, either.

There needs to be public ownership of certain resources and lands and services. The assumption that privatization won't result in the American people locked out of places they once could go freely is naïve at best. There's even a reverse privatization whereby cities build sports stadiums with money assessed and levied from taxpayers for that purpose, and then the sports team make the profits from the stadiums. Cities build stadiums to convince teams to come to their city. To hell with that. Let the team pay for their own damn stadium or stay where they are.

It makes no difference whether land is fenced off and guarded by the government or a corporation. It makes no difference if money is squandered by the government or a corporation. It makes no difference if I pay the government for a service or the government takes my tax money and gives it to a corporation to provide that service. It is all still the government.

Only children pull the blanket over their heads and pretend what's there isn't there. I don't feel better if some corporation funds a national park instead of the government. I don't especially feel better when there truly is no oversight into this process or real accountability.

It's bad enough our elections are a sham. But if certain politicians have their way, we'll elect a government that then farms out its duties to corporations. A privatized government is still the government. Many people have fooled themselves into believing the illusion that the market will correct the government inefficiencies and incompetence. But they refuse to educate themselves and learn it was often corporate inefficiencies and incompetence that led up to the government agencies being created. Yes, there are government agencies that need to be disbanded because they're no longer truly serving the American people.

Notice, however, I don't call for privatizing government agencies I think need to be disbanded. Either it needs to go away or not. Privatizing is not a solution. If there is a valid reason an agency needs to exist, like the FAA, then don't meddle with it by privatization. The learning curve could result in a thousand needless deaths. Privatization is a scam being sold by politicians getting bribes from the corporations that stand to profit from selling the property of the American people into corporate hands.

That's all there is to it.

Yes, it really is that easy to understand. There is no added "freedom," no cost savings, no better efficiency, either.

Let me close by saying this in regards to the corporate efficiency idea. In the 1800s there was no standard railroad gauge for some time. Meaning, the width between rails differed from railroad to railroad. So, true interstate railroad travel was nearly impossible. Was this efficient?

Of course not.

Corporations make mistakes. The railroads fought against air brakes on trains and safer coupling systems for railroads cars. This, at a time when trains were the sole mass transit system other than stagecoaches. Air brakes and better couplers would save hundreds of lives. Everyone knew that. But the railroads fought them because they said it was too expensive. They have them now, of course, but accidents happened and lives were lost until they capitulated and accepted them.

So, knowing that, does it make sense to go back to a past where we allow corporations to make decision regarding public safety on a cost analysis basis? They couldn't even make the best decisions that were in their long term best interest. They think in the short term, the profit margin. They never think about the long-term consequences of their actions.

Look what happened to Wall Street in 2008 and 2009. What happened to the corporate tough guys that were such paragons of efficiency and astute skillfulness?

Right, they all came whining to the government to save them. Who'd have saved them if the government itself was privatized and run by those people on Wall Street?

We'd all be living in caves right now.

Put that in your privatized pipe and smoke it.

CHAPTER NINE—ECONOMIC CONSEQUENCES

THE MOST DANGEROUS religion on the planet is not Islam. There are two billion Muslims on the planet. If Islam was as dangerous as right-wing hysterics paint it to be, the entire world would be in an epic world war right now.

As I have proven in previous chapters, Islamic terrorism is actually created and fostered by United States' meddling in the Middle East. The vast majority of Muslims are peaceful. But more importantly, the religion of Islam has its own Scriptures, the Quran, which provide important laws and precepts to govern behavior individually and socially. This is very important, in fact, it is critical to a healthy society, despite humanistic desires to bypass this fact.

Christianity has the Bible which provides important laws and precepts to govern behavior individually and socially. Judaism does the same with the Old Testament of the Bible and the Talmud. Buddhism does the same with written scriptures of its own. Interestingly one often finds precepts in the books of all these religions that are virtually identical. This means these precepts are universally acknowledged to demonstrate right behavior as well as wrong behavior that must be avoided. Now, this is important to remember, and we'll come back this point.

The most dangerous religion on the planet is Wall Street

Corporate Capitalism.

Make no mistake, this is a type of religion, albeit a highly primitive one, rife with superstitions and fetishes. It has its own priesthood, and practices a variation of human sacrifice that utilizes the original reasons for ancient human sacrifice.

However, unlike other religions, it has no book, scriptures, written precepts that govern individual and social behavior. It has no Bible to inform it of the difference between right or wrong. In all actuality, it steadfastly refuses any such moral codes to be written for it. Unlike people in the very distant past, Wall Street can understand the difference between right and wrong. But so long as right and wrong are not written precepts they must adhere to, they justify doing wrong through the dogma of their religion.

To fully understand this dynamic, we need to hear a bit of history. We need to understand what a Cargo Cult is. During World War Two, Imperial Japanese military forces were on several islands throughout the South Pacific. The strategy of the United States military was a campaign of what they called "island hopping." The U.S. would land and take an island, defeating the Japanese there, then use that island as a base to launch an attack on the next.

Soon, the U.S. was close enough to Japan to launch bombing raids on Japan itself with B-29 bombers. Each island that fell brought the U.S. military that much closer to Japan. Eventually it brought U.S. forces close enough to drop two nuclear weapons on Japan and end the war. None of this could have happened without an extensive supply line to feed and supply troops engaged in this campaign. To do that required tremendous resources in ships and transport aircraft.

Also, the supply line must be somewhat safe from attack. So the United States used some South Pacific islands as bases to resupply the island-hopping campaign. Some islands had landing strips and docks, and supplies were brought in and stored on the islands. Then they'd be sent where needed by ship or aircraft. This is nothing unusual. This is how modern war is fought.

Something highly unusual did happen, though, in the course of these events.

On some of those South Pacific islands were indigenous inhabitants that had never before even seen an airplane, much less understand such technology. To them, the aircraft was some magical spirit-being, coming down from the heavens. What's more, these spirit-beings then disgorged all manner of wonderful foods and gifts they'd never enjoyed before, or even seen. These spirit-beings just appeared out of the sky, bearing the magical, heavenly gifts of "cargo" as the strange men accompanying the spirit-beings called it.

These strange men would give them a share of the "cargo" (American troops always gave away food to civilians in World War Two) and the tribe could not believe their good fortune. Here was meat! Here were new, sweet fruits! Wonderful fabrics and clothing! Great tools no one had even dreamed of before! Medicine and medical supplies that were unheard of! Even these powerful drugs called cigarettes. All of it arrived regularly as "cargo." The thing that absolutely must be understood is that these people saw this as a vast improvement in their standard of living. To obtain food without such struggle, or have access to goods no one had enjoyed before.

What's more, they were growing accustomed to it and accustomed to having it. They wanted this and to keep this. No one thought it would come to an end. Cargo was arriving almost daily. How could it come to an end? Cargo seemed limitless.

Come to an end it did, however, when World War Two ended. Those remote South Pacific island bases were abandoned. The people on these islands had no idea that when the last aircraft took off, they'd never be back.

So, when time went by and aircraft did not return, they grew alarmed. How would they obtain cargo if the spirit-beings (aircraft) did not come back? From time to time, someone would see one of the spirit-beings pass high overhead, but it would never come down and bestow the cargo upon them. It was wondered if they'd done something wrong, or what must they do for the aircraft to return?

What they did was build several life-size models of these aircraft out of plant materials found on the islands. A religion sprung up around these rituals designed to beseech and convince aircraft to return to the island and bring cargo. It was thought the life-sized idols made in the image of the aircraft would demonstrate their devotion to passing aircraft and convince them to land. This is what was going on several years later when anthropologists discovered this and dubbed it all as "cargo cults." The entire premise of the religion was to obtain a return of the cargo by convincing the aircraft to return.

Now, modern Americans might laugh at this and shake their heads at such primitive superstations. Yet, Americans are all members of the biggest Cargo Cult in history: Wall Street Corporate Capitalism.

As I said in a previous chapter, our economy today is the legacy of the Cold War and, to some extent, World War Two. But it is mostly the product of the Cold War. The economy falls into the same boomtown dynamic as towns in the American West during the Gold Rush, as well as other gold and silver strikes of the late 1800s. Be that as it may, the belief system around the modern American "economy" and Wall Street has literally become just what I said: Cargo Cult.

Here's how it works. Americans are the islanders in the South Pacific, living self-sufficiently for the most part. One day, World War Two (the Cold War) occurs and aircraft (the Cold War economy) brings cargo (good jobs, high wages, suburbs, houses, new cars, consumer goods, television, freeways, new communities, money) to the islanders (the American people). The islanders fail to understand that this is a one-time thing that can't last forever, because they cannot see that. The cargo keeps arriving, so how can it end?

What's more, they've grown accustomed to having cargo and want to keep it. But, again, they will not understand that, when the war ends, aircraft must return home. The aircraft cannot stay there, nor bring more cargo. The war was why the aircraft came there in the first place. Without the war, the aircraft had no real mission there. But the war (the Cold War) does end and aircraft return home (defense jobs disappear and wages begin falling) and islanders grow worried they haven't seen cargo (high wages, good jobs, money, more possessions) in quite a while.

How can they bring back the aircraft (the Cold War economy) that will disgorge more cargo (high wages, good jobs, money, more possessions)? They have seen other aircraft pass overhead (the Dot Com Bubble, the Housing Boom). But they don't come down and give up cargo. So, the islanders come up with a system of religious rituals (corporate tax, economic stimulus programs, deregulation of corporations) that will flatter the aircraft (the Cold War economy) into landing and providing cargo (high wages, good jobs, money, more possessions) once more. The islanders build an image (the market) in the likeness of the aircraft and think it to be the same thing.

However, the image/idol is a creation of fiction, hatched in ignorance. It has no ability to take off, fly, or land like the aircraft did. But it is believed that if this idol (the market) is faithfully served, it will bring back the aircraft (the Cold War economy) when it sees the devotion the islanders have afforded it. No one wants to give up and go back to the way of life they had before the arrival of aircraft, despite the fact they truly have in reality. They've been without cargo for years now and must exist on what the island itself provides.

But they stubbornly cling to the idea about airplanes returning and bringing more cargo. They feel entitled to this and can't let go of it. Rather than enjoying the fruits the island provides, they keep watching skies and wasting time with futile rituals to appease and flatter a god that does not exist. So despite the fact their day-to-day needs are being adequately supplied by the island and also the sea, they reject that as being insufficient and demand the return of the aircraft and its cargo.

This all might be humorous if it was just some sociological quirk of the American people. Or, perhaps some fad new age religion.

Unfortunately, the very real phenomenon of an American Cargo Cult has severe consequences on American families and communities. Generations have been sacrificed on the altar of this cult, desperately trying to win back the cargo that is gone. A priesthood of Wall Street executives, corporate officers, government officials, politicians, and economic "experts" has arisen that effectively parasitize the American people.

Worse, some of them realized long ago that the aircraft are not coming back and keep that information to themselves. Instead, they grow fat on the offerings the Americans people make to the idol of the "market." Others in the priesthood believe the aircraft will return, and cling to the illusion of the idol convincing it to do so. The American people themselves clutch desperately to the belief that aircraft will return and, so, believe whatever the priesthood tells them and do whatever the priesthood tells them is necessary to get the aircraft to return.

As I said, that Cold War economy was a one-time "boom" phenomenon. It can't be duplicated. There simply isn't anything that requires such a massive scale program of manufacturing and subsequent economic growth. To use the economic growth ideas of 1958 and apply it to today makes as much sense as awaiting another carrot to appear in the hole from which the existing carrot was already pulled. But this is what government and corporate sector expects: economic growth on the scale the current wages being paid cannot support long-term.

This is what has created such massive credit card debt and what caused the housing crash. Corporations want to be the massive entities they were during the Cold War without the domestic manufacturing base to support that. They want the Cold War era profits and growth without the subsequently higher wages to support that. They stubbornly refuse to see these facts and admit this to themselves. Thus, they created this de facto cargo cult and mesmerized the American people into helping them cart this incarnation of delusion around with them. Wall Street, government, and so-called "economic experts" all say we need to let "the market" fix things.

What is this but an idol constructed to flatter the aircraft into landing? Or they invoke the words of economist Adam Smith and say the "invisible hand of the market" will point us in the right direction.

Is that so?

What if the "invisible hand" is pointing us to march lockstep over the edge of a cliff? But on the face of it, the belief in some "invisible hand" of a non-existent being is a primitive superstition, at best. The "market" is not a sentient being, nor is it some omniscient god that knows best. It can only do what living people direct it to do. To sit back and think some "invisible hand" will author the right choices is abdication of personal responsibility for the obvious failures of our economic system. The "invisible hand of the market" is a fetish no different than a lucky rabbit foot or a four-leaf clover. Yet we have banked our futures on these laughable superstitions.

In ancient societies, human sacrifices were performed for a number of reasons. But the main belief behind it was that their gods required it for a number of things to be provided by those gods such as good harvests, rain, victory in battle and prosperity. Also, human sacrifice would be used to appease and placate angry gods so those gods would not inflict even greater catastrophes than had already been suffered and which were thought to be the vengeance of angry gods. In some cases, there were gods markedly ambivalent with very unstable emotions that needed constant human sacrifice to provide benefits and abstain from violence.

Today, everyone sees this as horrifyingly repulsive. However, we enact these very same rituals within our society in the way we go about appeasing Wall Street corporations. We'll not just sacrifice people, but entire communities, even cities, so that the angry gods of corporation may be placated. What does anyone think is going on when a corporation says it needs to protect profitability and lays off several thousand people? They'll even call that making sacrifices, so the concept should not be lost on anyone. What do people suppose is happening when the entire manufacturing sector of on enormous city is moved overseas and the city withers and dies?

How is this justified?

Because this is necessary for the economy. Corporate growth and massive profits are necessary for the economy. So, if sacrifices must be made, then so they shall be. It isn't that these corporations are fighting for their very survival. It's that they are fighting for huge profit margins and ballooning growth, and to do that requires the sacrifices of others.

The ongoing problem is that the insatiable thirst of the corporations for profit and growth leads directly to more layoffs, job losses, and wage cuts. This, in turn, causes prosperity to depart from entire cities. More and more sacrifices are made for the economy but are never enough. The long-term problem is we've already sacrificed lots of people and towns and cities for the economy and the economy has not shown this to be working.

But we keep right on sacrificing more people and communities, expecting this to change. In the end, we will be left with gutted and blighted communities, a vast majority impoverished, and the economy will still be no better but will still demand even more sacrifices.

We need to now come back to a point I made in the beginning of this chapter. Humanity requires solid precepts that govern individual and social behaviors. Without these precepts, over time, society decays and falls into a morass of lawlessness and dishonest behavior. Competition for resources turns into a battle more akin to several wild animals tearing each other apart over a cadaver. Therefore, precepts were written to govern humanity. That these precepts came from God ultimately is important to recognize and acknowledge whether you believe in God or not.

Why?

Because God cannot be gainsaid or overruled in regard to establishing right and wrong behaviors. Obviously, humanity chooses to often reject these precepts and calamities happen as a result. Without getting too deep into theology, let me just say that a specific moral thread runs throughout all of the major world religions that have written scriptures they rely upon for moral guidance. These all state there are right ways to obtain money and wrong ways of doing that. All major religions are somewhat agreed in what the right ways are and what the wrong ways are. None of them justify destroying one's own community in making money. In fact, it is soundly condemned.

The problem we have, therefore, with the Wall Street cargo cult is that there is absolutely no set of precepts to govern their behavior. They have no scriptures in this religion to say what is right and what is wrong. Instead, Wall Street relies upon a vaguely inferred directive to grow the corporation and increase profits which carry no moral imperatives whatsoever that direct how it is accomplished. The government has laws, but it's not same thing. The law allows a corporation to do as it pleases with a factory in a city, regardless of the consequences to the city itself. People will justify it if the corporation closes the factory, saying, "It was business."

Even if several thousand people lose their jobs and, so, their income and houses, it is fine because it was "business." There were no precepts to say this act was morally wrong.

Actually, there are, but they are ignored.

But those precepts exist in a religious sphere well outside the cargo cult of Wall Street. There is no set of established precepts telling Wall Street that there is right way to make money and a wrong way to make money regardless of what the government allows. However, if the government attempts to pass laws establishing those right ways and wrong ways, Wall Street will fight that tooth-and-nail.

Many Americans will become convinced of that also and

object to the government trying to do so. Americans have become so desperate for more cargo, they will say or believe whatever the cargo cult priesthood tells them will bring back that cargo. Not that the government ever could successfully establish such precepts. They are some of the biggest worshippers in the Wall Street cargo cult.

The American people failed to notice that the aircraft (the Cold War economy) have not returned and it has now been several decades. Many sacrifices have been made to no avail. They are desperate for more cargo, but the cargo cannot arrive if the aircraft don't. In the desire for more cargo, the American people have thrown away established precepts of individual and social behaviors that are thousands of years old. Thousands of years of precepts that have served people well who have kept them, do not become archaic and obsolete in less than a few decades because people want more money.

There are many currently legal methods of making money that should never, ever be justified for any of reason. They have no benefit to a healthy society, they are harmful. There need to be established precepts that state that there are right ways to make money and there are wrong ways. Those precepts already exist too. But to be of any use, they must be followed and practiced.

When our society is as deeply divided and as fractured as it is, we need to sit down with all of humanity's established precepts and understand what the reasons were for them. When our families and communities are as torn apart and damaged as they are, again, we need to study ancient precepts so we understand that they were written for valid reasons. They weren't written to take away everyone's fun or deny rights to people. They were written to protect society from being torn apart and victimized.

Precepts warning against covetousness and greed should be obvious. When those precepts are broken and a man covets what his neighbor has, he'll do anything to obtain it. Be that lying, deception, cheating, or outright theft, he'll do whatever it takes. He could be a multi-billionaire, but if he decides he needs the money out of the pockets of a thousand poor people, he'll do whatever it takes to get it.

There isn't a precept in his mind saying "Hey, you aren't even supposed to be desiring what they've got." Other precepts command that vulnerable members of society, such as the poor, are to be taken care of and protected. Again, these precepts are discarded and ignored if a business can make money from victimizing them or blocking attempts to protect them.

Most of the business transactions and money-making activities of Wall Street would not be permitted if the precepts pertaining to such activities in the Bible were enforced. And that's just the Bible. Add in scriptures of other religions and there would be a solid brick wall of precepts forbidding the deceptions that originate in Wall Street. But what's more, the self-professed gate-keepers of allegedly Biblical moral precepts that they seek to enforce on society by law, the Republican Party, absolutely refuse to enforce actual Biblical moral precepts against Wall Street.

Amazingly, the Republican Party justifies, admires, and praises the breaking of Biblical moral precepts by Wall Street in pursuit of money. Let's look at the damage the Wall Street cargo cult does in society. We can already see that they will close factories and throw thousands of people out of work just to increase profits. This, in turn, leads to the decline and decay of large urban areas and often entire cities. The numbers of Americans falling into poverty is greater than the number rising out of it.

That alone says the economic system is a failure.

But, since the economic system has taken on the status of a religious cult, no one chooses to see this. Because there are no large-scale consumer goods being manufactured in the United States to drive a healthy economy, corporations rely on consumer spending alone to drive the economy. Or, rather, animate the corpse of the Frankeneconomy cobbled together from various cadavers. Therefore, it creates the desire in people to spend more money than they actually can afford to spend to acquire more things they truly don't need. This leads directly to debt and economic problems as result.

The Housing Crash was created by people trying to spend money they really didn't have, to buy houses they hoped would increase in value, creating money out of thin air. Without people increasing the amount of money they spend on consumer goods each year, the economy will crash. Some retailers bank their continued future on Christmas overspending alone. That alone should sound the alarm bells. We have serious social problems that result from the damage done to families and communities by the obsession with the economy. It is thought to be normal that parents work ten to twelve hours a day, six days a week, and have no time to spend with their children.

As a result, kids learn social values taught to them by the television. Then society wonders why there is teen drug abuse, teen pregnancy, teen crime and teen suicide. Generally, those things are prevented by a strong family. But to have strong families, the parents must be there to provide it. We've had a few generations like this now, and American society is unwilling to admit this to itself. Each generation born now is being inculcated with the desire for cargo. But not having actually seen cargo for themselves, they become disillusioned and seek escape.

Christmas is shown to these kids as a feeding frenzy of materialism and an avalanche of electronic toys cherished above any concept of family togetherness or cohesiveness. Some people are beginning to realize the cargo isn't coming, and that's what's starting to worry Wall Street.

The damage done to the social fabric is serious and manifests in mass shootings, road rage incidents, teen prostitution and sexual exploitation of minors, and widespread thefts and murder.

The very nature of what it means to be a human being is denied by many employers. Employees denied access to bathrooms except during lunch break, or forced to work while sick or be fired, for example. Such things deny the very humanity of those employees and are justified as smart business decisions to protect the bottom line.

When a mother has a very sick child and she cannot take her child to the hospital because her employer will not allow it, what does this say? This says the corporate need for profits has more social value than the life of a child. If the child died as a result of not going to the hospital, the corporation would not see itself with blood on its hands.

And that's the very problem.

People are denied proper wages that a person can decently live on, in order that a corporation can have a higher profit margin. Wealth is not coming to communities in the form of good wages, and prosperity is being robbed from them and carted away.

There has to be an equal balance between profits and wages.

If you as a corporation feel you are entitled to profits that basically gave billions of dollars a year to a handful of people, then the employees have just as legitimate a right to feel entitled to wages they can at least live on decently. But when employees receive a penny for every thousand dollars a corporation makes in profits, this is not a fair trade.

Consider it this way: suppose the corporation was told that they only deserved a penny per thousand dollars product value on the market. In other words, they had a product worth a thousand dollars, but some customer said, "I will only pay you a penny for it. Take it or leave it."

The corporation would claim it to be hugely unfair. Why, then, is it different with the labor of employees that helped create the thousands of dollars of profits? The CEO didn't create that. The corporation couldn't do it all by themselves because if they could, they'd have never hired employees in the first place. People accept the corporate excuses about this because they're told better wages (the cargo) will return when the economy gets better (the aircraft bearing cargo return).

Right now, as we saw during the Great Recession, Wall Street has awarded itself the distinction of being "too big to fail."

This is wrong. If they're "too big to fail," they're also too big to be allowed to exist. No private corporation or group of them should have been allowed to amass that type of power in the first place. This cabal should be permitted to hold the entire nation hostage and extort ransom whenever it wishes to do so? That this sordid collection of frauds, flim-flam men, and other parasites chart the destiny of the nation is a thing that should alarm everyone.

That such confidence should be placed in the hands of a terminally ill octopus that created the 1929 stock Market Crash, the Great Depression, the recession of the 1970s, the recession of the 1990s, the Dot Com Bubble, the Housing Crash and the Great Recession has no justification whatsoever. This octopus would have died during any one of those had the government not stepped in and resurrected it from near-death. That the octopus needs to be permitted to die during the next economic disaster is obvious. The octopus needs to die so it can get out of the way of other creatures better able to thrive.

The government acts like economic giants in the past haven't died and been replaced elsewhere in the world. If this octopus we call Wall Street cannot bring itself to do anything but almost die every decade or two, it obviously isn't healthy. Its tentacles continue grasping and pulling all the prosperity from communities in a desperate attempt to keep itself alive. The time has come for American communities to build walls to block the tentacles, and so hasten the unavoidable demise of the octopus. The Wall Street octopus is dying. It's been terminally ill for quite some time now, but the government and others are in denial.

The government doctor-shops for economic experts who will tell us, "Oh, no! The Wall Street octopus isn't dying! It's just a little sick right now, but if it's well-fed with prosperity of future generations, it will get better! You'll see! Then the octopus will create more prosperity!"

How do people believe in those fairy tales, over and over again? The news tells us that Wall Street stock is falling and everyone craps a collective brick over it. As if tomorrow, the shelves will be bare as a result or the sun won't come up.

Again, an entity with this kind of power needs to be gotten rid of, not encouraged. People in America seem unable to understand that Wall Street speculation is gambling with no fundamental difference from roulette or craps. Except these people gamble with people's jobs, or world food supply, or the oil it'll take another war to replace. Again, why are these people in possession of this kind of power?

This is insanity.

There will be another major economic crisis. The greed and gambler's fever of Wall Street guarantees it. They assure themselves that, no matter what, the government will save them if their mistake catches up with them. Because they're "too big to fail."

The American people must insist that Wall Street absolutely be allowed to fail. No more bailouts. One of two things will happen. Either Wall Street will suddenly find the money they need to save themselves (which they have in offshore accounts) and never repeat those costly mistakes again. Or they actually will fail and when their holdings go up for sale for pennies on the dollar, average Americans buy them and build a new, more community-based economy without some central control center dictating to it.

Because what Wall Street has is an economic dictatorship where it barks orders and every company has to jump and carry them out. So, when it's issuing catastrophic orders that will result in dictatorship, every company is carrying those out, too.

Wall Street is also Hitler in the bunker, issuing orders that only hasten his demise. Wall Street must be allowed to fail in the next economic crisis, which will happen a lot sooner than people think. The economy must shrink to realistic proportions and Wall Street obstinately refuses to allow that. Thus, economic problems will continue until there's a huge crisis that Wall Street cannot sweep under the rug. When that happens, Wall Street needs to be allowed to fail. When they say they'll take us all down with them, they need to be reminded we're already there. It's them who aren't. They're the ones with everything to lose. Let them lose it for a change.

What, are you going to lose your house if Wall Street collapses? How exactly will a bank that no longer exists foreclose on your house? I don't think supermarkets will be unable to find buyers for food. It's the people on Wall Street passing worthless pieces of paper between each other that won't find markets for pieces of paper anymore.

Unless they've got something of genuine value, they'll go bye-bye.

So what if the whole economic system comes crashing down? You can't build a new hotel until you demolish the old one sitting there. Let all the fat-cats in the financial sector up on Wall Street end up picking onions in Fresno, for all I care. They've parasitized this country long enough.

Until that happens, Americans need to understand their communities are pretty much being looted by Wall Street. Americans have a right to protect their communities from this predation and parasitization.

There are two ways to help accomplish this.

No, not by voting and getting involved in social justice causes. In the case of voting, Wall Street funds the candidates. The ways Wall Street can be somewhat locked out of communities is through community-based economics and underground economies. These two things keep the money in the community where it circulates rather than going to corporate headquarters a thousand miles away.

But first, reduce consumption overall. How much stuff do you really need? Possessions are to make life easier, add beauty to life, or serve a useful purpose. Building a life around possessions gets it backwards. You build a life and bring possessions into it on an as-needed basis. You can't let possessions possess you. Especially if you're spending money you haven't got to acquire them. That's what Wall Street convinces you to do so they can amass the wealth you had and leave you with possessions worth far less.

If you want to escape corporate slavery, you first have to stop being enslaved by possessions and the desire to accumulate them without a genuine need being present. The best place to find living examples of community-based economies is in heavily-immigrant ethnic neighborhoods such as Hispanic or Middle Eastern communities.

One thing you'll notice: there is a majority of locally-owned small businesses. You'll see virtually no chain restaurants. No one will eat in them, preferring locally-owned restaurants that offer better food at better prices. You won't see many Big Box stores. People in these communities, for the most part, prefer to shop at smaller stores owned and run by people within their community. They know those stores will have the distinct ethnic foods and products they need, whereas the corporate stores may not.

The smaller stores offer better prices because the people within the community won't pay beyond what they can afford. They weren't brought up with the idea of living beyond their means. The stores need their prices to remain competitive or someone else's will be, sooner or later. But the biggest fact is the shopkeeper is a member of the community and has social obligations to them. He can't run around screwing them and not expect to have to answer for that someday. He wants to keep trust and so people do trust him. He doesn't answer to a CEO a thousand miles away ordering him to engage in deceptive practices to enlarge the profit margin. He answers to his community.

There is a big difference.

When you go into these ethnic neighborhoods with an abundance of locally-owned stores, you've also seen the way America was before the corporations took over. They're proving that a community-based economy can be done. People act like these immigrants are this great threat to America.

I say they're really the ones who embody what really was

America before we sold ourselves into slavery to Wall Street. The real threat to us is coming from these so-called great Americans up on Wall Street. Those are the people destroying our communities. The immigrants coming here are building communities, often seen in places gutted by corporate predation. So, in order to build a true community-based economy, we need to go into these ethnic neighborhoods and learn from them.

We can't try and all of us do this on our own here without input from other places and people. This is how local has become another expensive trend in some places. Someone opens a shop and expects that he's entitled to the same profit margin a Wall Street corporation gets. That's not how it works.

Hispanic and Middle Eastern stores aren't doing that to other people, so just because a shop is locally owned doesn't justify wildly higher prices. The worst thing that can happen to a grass-roots movement is for it to become a trend that gets co-opted. That's what happened to organic food. A true community-based economy serves the community with affordable goods it needs and is sustained by the community that shops there as a result. The concept of an underground economy is one that is somewhat controversial. By underground economy, I am not talking about a black market where illegal goods are sold.

I am talking about an economy where individual citizens buy, sell, and trade among one another without government interference, hassles, and red tape. Since the government has gone well out of its way to create an uneven playing field that favors the corporations, citizens should seek to level that playing field whenever possible. The opportunities to create true markets through the use of clandestine swap meets, impromptu flea markets and yard sales are limitless.

In an underground economy, an artisan can sell crafts made with his own hands without the risk of a storefront business, or the loss of money doing business that way. He sells out of his pickup truck bed. Thwart his store and he can pick it up and move it to wherever the market is or market is strongest.

This idea is to basically resurrect the old public markets and fairs held on public commons centuries ago. This is already happening, but the concept needs to be greatly expanded to go beyond craft fairs, conventional swap meets, and farmers' markets. There are lots of people with merchandise to sell but no way to sell it. This is not to say people ought to go about it in a way to challenge local small businesses.

However, everybody has a right to earn living. If they've found they are locked out of that by partnership between government at all levels and corporations, then they have the human right to sell legitimate merchandise in a true free market.

No business license? So what?

The point is to lift people into self-sufficiency, not hamper that process. The underground economy operates without licenses, regulations, and taxes. There is no valid reason such things should be levied upon citizen engaging in an open air, face-to-face transaction trading in legal goods and services. If a person finds discarded wood and carves small animals from it, then sells these for cash on a regular basis, why should he be at all discouraged from that with licenses, permits and so on? He is selling the fruits of his skills and talent.

The government imagines it is entitled to a share of the proceeds in the form of taxes, so the government actively tries to discourage true free markets because it cannot collect taxes from them.

But again, historically, human beings have bartered, bought, and sold in open free markets without government interference for thousands of years. The government has no moral right to step between citizens attempting to conduct transactions buying and selling legal merchandise. If they wish to regulate established stores in actual buildings, that is one thing. But if people meet in open air space to trade, this is what a true free market actually is. The government can deny that all they want, but they can't deny thousands of years of human history.

True free markets building an underground economy to stop

the flow of community money to Wall Street is an act of economic freedom. True free markets can begin to siphon off the money otherwise headed to some corporation and keep it in the community where it belongs.

Should the government complain, it should be remembered that laws against true free markets are difficult to enforce, at best. Without receipts, it's difficult to prove how much money changed hands or what the merchandise was worth. These free markets already exist. But communities need to expand them and find ways they can be used to benefit the community even more. The main idea is, rather than buying a new stereo from a Big Box store, buy it used from a member of your own community.

I'm not saying community-based economy and underground economies will create paradise overnight. I am saying that we have options. We're not as helpless as we think we are. We might be forced by necessity to work for a corporation. But they can't force us to spend all our money with them.

We choose that.

We choose to go into their Big Box Stores and chain retails and buy all that crap. We choose to spend money we really can't afford to spend. We're the ones without patience to wait and find it used. We're the ones who are just as greedy to accumulate more unnecessary possessions as Wall Street is to accumulate more billions of dollars they don't need.

The kids don't need this or that computer game or a brand-new cell phone. Besides the Wall Street cargo cult, we've also got the "cult of the child" here, where people buy their kids everything they ask for. Do you know why they often do that? Because they don't spend enough time with their kids and they know that, so they feel guilt and try to buy their way out of it. And buy the affection.

That does not work.

The reason you're not spending enough time with them is either you're working long hours to pay for all that crap you bought them, or you're spending too much time in front of the television. If you're working the long hours just to survive, the kids obviously shouldn't even be asking for computer games. We've got our priorities backwards in America, again, as per usual.

The corporations market direct to the kids so they'll nag the parents to buy the products. The parents need to grow a backbone and re-establish control over the household budget. It never should be about what kids want. It should be about what the Family needs.

And that often isn't things. It's time.

People need a realistic assessment as to what they truly need to be content. This economy we have right now causes more people to fall into poverty every year and fewer to climb out of poverty each year. That's a candle burning at both ends. And, for what? A bunch of economic gadgets bought on credit?

The economy will collapse. It's not an "if" question, it's a "when" question. It could be ten years away. But, if you learn how to be content with what you've got, you won't be disappointed when the economy is no longer able to deliver more.

It really is up to you.

You are not totally helpless and you are not totally at their mercy. You are the one who decides to buy what television tells you to buy.

Or not.

CHAPTER TEN—SCAMS EVERYWHERE

WHEN IT COMES to dealing with corporatie Big Box stores, supermarkets, chain establishments and the government, I live by what I call "Jack's Rule Number one." Jack's Rule Number One is: "Always assume it's a Scam." If it sounds too good to be true, then it isn't good or true.

We are living in an era when corporate retailer sleight-of-hand scams are at an all-time high. It's a tough economy, so they're doing whatever they need to do to convince you to spend an extra dollar without offering anything extra for it. I've got to hand it to them. They are good. You've really got to keep your eyes sharpened to a razor's edge to catch them in some cases.

Take for example a certain supermarket chain. Every supermarket has their "specials" they run and they have brightly-colored price tags on the shelf where the sale product is sitting. Now what this chain does is they have this brightly-colored tag for, say, milk. It says "ONLY $1.99 EACH!"

Wow, good deal, huh? But in tiny little letters below that, it says "when you buy three." The letters that say the milk is $1.99 per gallon are about an inch tall. The letters that say "when you buy three gallons" are less than one quarter of an inch tall. Below that, in smaller letters than those, it says "Regular price $3.99 per gallon."

What do you think happens nine times out of ten? People grab the jug seeing only the huge letters saying it was $1.99 a gallon. They don't notice the smaller ones saying they need to buy three gallons at once to get that price. And, really, who buys three gallons at a time and has room in their fridge for it all? What happens is the milk gets scanned at the $3.99 price and people don't notice it because they're not paying attention. Often, they won't even check the receipt at home and catch it. Even if they do, they'll just assume that maybe the sale had expired. Besides, going back to the supermarket to return the milk for a refund would be a waste of gas.

Now the supermarket does this with countless items, throughout the store. It's all perfectly legal because the law just says prices must be correctly marked, not that the sizes of the letters must all be uniformly the same size.

Another common scam is to advertise something like a seven-bone pot roast at $2.40 a pound. Well, you'll make a trip to the market for that, right? Except you get there and find out the only sizes are these huge ten-pounders and they've only got two or three. If you want it, you have to buy the one big enough to feed a family reunion.

As I said, always assume it's a scam. They got you into the store, and they do have smaller seven-bone roasts, by the way. Those smaller ones cost $3.50 a pound. People will mistakenly buy those recognizing the distinctive appearance of a seven-bone roast and assuming the $2.40 per pound price applied to them all. They did not notice the sale flyer that arrived in the mail with huge lettering that said "SEVEN BONE BEEF ROASTS ONLY $2.40 PER POUND" also said in tiny letters under that, "on selected sizes."

Again, people won't pick it up when they snatch up the smaller roast at $3.50 a pound, it'll all go through the checkout line and they won't even see it on the receipt. Or, if they do see the difference in prices at the meat display case, they'll say, "Oh, well, I have my heart set on a roast, so I'll just pay the extra for the smaller one." This scam pays off handsomely every time. And this is just one small example of typical retailer scams.

A variation on this scam uses optical illusion to gull the masses into paying more for the same. Here's how it works. All of America loves the "All-American Pickles," for example. Let's say that they have a distinctive jar and label everyone recognizes, it is a 32-ounce jar, and it usually sells for between $3.99 and $4.25 per jar at the supermarkets. But now Big Box Grocers decides they want to look like they're selling bigger "family size" items that cost a little more, but are a better deal because you get a lot more. So here's what Big Box does. They send a guy down to All-American Pickles and say, "We'll give you this nice, fat contract with guaranteed purchases every month. But we need you to make a 40-ounce jar. Same basic design, but fatter and 8 more ounces." Well, All-American Pickles doesn't give a care. They're being offered a blanket purchase order worth its weight in millions of dollars, and they can source the bigger jar very easily.

So, here comes Big Box Grocers selling these 40-ounce jars of All-Americans Pickles that also has a label which says "Family Economy Size." And the price of this jar of pickles is $7.99 and people snap them up. They're only getting one or two more pickles for about twice the price of the 32-ounce jar. But it looks like a good deal because it's priced at $7.99, and not eight bucks. An optical illusion on price. Gee, and it even look like more, too! Look how big and fat the jar is!

Only, what, three bucks or so more for twice the amount! But is it really twice the amount? No, it isn't. It only looks that way. It's an optical illusion. No one but Big Box has that size jar of All-American Pickles because the jar design is proprietary to them. That way, no one can compare the price with another store. The reality is, a person could buy two 32-ounce jars of All-American Pickles at the supermarket, get 64 ounces of pickles, and pay pretty much the same price as Big Box's 40-ounce jar. Most people will not catch this. They will only see that the jar is technically bigger, the label says it's a "family economy size," and they'll also not have seen it available anywhere else.

They will conclude, in their minds, that Big Box was able to negotiate a lower price with bulk packaging. Thus, they will usually never detect the swindle. Over time, they'll even grow attached to that size of jar and prefer it over the old style 32-ounce jar that the supermarkets sell. Various Big Box Stores stock all kinds of allegedly bulk package products that are actually just cleverly packaged in slightly bigger packages to create the optical illusion you're getting twice as much for your money.

Sometimes, they even ask All-American Pickles for a 32-ounce jar, but one taller and thinner than the one the supermarkets sell. Or one shorter and fatter. This present the optical illusion of more and, thus, a 32-ounce jar of pickles that sells for $3.99 at the supermarkets can be sold for $4.50 by Big Box Grocers. People will pay it without a second thought. It looks bigger. It looks like family/economy size bulk packaging the Big Box promotes itself as selling. So it must be. The label will also say New Size to confirm the deception.

That's just one small example. The truth is, nearly everywhere you turn in the United States, there is some kind of deception going on in regards to chain outlets, corporate retailers, and the elections. The same advertising and marketing agencies serve all of them. The same public relation firm serves all of them. This is the world of advertising and marketing and it has permeated every aspect of American society from shopping to politics.

Of course, there is nothing inherently wrong in selling your product or promoting your political candidate. But as I said in a previous chapter, there is a right way to accomplish that and there is wrong way to go about that.

What must be understood is that if a supermarket or a political party needs to engage in deception or subterfuge to sell their products or promote their candidates, what they're really saying is people wouldn't opt for them if they really knew the truth. Or weren't conned into going for it. In other words, their business and political candidates aren't strong enough to run on their own merits. So, instead, false merits are dreamed up for them by marketing agencies.

To fully demonstrate the deceptive abilities of advertising and marketing, we need to briefly explore what's called public relations agencies. A public relations firm helps with the public image of a company's products or a political party's candidate. Now, both of these things are, in truth, actually the same thing in this day and age. They are sold and marketed to the American people by the exact same methods. You'll even see news articles asking if people trust the Clinton brand name now, and so forth. Thus, we see there is literally no difference between Senator Sneed and Jolly Time Potato Chips. With the public relation firms, the same tactic is used to promote either one. It's about getting the brand name out there.

Anyone can run ads. But getting the name out there means in news articles and so forth. Here's how it works. Let's say that Jimmy Smith Frozen Pot Pies wants to get more people buying their new buffalo meat pot pie. They've been advertising the hell out of it on TV and in magazines and sales of it are still flat-lined. Well, they were certain this new product would be the one to attain that 20% growth they needed to fulfill corporate mission protocols. So they can't just give up and pull the plug on it. Too much product is already out there.

Therefore, they contract with a public relations firm to write what will appear as a news article when it's sent on the wire. Basically, public relation firms can write news articles and put them out on the wire for newspapers to pick up and publish for free. Now, you're a newspaper struggling and here's an article you can print for free, no charge and no need to pay a reporter. Of course you pick it up. Your boss is under the gun to increase the profit margins just as much as it is for Jimmy Smith Frozen Pot Pies.

This is why you can look through tens of newspapers, all different, across America, and find the exact same news articles extolling certain products, foods, or consumer goods in all of them.

What Jimmy Smith Frozen Pot Pies gets when they hire Baxter Public Relations is this: Baxter has a staff of writers skilled in writing the same type of propaganda the Old Soviet Union used to write. What they do is write an article pointing out the new trend in America of frozen pot pies. But they phrase it as a question so they don't get caught having to prove it. This also works subliminally to convince people to get in on the trend while it's just beginning so as not to appear a Johnny-come-lately out of touch with what's hip and cool. So the article will be titled: *Frozen Pot Pies: the New Trendy Food for Comfort Foods*. By doing that, they've also gotten across the message that the frozen pot pie is a piece of Americana, and a comfort food of down-home status.

The article will discuss how Americans, overworked and with hectic schedules, still long for home-style meals. And frozen pot pies can deliver that. Then there will be a bogus interview with Jimmy Smith Frozen Pot Pies CEO, as if a real reporter had actually gone out there and interviewed the dude. Most people will think that's what actually happened, too, because they don't know a public relation firm wrote article. Not the newspaper and not a major news agency whose articles are out on the wire, either. Sometimes, news agencies themselves pick up these articles and put them out on the wire as their own.

Thus, the article has an interview with The Jimmy Smith CEO who delivers the punch-line. He tells us that sales are brisk (whatever that means) and gosh, they just released a new buffalo meat pot pie that he's certain will take off. He'll talk about how no one else is doing buffalo pot pie even though buffalo meat has been a trend for quite some time. He'll say they've been shipping thousands of these pot pies. Of course, he does not say they ship thousands of the pot pies anyway. He'll assure everyone the same vegetables are in the pot pie and the traditional gravy and seasoning recipe has not changed one bit from the original handed down from Jimmy Smith himself. But the buffalo meat is leaner, healthier, geared towards Americans who want a healthier lifestyle but with a home-style cooking flair they don't always have time to make with busy schedules.

Yes, the CEO will regale us with all of this and, hilariously, he didn't necessarily even say it. The public relations firm wrote it, showed it to him, and he approved it. This is the exact same method by which the campaign speeches of political candidates are written. So, the article goes out and is picked up by newspapers across America. People read it and while shopping, they see the Jimmy Smith frozen pot pies and decide to try them.

Very conveniently, they happen to be on sale at a good price (when you buy five of them of course). Then, next week the public relation firm follows up with another news article. This one is a human interest story about Janet Jones who is the head chef at Jimmy Smith Frozen Pot Pies. She'll tell us how she personally makes sure every pot pie has the high quality that Jimmy Smith insisted upon way back then.

It doesn't hurt that the CEO has given her a gratis two-week paid vacation and bonus to say what the piece of paper Baxter wrote says. What's she going to do? Say no? She knows damned well she might lose her job if she says her background is not cooking but chemistry. Or that Jimmy Smith also manufactures the store brand Pot Pies sold for a lot less, and that there's no essential difference besides packaging. That's how Jimmy Smith captures all the sales. And with the public relations firm, they'll capture a lot more.

Thanks to the efforts of the public relations firm, pot pies do take off as a trend in America, albeit one wholly created by clever advertising masquerading as news articles. Thus, Jimmy Smith launches a whole new line of gourmet pot pies that are nearly double the price of the traditional ones, and people fall for the scam and buy those too. They also launch a line of much smaller personal lunch pot pies that cost the same as the larger ones. But marketed for the "busy office worker who still wants that home-made flavor" and blah-blah-blah, people amazingly fall for the scam and buy those too. Big Box Grocers approaches Jimmy Smith with a plan to produce an economy size six-pack of pot pies. The pot pies in the six packs are smaller than the regular-size pot pie. But the price of the economy pack makes it look cheaper to buy than six regular size pot pies separately. In fact, the price difference between six regular pot pies and the economy size is not that great. But people fall for yet another Big Box Grocer Packaging optical illusion.

You wonder why your grocery bill is so high when it seems you're getting less? It's because you are. And this is how it's happening. The truth is, this is what's known as the "Tuna Can Syndrome." Back a few decades ago, tuna came in a seven ounce can. Then the can was reduced in size to 6¾ ounce and kept at the same price. No one even noticed a can smaller just slightly. Then the can dropped to 6½ ounces. Then 6 ounces. The prices were always the same. But you were getting less product.

The can is now 5 ounces and you're paying the same. You can reduce the size of a can in small increments over time, keep the price the same, and no one will notice it. Even better charades are done with frozen microwave meals. Take a good look at most of them and you'll notice an abundance of cheap ingredients. Pasta, dough, potatoes, carrots, rice, and corn make up the bulk of many of these meals. A good example is a pot pie. Let's say that pot pie is $4.00. Okay, well in it is about two cents worth of potatoes, a penny's worth of carrots, about a penny's worth of peas, and about fifty cents worth of meat, flour, and the various food chemical fractions that make the gravy. Then you've got about a quarter's worth of packaging.

The process that puts it all together is automated, so labor comes down to about a dime. Basically, you can assemble the pot pie for a buck, give or take a nickel. But it's convenient, right? We still have more of the scam to discuss. These processed food microwave meals do not actually contain the same amount of food most people would eat if they cooked a meal. In other words, if you made spaghetti, you would eat a bowl full. But the microwave spaghetti dinner (that costs several times over what home-cooked spaghetti costs) only fills that bowl half-way. So, an hour or so later, what do you do sitting in front of the television? You grab snacks, also highly processed foods from the same food corporation conglomerates. With the snacks, they can get you to pay two to three dollars for corn or potatoes worth about a dime. If that much.

In front of the television, you unknowingly eat more of those snacks every time you see snack foods advertised because those push the "gee, that looks good, I'm hungry" button. Then America wonders why there's an obesity epidemic and why their food dollars don't go as far. Well, when you rely on processed microwave meals as dinner, you need to make up the deficit with snack food not much later. People that eat home-cooked meals may snack afterwards, but it is a true snack consumed in moderation. It isn't something filling up the void left by a microwave meal with less food than being served in United States prisoner-of-war camps for captured German troops during World War Two. And we were on rationing then, on top of that.

The entire premise behind all scams is this: How can we supply the very least while extracting the greatest amount of money from the customer? Advertising and marketing are not about competition between brands in the marketplace. They'd like you to think that. But what marketing does, usually, is convince you to take a course of action they want you to take without fully explaining why you should. Nowhere is this more evident than in the world of American politics, home of the Ultimate Scam.

Look at the 2016 presidential election campaigns. Now, the economy is in the commode and it has been since late 2008. People fail to understand we have not recovered from that. That damage has not been repaired. Okay, so what do the Republicans seize on as their topics? Iran, for one thing. Logically, what has Iran got to do with our financial situation as average Americans? Even were they able to field a nuclear weapon, which is highly unlikely, they could not pose a serious threat to American cities. To suppose Iran is as important an issue as whether or not one will have a job next year is beyond belief.

Yet, working Americans will fall for this scam every time, just like they did with Iraq. Who was also said to be building a nuclear weapon, as we recall now with chagrin. Truthfully, these Republican candidates made to their audiences the same case the Imperial Japanese military made to attack Pearl Harbor. "If we don't attack them now and cripple them, they'll become a bigger threat to us later. Therefore, let us attack them now while we can."

Of course, this led directly to a war Japan then lost. A war which also led up to the invention of these nuclear weapons we're worried about other countries getting a hold of, by the way. The reason we think those countries will use nuclear weapons the moment they get a hold of them is because that's what we did. The Republican candidates also whip up paranoia and bigoted fear against immigrants. These immigrants usually are Hispanics, Middle Eastern, and Muslims. With the Hispanics it would usually be broadcast that they're illegal aliens that come here to steal our jobs and mooch off of our social programs. Also, that they sneak across the border to have babies born on American soil that are, therefore, born American citizens. The parents, though here illegally, then have a legitimate reason to be here. These babies are called anchor babies by the Republicans.

Firstly, Mexicans have the same legitimate claims to live in the American Southwest as Europeans that came over here as immigrants do. Those Europeans were immigrants that only become Americans when they arrived here. It needs to be understood that Mexicans were already living in the American Southwest long before it was United States territory. The American Southwest was once part of Mexico until Mexico lost most of it to the United States in the Mexican-American war. Mexico sold the remainder to the U.S. government after the war, deciding with the U.S. government the border we have today.

But the border was no different than any other border drawn on a map with a pencil after a defeated nation lost the territory in a war. Remember that's how Middle Eastern countries were created after World War One. You can't just say your pencil overrules the people that lived there for hundreds of years before you even got there. Mexicans, in truth, are not immigrants to the American Southwest. They are the native, indigenous (to some extent) population of the region. It's the Americans that arrived to the Southwest by wagon train and had their own anchor babies there who are the immigrants. Again, a pencil does not confer magical powers on to a map that Europeans themselves drew in the first place.

Now, here it is about 150 years later, the offspring of European immigrants sit here whining about Mexican immigrants whose ancestors had long been here before the Mayflower arrived. Those people forget their immigrant grandparents and great-grandparents were universally despised, hated, and told to go back where they came from by Americans already here, too. And accused of being illegal aliens on top of that. I also don't see all of these red-blooded Americans lining up to pick onions in Oxnard. Or standing on street corners trying to get picked up for day laborer jobs. But Americans fall for this every time, thinking all the skilled tech jobs are being snapped up by same guy that just hoofed it across the border from Sonora last week.

Notice these Republicans never call for jailing corporate executives with companies that knowingly hire illegal aliens. No, instead, they'd rather punish the victims of those sweatshops that no one else was willing to work in. About the social programs, how exactly do people without American citizenship prove citizenship to the welfare office? With fake identification? Well perhaps, but let me say this. The United States government gives billions of dollars of aid to Israel alone. Why, then is it okay to give tax money to those foreigners, but not ones that are literally our neighbors. Really, what difference does it make if some man in Africa got a dollar in U.S. aid or some Hispanic man went and got that dollar from a social program?

We act as if these are not human beings we're talking about here. Social programs that provide food, honestly, put money into that economy those same Republicans are saying we need to encourage the growth of. People take food stamps to the store and buy food. How is that, again, any different with taking the same amount of money from the food stamp program, buying corn and wheat, then shipping it over to Africa as U.S. food aid. These same Republicans also overwhelmingly support U.S. military aid to Israel which is like a food stamp to get weapons. We basically give Israel weapons stamps that they use then to purchase helicopter gunships and other weapons from American defense contractors. That's how it works.

If you're going to insist taxpayer dollars not be spent on anyone without U.S. citizenship, then let's is fair about it. Let's cut off all these other countries, Israel and NATO on top of that. Look at the scope of that scam. They convinced Americans to be outraged over a few bucks going to a Hispanic family that buys beans, rice, and a few other groceries. Everyone's in a lather, screaming to deport them. But we then sit and cheer when the government gives hundreds of billions of dollars to Israel who then buys weapons from American defense contractors that then pocket the money. People fall for this scam every time.

Not only that, but the Republican Party successfully convinces mostly working-class Republicans to turn against and despise people just as poor as they are, simply because they're Hispanic. While, at same time, mistakenly believing those Hispanics are victimizing them when it's actually the Wall Street corporations the Republican Party is in bed with that's victimizing the American people as a whole.

As far as Middle Easterners go, this is mostly directed to the Muslims. But few Republicans take the time to find out that not all Middle Eastern people are Muslims. Actually, there are quite a few Christians among Middle Eastern populations. But, of course, the Republican Party appears to have forgotten that this was the birthplace of the religion, after all.

All kinds of misperceptions about Middle Eastern people, and Muslims in particular, flourish thanks to the collective ignorance of the Republican Party. First we heard the hysteria about the Muslims wanting to force Sharia law on Americans cities. Sharia law being Islamic moral codes enforced by law. The fact is, there are several Middle Eastern nations with governments that do not practice Sharia law. But there never was any Muslim group in the United States demanding that American courts practice Sharia law.

This was typical press release hoo-ha coming out of right-wing think-tank public relations firms. That's who authored this nonsense, based off of a small-time story about a Sharia-based mediator group in Islamic communities that gave civil decisions. Basically, it mediated disputes between neighbors who voluntarily opted to use the Sharia-based system to decide who was right. This was not a criminal justice court. Nor did it enforce moral codes in the community. It was no different than the small claims court television shows Americans think to be so great. By the time the right-wingers got done doctoring it, you'd think Muslims were out to ban bacon and to force every woman in America to wear a hijab.

However, the scam was rather easily detected. At the same time arose a dispute as to whether or not Christian-owned businesses had the right to refuse to serve gay customers. The Republicans overwhelmingly backed the alleged right of Christians to discriminate against gays. They called this religious freedom.

There's that "freedom" word again being used to describe everything but that. The thing is, though, saying that there should be a religious freedom law that allows Christians to legally discriminate against gay people is saying you believe in a Christian version of Sharia law. So, they feared Muslims forcing their moral codes upon them, but approved of Christians doing so. And wrote laws to that effect! Nobody even realized the scam!

The scam was two-fold. First, how do we inculcate fear of a

certain group of people so American people will support more wars against them? Because the Iraq War had made Americans very hesitant about more military action in the Middle East. The Republican Party supports the corporations that profit off of those wars. Second, how do we scoop up the votes of the evangelical Christians who'll also support our pro-Israel policy we're spending hundreds of billions of dollars on? That's how you can pull out a two-headed nickel, ask the American people to pick a side for coin toss, and the American people will call "tails" every time. Even seeing that is a two-headed nickel, they'll call "tails" every time.

Not that the Democratic Party is any better. Actually, they have better advertising and marketing connections. There were scads of newspaper articles about the high cost of health care, and at least one movie about it, in the lead-up to the 2008 Presidential election. Everyone understands the ads for Obama as saying he would deliver a universal health care system. That would not force you to participate in it, too, because there were already people refusing to go along with such a thing. This was being constantly broadcasted and the Republicans were already whining about socialized medicine.

Everyone knows what we have.

An awful system of private health insurance, but one you are required by law to buy. This invokes the principle behind the scams I told you about earlier: How can we supply the very least while extracting the greatest amount of money from the customer? And that's what they did. Rather than pay for universal health care, they just forced us to pay for private health care insurance and covered part of the cost. But it got him elected, didn't it? Do you think he'd have gotten elected if he'd said he was going to sign a law requiring you to buy private health insurance or lose hundreds, even a thousand, dollars of your tax return rebate if you don't?

Obamacare was a brilliant scam, I'll give that to them.

With the stroke of pen, the profit margins and holdings of

gigantic private insurance companies ballooned overnight. What's more, they had conned the American people into going for it. Obamacare is the perfect textbook example of how American election scams operate.

Contrary to popular opinion, the true intent of the scam is not election fraud or rigged elections, though that certainly occurs. The true intent is to present the scam as a great thing, getting you to buy it. Once home with it it's too late to take it back for a refund. Therefore, deception obviously must be used to get you to think the government will give you free health care. They cannot tell you what they really plan to do or you won't fall for it.

Anytime the government or a political campaign promises something to you, remember: Always assume it's a scam. It's not being overly cynical or paranoid to look critically at the motives of the government, elections, and corporations. Everything they do should be assumed to be a scam of one kind or another until proven otherwise. Look, they have not given us sufficient reason to think otherwise. Time and time again, they've run these scams and we only discover them too late to do anything about them.

Like the Housing Boom scam that only was revealed as a scam when we fell into the Great Recession as result.

Like the Iraq War scam that was only revealed as a scam when we were ass-deep in that war with no way to truly win it.

Like the Obamacare scam that was revealed as a scam only when we were being forced to buy private insurance by law with no way to reject that law or its provisions.

Like the Syria regime-change scam that was only revealed as scam when it blew up into a major war and the birth of a deadly terrorist army we had created.

Like the Big Box and chain retailer scams by which they go into communities and "price war" the small shops out of business. Once the mom-and-pop stores are gone, the Big Box and chain stores jack up their prices higher than the mom-and-pop stores had. But now no one has a choice except to shop at the Big Box because all the local stores are gone. They fell for the scam thinking those low prices would last forever, so they betrayed their own neighbors.

These scams operate twenty-four hours a day, seven days a week. They do not sleep. There is a constant barrage of input to overwhelm and break down your resistance to: "Buy this! Eat that! Shop here! Vote for McDweeb! Take this medicine and you'll find life worth living again! Wear these shoes! Drive this car! Your wife should look like this! Your kids need these computer games! Drink this beer! Vote for McDorkle! This ad paid for by the Campaign to Elect Doofus! If you can't sleep you should take this pill!"

And on and on it goes, non-stop, an endless march of marketing mediocrity everyone sits there mesmerized watching. They don't realize they're being brainwashed. Look at the calls to privatize Social Security. This comes from the Republican Party. They smear Social Security as an entitlement as if people are just awarded this money for free and haven't paid into it all their lives. If the Republican had their way, they'd raise the age you could draw Social Security to 100 so few would live to collect it. The Republicans like to say Social Security is running out of money. Right, that's because the government loots the Social Security cash box to get money it doesn't otherwise have to buy more weapons it doesn't need and fight wars it has no business fighting.

Therefore, the Republicans say the solution is to privatize this system. Look at it logically and with an eye of reality. If you are CEO of an investment firm that handles retirement accounts, then one day the government just scrapped Social Security, wouldn't you realize people will have no choice but to invest with you? So why would you need to offer much at all to get them to come to you?

More to the point, would you give a care about how much money they ended up retiring with as long as you made profit margins go up each year? And when the economy takes a dive, like it does every year, you can simply pay nothing or little into the accounts while pocketing your own profits. "Hey, the economy is bad, so we can't pay the matching funds into your account. Sorry." Come on, doesn't even one person wonder why these Wall Street fat cats are lobbying the Republicans to privatize Social Security? Does anyone actually think they care about retirement income of senior citizens? I mean, here's a scam so obvious you'd have to be a 10th century peasant not to see it.

Social Security is not about running a retirement savings system where they have to make huge profits each year, with those profits increasing every year on top of that. That's basically what a 401K is. So, Social Security can have people pay into it and they're assured as to what they'll get in the end. But with a privatized system, it'd be run by investment firms needing to make profits. It'd be the same stock market based system as a 401K. Therefore, people could lose money from it just like they did with 401K plans during The Great Recession.

You can't lose money on Social Security like a 401K plan does. And people think a privatized Social Security would be better? Yes, they do. Why? Look at the scam. The way privatized Social Security is sold to the American people is that they'll be able to make more money if they can control their own money. This is a wining gambit. Promise more money and you appeal to the desire of people to get more for less.

As I said in the very beginning of this chapter, if it sounds too good to be true, it isn't good or true. And after Wall Street nearly collapsed in 2008-2009 without the government riding to the rescue, how can they offer a better retirement system? Think about that realistically. Here's Wall Street, which says it has a better retirement system, getting its ass pulled out of the fire by the government who runs the Social Security system they criticize.

Let's say they did privatize Social Security and Wall Street ran it. And they typically blew all the money on bad investments and came up empty-handed on peoples' retirements. Guess who'd have to come up with the money to make good on those retirements and make sure old people got their checks? Government! So why not have just stuck with Social Security, people would say. Why? Because you all fell for the scam and thought privatized retirement accounts would give you more money than Social Security! Really, people need to wake up. These scams are not that difficult to detect.

"But experts say privatized Social Security will be better! They've proven it!" Oh, they've "proven" it, have they? Let's not forget experts told us the Iraq War would be a cakewalk, remember that? Oh, and they "proved" that also, before it began.

The experts led us right into the crash of the housing boom that resulted in the Great Rescission and the near collapse of the Wall Street. Most experts are professional college students that have never had a real job in their lives. They just sit in universities, collecting more initials to write after their names. Oh, they're all highly educated, but without common sense.

Book smart, but can't change a tire if their lives depended on it. They go from think-tank to university to politics, making educated guesses about things they've never actually experienced or seen. Experts on war who've never even been in the military. My gosh, we've got a Secretary of Defense like that. Yes, another expert, and look what we've got to show for it.

Experts on retirement savings accounts who have never had to live on a fixed income and whose family is very wealthy. These experts are the confidence men leading us into the scams like barkers on the carnival midway row of bogus games!

My gosh, people, doesn't anyone remember the old television commercials of the 1970s? "Nine out of ten doctors recommend switching from butter to margarine!" "Experts agree that margarine is healthier than butter!" "The result is in! Heart health experts agree margarine is better for heart health, hands down!"

What did we find out but a couple decades later? That the reverse was true! That butter was healthier and that margarine full of hydrogenated fat was actually not healthy! But the dairy industry didn't have the political clout the Big Agri corporations had when selling the corn that margarine was made from. Corn was subsidized by the Government.

Damned right the experts wanted you to buy margarine. But if you didn't ask why butter, a food eaten without problems for thousands of years, suddenly became bad because these experts said so, then you fell for the scam. But you wouldn't know it to be a scam unless you had trained yourself to carefully approach the claims of any advertising and marketing with knowledge that you're being lied to. The experts have made a living off of methods to cleverly craft lies that can hide the true nature of whatever it is they promoting. The experts even said atmospheric testing of nuclear weapons was harmless. Don't forget that.

After my Rule Number One, comes Rule Number Two. Jack's Rule Number Two is: "Figure out a way around the scam." Most of the time, what you see advertised in supermarket sales flyers aren't always the best prices in the store. Often, it'll be things not advertised that are the best prices. The "sale" is trying to move more expensive stuff by convincing you it costs less. But you'll usually find lots of things for cheaper if you just ignore the flyer and look.

For example, say you need meat. The supermarket flyer says these pot roasts are on sale for $3.50 a pound. But I've only got $10.00 to spend and a three-pound roast has already gone fifty cents over budget. Looking around, I see chicken thigh over here at $1.29 a pound, which is already cheaper by far. Looking closer, there is a 50 % off sticker on them, which drops the price to a little over sixty cents a pound. I can get plenty of meat and have money left over for vegetables. So it's chicken and not beef, so what? Meat is meat. The supermarket tries to get me to think pot roast is the best deal going. But if I don't just accept that at face value and assume I'm being scammed into thinking that's what they want me to think, I'll look closer and find the better deal on my own. I found a way around the scam.

The other thing is the nature of big chain supermarkets

themselves. They have to be all things to all people.

But when you're the jack of all trades, you're the master of none. The supermarkets themselves pushed out the local bakers, butchers, and greengrocers back in the 1950s when they began to really flex their muscles. It seemed more convenient and prices were lower. That was then. This is now. Right now, the truth is, if you're not shopping in ethnic groceries stores, you're paying way too much. Look, immigrant communities don't have scams to run when it comes to selling food. They have to sell at good prices or someone else will.

But don't take my word for it. Go to a supermarket and price olives in jar, lamb meat, and tea. Now go to a good Middle Eastern grocery store in a predominantly Middle Eastern immigrant neighborhood. The price difference will amaze you. See, the Middle Eastern grocer hasn't got a chain of distributors, executives, and a CEO all with a hand out for profits. He hasn't got someone hassling him to gee the margins up and so he's got to raise his prices. And on spices, no one can compete with Middle Eastern grocers, hands down. Generally, if you make the rounds to the Middle Eastern, Hispanic, and Asian grocery stores, you'll save hundreds of dollars on your food budget in a year. You'll also find your neighborhood greengrocer or produce market often has lower-priced fruit and vegetables than supermarkets.

Now, I am not talking about these community farmers' markets where organic fruit and vegetables come from boutique and hobby farms. Those are usually unrealistically priced. People say, "Don't you support local agriculture?" Yes, I do, but only up to a point. It needs to be affordable to the working people or it just becomes another trendy limousine liberal fad like electric cars no one but the wealthy can afford.

Listen, scams are scams and local movements and green culture also has perpetrated some of the biggest scams. I am sorry, but potatoes don't cost five dollars a pound, regardless of what color they are. They are not that difficult to grow. If a person has ten dollars to spend, he's better off buying ten pounds of broccoli or cabbage at a buck a pound from the non-organic greengrocer than two pounds of the same from the community farmers' market. The community farmers' markets are a good idea in theory, but they've been overrun with elitism and a boutique mentality so overwhelming at natural foods markets.

Get prices where the working people can afford them or you haven't got a viable solution. What you've got is a marketing gimmick and one ripe for scam artists. Again, shopping local doesn't mean buying into expensive boutiques and markets that have usurped the local name to run their scams.

You have to understand that nearly all foods and trends that involve products or activities where products can be sold were created by advertising and marketing, with the help of product placements in television shows. When grass roots fads and trends arise, it takes about one year for corporations to co-opt it and cash in on it.

The same with political movements. The Tea Party, of course, got co-opted by the more extreme wing of the Republican Party. And the Occupy Wall Street movement got co-opted by the Democrats. The term natural food was started by counter-culture hippies in the late 1960s and early 1970s. They started co-op grocery stores that they called natural foods markets, that being, a "back-to-the-land" philosophy on unprocessed foods. It didn't take long for the corporations to grab hold of that and meat raised in factory farms is labeled as natural as are all manner of processed food. Getting around the label is key.

To find a way around the scam, you have to totally disregard what you're being told about it and look deeply into it to see what it really is. Not every single business is running a scam. But you can't afford to go thru life in the current United States thinking you are being told the truth on television and in magazines.

If it seems a corporation is spending a great deal of time and money to convince you of something, you can be damn sure there's scam in it somewhere. It goes without saying when a politician is doing that, there is scam going on. Ask yourself,

"Why are they spending all thus money to convince me of this? Who is paying for it up front? More importantly, who is paying for it behind the scenes that I do not know about? And what is their true, but hidden motive?"

Even a lot of allegedly independent political organizations, social justice groups, environmentalist groups, and various right-wing causes are getting dark money out of deep pockets. Let's say, for example, the Republican Party wants to make inroads into a traditionally Democrat-controlled city. In the next city election, you'll see all these snazzy signs popping up all over the place, blasting the Democrats for all types of social ills. Now, these signs cost money. A lot of money. Who's putting up the money to pay for that? And what is it they want out of their investment? Obviously, there's a scam afoot to be spending all that money to try to win some local election.

Or, let's say all these billboards start appearing sounding the alarm about global warming. Others are calling out for the passing of a law to provide tax rebates for people that buy renewable energy products and systems. Magazine ads appear in all the liberal-oriented magazines, television ads appear with liberal celebrities sounding the alarm about climate change.

Okay, now, none of this is free.

Billboard space costs money and so do television commercials. Why is so much many being spent to convince you the planet is getting warmer and that renewable energy is the solution? It all revolves around lobbying effort for a tax rebate to encourage people to purchase renewable energy systems for their homes. A diligent investigation that can be accomplished in five minutes on the internet reveals who is paying for all of this marketing.

It's a conglomerate lobbying group composed of solar panel manufacturers, small wind turbine manufacturers, battery manufacturers, and the distributors of these products. Why are they going to that trouble and spending that kind of money? Is it because they're trying to promote green energy? No. The green they're concerned with is money.

You see, renewable energy systems that can supply most of the home's electricity needs are very expensive. So much so, many people can't afford them.

That's why you see so few homes in the United States with solar panels on the roof, even in desert cities. But if you could get the government to basically subsidize the purchase and socialize the profit margin to be paid for by losses in tax revenue, it might increase sales. Especially if you're telling people the very planet depends on it. Americans might not see the justification to let people write those purchases off their taxes otherwise. The loss in tax revenue means something else will suffer from budget cuts. Maybe education or social programs.

Or, taxes will need to go up later the more that tax rebates become a way to socialize profit margins so the American people basically pay for it. Is this a scam? Yes, of course it is.

First off, where is the investigation into the profit margins these companies make? Perhaps the prices could be lowered if the margins weren't so high.

Second, where are the American jobs that benefit when most solar panels are manufactured overseas? Why should the taxpayers subsidize foreign manufacture?

Last, the whole premise behind tax rebates to purchase any products is basically forcing tax payers as whole to pay for your toys. This is wrong. Pay for this crap yourself. Why should we subsidize corporations? Let them find a way to build the proverbial better mouse trap. But if the government has to pony up the cash to make it affordable, it isn't a realistic solution at all. It's just another scam to sell crap and get someone else to pay for it.

There is a third and final rule. Jack's Rule Number Three: Defeat the scam. This is not as difficult to do as you may think. One easy method to avoid being exposed to scams is to cut off the access flow by which they are conducted to you. How? Turn off the television set! Get rid of cable television. Stop buying and reading the magazines in popular circulation.

Understand that all fads and trends are scams. If everyone has to run out to buy this new electronic toy on the market it is the manufacturer of it that started that fad. If people are continually badgering you with questions about if, when, or have you bought any certain thing somewhat new to market, it is because they themselves are being bombarded with advertising for it from the purveyors of the scam. The scams often generate their own peer pressure because the product is portrayed as cool and everyone in America often falls victim to wanting to be cool. They try to help those around them be cool and, if they refuse, often ostracize them.

It all really boils down to this: everyone knows what he or she needs to get through life. People make autonomous decisions about that every day in regards to what to eat, what to wear, and so forth. If some marketing agency is feverishly bombarding you with advice on what to eat, wear, buy, or vote for, it's probably not anything you genuinely need. Humanity did not sit around for tens of thousands of years saying, "Gee, I wish someone would hurry up and invent statin drugs to save us from this genetic design flaw of bad cholesterol!"

Nor did humanity sit around for tens of thousands of years saying "Gee, I wish someone would hurry up and invent vitamin water because plain water isn't healthy enough." Bottled water itself is one of the all-time greatest scams ever born. They can get you to pay two dollars for less than a penny's worth of water they drew from a municipal tap, the same as serves your house. Again, if someone has to keep pounding the message to buy something, it's a scam.

If a politician appears to be obsessed with something, he or she is up to something you're not seeing. Use your mind. That's what it's there for. Make your own decisions, No one needs to run ads telling you to run out and buy cabbage. Everyone knows it's good food. Bet let some corporation come up with a boiled cabbage microwave meal and they'll spend millions of dollars in advertising to tell you that not only is cabbage good food, but eating cabbage is cool and the new trend. And the experts all agree people need to add more cabbage to their diet. Plus, it's gluten-free (which is yet another scam to sell gluten-free products).

The food sector alone is responsible for countless scams, turning the simple act of eating into a socio-political nightmare. People broadcast their dietary choices (vegan, vegetarian, etc.) on bumper stickers and t-shirts as if it's the same thing as being Catholic or the member of a political party or an ethnic group. Perfect suckers for all the marketing gimmicks coming out of the growing vegan/vegetarian processed foods manufacturers. Hey, you guys, processed food is processed food whether it's vegan or not. Potato chips are vegan.

Again, always assume it's a scam. You just don't dole trust out to everybody on Wall Street and in government offices. That's what healthy boundaries are for. Trust is for family, neighbors, friends, people you actually know. Trust is earned.

So, when Acme Vitamin Water is telling me I need to drink vitamin water to protect my health, do I trust that as factual? Of course not. If you drink plenty of water and eat a truly balanced diet, you are getting everything you need as a human being.

Not to mention that for the price of the one bottle of vitamin water, you could buy enough multi-vitamins to last you for a month. The entire system survives by convincing people to buy things they do not need (or at least, not in such great quantity) and to vote for things—and people—that truly do not and cannot benefit them. The entire system revolves around this.

If people stopped buying what they were told to buy and voting for whom and what they are told to vote for, the entire system would fall into a panic.

And that is the only event that would cause them to truly listen to us for the first time.

Jack Perry

CHAPTER ELEVEN—OPTING OUT

HAVING NOW COME this far in the book, you may wonder, "So what, then, can I really do? If the political system itself is corrupted, Wall Street is in total control of the country, and all kinds of scams come out of them both, what hope is there?"

In this chapter, I'll talk about my own personal solution to dealing with it. It is not a political movement. It's not a social movement. Both of these things end up co-opted and compromised when taken to a national level. We need to stop thinking bigger and start thinking smaller. It's time to stop trying to change the country and just change ourselves. It's time to stop caring about politics, government, Wall Street, and the economy.

Imagine they gave a system and nobody came. The power you have, the one thing you can truly change immediately, is to refuse to participate in the system as much as possible. I call this Opting Out. Since we know the elections and candidates are a sham, there's no point to getting involved in voting. Opt Out of the various political groups lobbying for every cause from gun rights to environmentalism.

Notice that just giving those people your address results in scads of junk mail begging and badgering you for donations. That's why they exist: to make money promoting some social or political cause which generates publicity for more fundraising efforts. Opt Out of mindless consumerism and the enslavement to Wall Street to support the addiction of possession accumulation. Don't buy things that, in the end, are not essential. Then Opt Out of the rat race, where you're working harder and longer to make more money to be able to spend more money buying more crap you don't have time to enjoy because you're always at work. Find out how much you really need to have enough (not more, more, more) and stick to that. Opt Out of increasing demands for your time.

I am not preaching asceticism or Luddism here. I am saying that we're being sold on a scarcity mentality when, in reality, plenty already exists but we do not see it or choose not to see it. We need to begin by returning to how we define wealth and prosperity.

Let's begin with wealth. Do you suppose that if you're not in possession of large sums of cash that you're not wealthy or possess no wealth? Okay, now do this. Take a look around and take stock of what you've got. I mean got, not just own. They're not the same thing. I can own a Bible but still haven't got the meaning, you see. So, what've you got? A roof over your head? Food to eat? Clean water to drink? Water to bathe in, and hot water at that? Electricity? A bed? A stove?

Okay, if so, do you realize that millions of people in the world don't have all of those things. Hundreds of children and infants die daily because of that. Emperors and kings in history didn't have clean water. And without water, there is no life. If you can draw a glass of water out of your tap and safely drink that, you are in possession of wealth. Don't think so? Go into the Mojave Desert without any water, but a wallet full of money and see what happens in three days. If you have all of the things I just mentioned, you possess wealth. All money is for is to buy those things. Nothing more.

Money isn't some magical amulet that confers happiness on its owner. Having more of it than you really need cannot create more happiness. It then becomes just another thing to keep track of. Now, look again. If you can add to all of that the following—reasonable personal health, family, friends, and strong spiritual practice—you have a tremendous wealth that even some billionaires haven't got. See, they own things but they haven't got things. A rich man can get any number of women willing to marry him because he's got money and they want it. But for all of his vast millions of dollars, he cannot buy the love of a woman. It cannot be purchased. It's not an object or a thing to be possessed. It has to be given. In his heart, he will know that should he lose his money, he will lose his wife also because she does not truly love him. Thus, his heart remains alone, for all his money.

Likewise, for all the money now at her disposal, it does not bring love to his wife, either. In her heart, she knows she does not have love. In truth, their relationship is closer to a form of prostitution than marriage. If two poor people love one another, they are far wealthier. They have what cannot be purchased for all the gold in universe. For all of their money, rich people will all come to death and exit this world without it. Once dead, it becomes the property of someone else. The huge mansions they built, in time, fall into ruin and return to the earth from which their building materials come. Their fancy, expensive clothing is eaten by moths or given away to beggars. Many of their cherished possessions are discarded and wind up entombed in landfills with rubbish. The great companies they built and devoted their lives to are mismanaged and go bankrupt. So, too, does every whit of their legacy pass away.

The rich have no power to save themselves or their possessions from eventually passing away. Therefore, it is plain to see that the obsessive desire to accumulate vast possessions merely to own them is a futile life. All of those things, and the person who accumulates them, will return to the earth from whence they came.

Therefore, genuine wealth is enjoyment of what you've already got. Spending large amounts of time merely to accumulate more subtracts time from which one can enjoy what one already has. Time is not money. Time is wealth. Money and wealth are not the same. A trillion dollars cannot purchase one second of a person's life back or add one minute at the point of death. The rich man, who spent his entire life pursuing more money, thinking he'll stop to enjoy it when he is old, is a fool. He traded what he actually had, which is time, to obtain more of what he already has, which is money, gambling on having something he might not have in future, which is more time in old age.

If a person has a spiritual practice, that is priceless in and of itself. When one, after death, passes into eternal life, of what value are vast riches that not only do not follow one into the afterlife, but would have no meaning or use there anyway? Obviously, the afterlife cannot be purchased for any amount of money. Regardless of what occurs in the afterlife, it is plain to see that money and possessions cannot be carried into it. They remain here when the owners die. We can all see that, and this has been common knowledge for thousands of years. Since the spiritual body has no need of possessions, is eternal, and exists in an infinite universe, the desire to accumulate possessions upon a speck of dust in that universe only to leave them behind is meaningless and pointless.

A spiritual practice, though, bestows a true and priceless wealth since one's consciousness can be carried into afterlife. The entire practice of accumulating vast possessions and calling it wealth is like children building sand castles on the beach when the tide is out. When the tide returns, the sand castles will disappear and return to the sand once more. This is why most major religions call accumulating vast possessions and riches and then clinging to that, futile. A spiritual practice doesn't cost any money and that should clue everybody in as to why the obsessive accumulation of riches is pointless where it really counts. The richest in the world will leave this life without a single penny.

Therefore, we can see that what America is telling us is that wealth, which we should chase after and squander our lives in pursuit of, is not real. True enough, poverty is not an ideal. But once one has enough, how much more does one need? If a child in a sandbox grabs all of the toys, monopolizes them, refuses to allow other children to play with them even when he isn't playing with them, and declares they're all "his" and refuses to share, we call that child a "spoiled brat."

Yet, when an American executive, a CEO, or Wall Street corporation does this, we idolize them for it and call it good business. What, therefore, are we truly teaching our children? Now, am I saying their money should be seized and redistributed to the poor? No. I am saying that this behavior should not be encouraged. Nor should greed at all be encouraged by saying all Americans are entitled to some unrealistic standard of living, be they rich, poor or middle class.

But we also must understand that a thousand people living in poverty so that one man can be rich cannot be justified. That doesn't mean take away the rich man's money and give it to those thousand poor people. That is not a solution. What I am saying is that when it became evident this man was getting rich by people falling into poverty, he should have been stopped at that point and told he had enough. Let those other people keep what they need to live. Of course, we're not there yet as a society. We're not at the point where we can put up speed limit signs and stop signs on the road to becoming rich, so it can be made safe for society as a whole. But if we don't start moving in that direction, in time, our society will fail.

Wall Street needs to come to a decision. Will you lower the prices on all essentials and ensure prices remain affordable based on current wages? Or will you return an abundance of long-term good-paying jobs by which prices and wages correct themselves automatically? You need to come to a decision and pick one of them. You cannot continue refusing to do either one of them and expect to survive once the number of working and non-working poor rises to about 60% of the population, which is where it is rapidly heading.

A revolution does not suddenly happen.

A series of causes and conditions leads up to one. When the causes and conditions arise within the United States, there will be one. A revolution in the United States will occur from economic causes and conditions, not political. A certain gun could be banned or gay marriage could be banned and there won't be a revolution over it. Civil unrest, maybe, but the majority of people won't take to the streets. Let the majority be unable to buy food or pay the rent, that's when you'll have revolution here. However, so long as the American people are in agreement with Wall Street as to what wealth is and how it can be properly attained, Americans will continue to fall into poverty.

If Americans themselves cannot properly define wealth, they cannot properly demand their share of it. Until we come to a realistic perspective about what wealth really is, social justice movements such as raising the minimum wage are doomed to fail even when they succeed.

Let's turn our attention now to prosperity. What is it? What does it do? How do you know you have it?

First of all, prosperity is not something owned. You either have got it, or you have not got it. Again, "got" and "own" are not the same thing. You can own wealth to some extent. But there is no way to own prosperity. Prosperity is a state of being that a series of causes and conditions leads up to. Prosperity cannot be created by politicians or some nonsense economic stimulus plan or mailing people a bunch of checks like Bush did. Prosperity has to be created by a community through a cooperative process. For that to be possible, there need to be stable, long-term jobs that pay a decent wage. No, you can't create prosperity by increasing the minimum wage on a bunch of fast-food jobs. Prosperity is a long-term project a community has to work at. But first we need to understand what prosperity is.

Consider the following: a husband and wife both have high-paying jobs. However, each works a ten-hour shift and comes home exhausted. They have a beautiful house, new cars, and their kids have every electronic device they ask for. But the kids hardly see the parents and the parents make little time for the kids. In time, the kids end up abusing drugs and one dies in a drunk-driving accident while another gets pregnant at sixteen. Can this family be called prosperous?

A mountain town attracts rich people looking for second homes in the town. The town thinks this will create prosperity because of jobs created to build homes, more property tax revenue, and more customers for local stores. However, with all of that, property value goes up and with that goes up prices and the costs of living in the town. In time, the long-term residents of the town live in increasing poverty or must move away to someplace they can afford to live. But the homes of the seasonal rich residents portray prosperity in the town. Can this town be called prosperous?

A city succeeds in increasing minimum wage. Workers with the higher income begin buying new cars and even smaller manufactured homes with mortgages. But soon the cost of the increased wages drives up prices. Over time, the workers find they're back to Square One again, except now they've got car payments and mortgages they can't afford. A few are able to find second jobs to try and make ends meet and work twelve or more hours a day. Can these workers be called prosperous?

A teenager wants a video game for Christmas that costs $100. However, his parents can't afford it. Instead, they gave him a new coat, which he really needed because his old one didn't keep him warm enough. His grandfather gave him a new Bible as a gift. Angry, the teen took the new coat and the Bible to a swap meet where he was able to trade both for a very used video game he wanted. Once home, he discovered the video game didn't work. A winter storm with freezing temperatures was on the way, and he was stuck with his ragged old coat now. Then his grandfather called to ask him if he found the $100 bill he had tucked in the Bible. Can the actions of this teen be called prosperous?

These are all parable examples of how people, time and time again, fall into deeper holes chasing what they believe to be better or more prosperity. Prosperity is not a thing to chase like higher wages or more possessions.

It is a state of being in your community.

You can have all the things in the world you ever wish for, but if you can't step out your front door without being accosted or assaulted, it does not mean anything. Prosperity is when people have relatively good, stable jobs that pay enough to live on and have enough.

It's a community that is relatively safe, healthy, has good schools, has opportunity, and offers a place that a family can be kept together.

It has good homes to live in, clean water, food and community activities that bring people together.

It has active spiritual communities within it without strife and hostility between them.

It has a majority of locally-owned businesses.

It has a community government composed of people that actually live there and either grew up there or lived there at least a decade. The local government puts local matters and people before all else. If a corporation wants to come in, the corporation must prove how it will add to the prosperity of the community and not harm it.

It's a place where people are happy to live. Without most of these conditions coming together, prosperity does not exist.

You can't have prosperity when you've got a high crime rate. You can't have prosperity when most people are unemployed or underemployed. You can't have prosperity if local government is a bunch of carpetbaggers kissing corporate asses to come and pay no taxes while sucking the local aquifer dry. At the same time, you can't have prosperity when the opportunity to create it is there, but the residents are too lazy to get off their asses and help create it.

You have to be involved in your community, even if that's just reaching out to your next-door neighbors. But just plopping your ass in front of the television set and expecting the rest of the community to create community for you is a bunch of malarkey.

Prosperity is a community effort of a community that takes care of one another. A bunch of wild beasts tearing each other apart for an extra fifty cents an hour will never create prosperity.

It doesn't take everyone being rich to create prosperity. Being rich doesn't create it. They'll squat in heavily-guarded, fenced fortresses they call homes. They can't even see their neighbor's house, much less talk to him over the fence. A community must exist for true prosperity to be possible and prosperity must be created so the community can continue. This is a symbiotic process. You cannot have one without the other.

Again, prosperity means a safe, stable community where people have enough to live on and have access to healthy activities and interact with one another. It's hard to build that when everyone is working a ten-hour shift, six days a week and barely getting by. No one has time to volunteer at the recreation center. So the kids are off doing drugs and breaking into houses. It is imperative that once you have enough, you stop there and start giving some back to the community. It's not the government's job to build you a community. It's their job to enforce the laws and provide clean water and so forth. And if you think the corporations will build you any kind of a community, worth living in, you are sadly mistaken.

Ask half the people even in a medium-sized city what free or low-cost activities or programs exist there. They won't know. But those are the very things that provide fun, healthy activities that don't require constant inputs of cash and endless shopping. "There's nothing to do because I haven't got any money." Malarkey. There's a public library, there's probably a recreation center, there's a park. There are free activities at the rec center, there are chess clubs, and there are churches and mosques, and so on. Those are all things that create community.

If you create a community that takes care of one another, prosperity is being created. You have to look beyond the assumption that prosperity is about having lots of money. It isn't.

When I say Opt Out, I'm not saying build some gated

Regime Change You Can Believe In

compound in the middle of the Arizona desert and live there alone. If that's what you want to do, who am I to judge? What I'm advocating is Opting Out of wasting time with what we know to be futile, because that then frees up time to act where it can bear fruit.

In the community.

The nation as a whole will never be changed at once across the spectrum. It will only take on a slightly different version of the same thing every election cycle. Communities need to create prosperity and community for themselves and stop waiting for the government or Wall Street to do that for them. On an individual basis, this means understanding that if your life has no meaning, accumulating money and possessions will not give it to you. Neither will political power or owning a major corporation.

Define what wealth means to you. Look around at what you've already have. Do you need more? What are you willing to trade for more? Spending more time at work? Your marriage? Your kids' love? What is "more" worth to you?

Saying "I have enough" gives you that permission to lay down your tools, rest, and spend time with your family and community. That's where real life happens. If people think their lives should be defined by the products they buy, I feel sorry for them. Take away all those products and what have they got left of a life? Nothing at all. Opting Out means turning off the television set. Getting rid of the barrage of marketing and advertising. Some people say: "What is wrong with wanting my kids to have a nice Christmas?"

Okay, define "nice Christmas." Do you know what would have been a nice Christmas for a lot of Americans kids in 1944? Dad home for Christmas and not lying dead in some Belgian forest or Pacific Island. Christmas was first a religious holy day. Because of that, it was also a traditional time of family and community togetherness. Over time, a handful of gifts were exchanged. But it was never about the gift-giving alone up until recently as far as the history of Christmas goes. It's Wall Street telling you it's all about the gifts. Because they've so painted themselves into a corner with their short-sighted greed, they rely on Christmas sales to show a yearly profit. So, what, are you opting into that to enrich some fat cats? And since when should kids run the house?

Opting Out means refusing to participate in divisive politics of one side against the other. Hey, they're all a bunch of baboons, okay? Let them destroy one another, because that's what they're doing. Opt Out. "What? Don't vote?!" That's up to you. But if you know you're being scammed, why bother? Do you think it matters whether one or the other wins? If you've got to vote, the place it matters is local elections. That's where the politicians originate. Start demanding better local officials. Maybe we'll start getting better senators and congress people. You know, if a community holds its leaders to a higher standard, it'll carry upwards eventually. But you're not going to change anything for the better with presidential, congressional, or senatorial elections. They're all in bed with Wall Street.

Opt Out of activist causes that go round and round the merry-go-round. Let me spell it out for you. You are not going to able to ban guns, meat, Muslims, gay people, abortion, Christianity, or any number of things. It's just not going to happen so why are you wasting your lives fighting such futile battles? "Well, I'm an environmentalist and I'm fighting for the planet!" Oh, are you now? So all those CDs and DVDs in your collection, where did those come from? I take it that you've got a cell phone? Who made that? Do you know how much electricity it takes to make fake soy cheese versus plain old milk cheese? How is the grain you eat harvested? By a thousand men with sickles? I doubt that. So get off the high horse.

Generally, activist causes from gun rights to environmentalism are scams to bilk the dupes out of money. They hire professional lobbyists who never worked a real job in their lives at a hundred grand a year in salary. And you sign checks and mail them off to those con artists. One very well-known environmentalist organization got hold of my mailing address once. They sent me so much junk mail whining for donations over the course of a year, it probably amounted to a tree worth of paper. How environmentally sustainable is that? Opt Out of that and spend time and money with your family and community. These activist groups will roll merrily along without you until the wheels fall off, along with the rest of the political system.

Opt Out of the need for constant entertainment. This may come as shock to some people, but life in the past didn't come with a soundtrack. If you need to hear music constantly, watch movies and television constantly, and play computer games in between that, stop whining about not having any money or not being paid enough. I am tired of hearing people whine about low wages and they have ten times the amount of stuff I've got. I live within my means and I don't buy stuff I don't need. If you "need" to buy all those CDs, DVDs, and computer games and then haven't money for food, whose fault is that? You buy that crap after you've paid rent and bought food. Too many people out there are just digging their own holes deeper.

I am not denying employers out there don't pay a living wage. But if you go and waste the money you do get, how is that any better? The employer will say, "Well, if I pay them more, they'll just buy more computer games with the money." Stop buying into the need to be constantly plugged in to some electronic device. My word, it's like everyone runs around engaging in electronic masturbation. Opt Out of it.

Opt Out of buying anything you don't really need or can't afford. Yes, owning a house is nice. But if you can't afford the payments without severe hardship, it isn't worth it. To do what? Get it paid off when you're 75, retire, collapse into your home in exhaustion and die the next year? Then whose house will it be? "Well, I don't want to end up in an old folks' home!" Yeah, well, there's no guarantee you won't if your health declines, even if you own a house. Fall and break your hip in there and it might be the government or your kids that put you in an old folks' home despite your objections. There is nothing wrong with an old folks' home if it's run right. Some of them are better deals dollar-for-dollar than some condominiums with housing association fees. Hell, everything I've got that I treasure fits into a suitcase. I could pack that into an old folks' home with room to spare.

Instead of buying things, go places. See America. See the world, while there's most of it intact. Learn new things. Teach how to bake bread. Participate in a chess club or a meditation group. Watch how quickly you don't have time for television and thus, stop buying so much crap the TV pounds into your head to buy.

Opt Out of military service. The military is the ultimate scam. They basically convince you to agree to being a slave they can order to die. Didn't know that, did you? Yes, if you enlist and get shipped off to a war, and in battle are ordered to do something that you know will result in your death, guess what? You've got to do it! If you refuse to do it, it's called "disobeying a direct order." It's against military law, you'll be court marshaled, and they'll put you in jail for years.

Oh, I know it all looks so cool on TV, doesn't it? The recruiter promises this or that. Well, go online and look at photos of the graves of soldiers that died in Iraq and Afghanistan. They all thought that, too. But employers value vets, right? Nope! There are lots of unemployed vets out there looking for work. When employers do layoffs, they pick the people getting the biggest paychecks that aren't executives or corporate officers. That's how it's done. It doesn't matter if there's a guy working there who won three Medals of Honor, they'll lay him off in a second if it saves them a buck. And do you think the government actually cares about that? They're done with you. They don't need you anymore. They're busy trying to convince more high school graduates to enlist and die in another one of their pointless wars.

"But what if I need a job?" So that's a good reason to go shoot and kill other human beings that haven't done anything to you before you enlisted? "Sorry I had to kill you, but I needed a job and the army was hiring." Right, anyone can enlist who is qualified, but they tend to leave the killing people for nothing, or losing a leg, your mind, or your life out of the recruitment pitch. Opting Out of enlisting in the military is one of the most important things. "Who will defend the country?" Well—let them hire private military contractors to do it since they're all so keen on this privatizing thing. Or let them send their own kids to fight, for a change. Nobody out there wants to conquer the United States. They can't afford to take on the debt.

The government and Wall Street crave and need people opting into their system. They need products bought, political campaigns staffed and paid for, televisions watched so people will run out and buy more crap and vote for more idiots. What if you just disconnected yourself from it all? Stopped voting, stopped buying crap, learned how to make things instead of buying them, stopped serving in their military and fighting their senseless wars for them, stopped caring about their silly political causes?

What if you pulled the plug on the television, stopped caring what magazines said, or stopped caring about fashion trends geared to sell expensive clothes coming from Third World sweatshops? What if the quality of life and relationships was more important than the mountains of merchandise we go into debt to buy? And even if we don't go into debt to buy it, what is the true cost of it to our families? What's all this insatiable consumerism costing us as far as our families and communities? Yes, it's costing the planet, too, but not even the environmentalists have the guts to opt out. At the end of the day, their political action groups still run on gasoline, electricity, and paper.

Sometimes, the best course of action isn't. Sometimes, the best thing to do is nothing.

Nothing.

All we're doing is digging this hole deeper and deeper. No, some career politician is not going to save us. No, some Wall Street malarkey about "We're the job creators" is not going to save us. No, some activist group full of granolas on one side or another full of tight-assed conservatives on the other is not going to save us. We can't spend, buy, picket, or vote ourselves out of the mess we're in. The only thing that can be done is to Opt Out of it and refuse to keep propping up the system. Because when it finally collapses—which it will—the only ones who survive will be strong communities who learned to do for themselves. Communities that didn't sit there and wait for the federal government or Wall Street to tell them what to do.

The "market" is not going to save us either. The superstitious belief in the invisible hand of the market is partly what led is into this nightmare. The invisible hand of the market is as ridiculous a superstition as a lucky rabbit's foot. That people believe in it is almost like the beginning of another Wall Street cargo cult.

You have to have a market based on moral precepts of behavior within a healthy community. There's a lawless region between Pakistan and Afghanistan where weapons and drugs are sold and life is very cheap. Well, that's a market. So you can't say, "Just let the market fix everything" and absolve humanity of responsibility when things like recessions happen. The market exists to serve humanity, not the other way around. But America does have this the other way around. Americans serve the market like slaves to a tyrannical god which demands human sacrifice.

Opting in to all of this is how corrupt politicians get elected and tragic wars start. We buy into this falsehood that Wall Street knows best and sit back as they impoverish the entire nation. We then send young men and women off to die in wars allegedly defending this so-called way of life.

Everything has consequences.

Everything has a cost.

People act like this state of affairs can continue forever. Well, whatever.

But if you're tired of this state of affairs, there is a simple solution.

Opt Out of it.

CHAPTER TWELVE—PROGRESS?

HAVE ALL OF these computers, cell phones, technology and other assorted electronic trinkets made our lives any easier? Have the mushrooming numbers of government agencies and laws from city to federal truly improved the quality of our lives? Have the automated-response customer-service call-centers demonstrated any vast superiority over the old human-based system? Has the endless heavy barrage of overstimulation by constant streams of music, video, advertising, and computer graphics given us peace? Have the endless choices of the same thing in consumer goods and chain restaurant foods enriched our lives?

The government, the media, and the corporations all keep selling us on this thing they call progress. The basic premise of this goes unspoken. So allow me to explain what they mean by progress. They define that as meaning: never be satisfied with what you have, the way you are, or what gives meaning to your life. You should always be striving after more—never rest until you're more than what you are, and things in the future are what'll give us meaning in our lives.

However, what has been forgotten is that progress was originally supposed to make life easier, not make it more complicated. Progress was never supposed to be an excuse to drive a wedge between human relationships, or take the place of them. The same goes for technology, since technology is the army that carries out the orders of progress, the leader of it all.

269

We have arrived at a point where progress is being made but no one can tell us what end goal progress is being made towards. "Good news. We're making a lot of progress!" Okay, towards what? "Uh… well, um, I don't know actually."

When you're trying to eradicate childhood diseases, for example, and vaccines have been invented, you're making progress towards a genuine goal. There is a social value in that progress. But if you invent some electronic doo-dad that people become spell-bound by to the point they walk into oncoming traffic and get hit, how can that be progress? Or if you invent some type of media by which people become wholly engrossed and ignore genuine human relationships, how can that be progress?

Where's the social value in that?

Everyone has called, at some point, a customer service helpline and gotten the usual automated response leading them to a menu. There they press a button to select their needed option. This leads them to yet another menu, to select yet another option. Often after navigating this labyrinth of button-pushing, and recordings, one is no closer to a solution than before calling. So, one finally presses the button to speak to a live human being. Where you wait several minutes to an hour to do so, because everyone selects that button. In the old days, you called a number and a human being answered. You said what you needed, and your call was transferred to another human being who answered your question. What was so hard about that, that they had to make it easier by making it even harder than before?

My wife and I were sitting in this local Ethiopian restaurant. We're talking and I see this young couple sit at the table beside ours. Before he's even plopped his butt in the chair he had gotten out his cell phone. He's sitting there texting, and the young woman is trying to get his attention and have a conversation with him. However, he's engrossed in typed messages to people who could be a thousand miles away. Rather than have a meaningful conversation with the human being right in front of his face, he's having a junk food conversation with people who aren't even there. Our food came out and it was simply beautiful. A pleasure to see, smell, eat and even touch because you eat it with your fingers. Here's this wonderful experience to share with the person across from you, as my wife and I were doing. I glanced over one last time and their food had come out. He was absent-mindedly eating with one hand texting with the other, fixated on the cell phone. The young woman had given up on trying to have any shared experience with him and concentrated on the food. See, here's this beautiful wonderful food and he can't truly enjoy it because he thinks these texts require his attention. So he lets a machine run his life and demand he do this or that thing. He's enslaved by it.

Not to mention people now expect to be able to get a hold of you twenty-four hours a day, seven days a week. When I was a kid, phone calls weren't made or answered during dinner. And if someone called after ten at night, there'd better be a damn good reason for it. As in, an emergency. And when you went out the door, the phone stayed home. Because it was plugged into the wall. Now a family will sit together to eat a meal at a restaurant and all of them will have their faces buried in cell phones and not a word spoken between them. Can this be called progress?

People, well, some people wonder why our society has not produced another Walt Whitman or Henry David Thoreau, or John Steinbeck. Those are all great American writers—the world greats in literature. Why, then, do we not see more writers like them? Because our society is nearly incapable of producing more and doesn't have the attention span for literature. Obviously, this doesn't apply to everybody. I am speaking about the society of mass media. Look at what passes for music. Can anyone see another Mozart arising from that? Half the music today is produced by machines. Is this progress as a culture?

We have a government that has been unable to win a major war since 1945. Yet, it goes around looking for wars to get into or, failing that, starts one itself. All of that knowing it won't win that war, too. Some people say "war is good for the economy," because popular folktales say that getting into World War Two lifted the United States out of the great depression.

If people cannot understand the difference between Afghanistan and Iraq and the Germany and Japan of 1942, they need to park themselves behind some history books for several weeks. We're not building endless waves of B-17, B-24 and B-29 bombers to go challenge a handful of renegade Taliban hiding behind rocks in Afghanistan.

The wars in Iraq and Afghanistan are the longest wars in American history. So where is the prosperity from the "war is good for the economy" theory? Those wars were, and are, long (Afghanistan is still going on!), so you'd think everyone in America would be tycoons by now! And the reason Iraq dragged on as long as it did until we walked, and Afghanistan is still going on, is because the government has no idea how to win a war. How can this be called progress? Progress would have been the ability to win a major war quicker than the ones preceding it.

Technology was supposed to make work easier, thus shortening the amount of time spent at work and increasing the amount of time families spent together. Plus it would increase leisure time and time spent in wholesome pursuits. That's what they said, way back when.

Did that happen?

The answer is a solid no. The amount of time spent at work has drastically increased because technology makes it possible to do that. The amount of time spent at work has also increased so people can pay for all of the technology they bring into their homes and devote the rest of their time to, rather than their families. The increase in leisure time never came, but what leisure time there is gets spent in front of the television, at shopping malls buying more technology to devote time to, or playing computer games. Artistic pursuits? Only if you can buy a kit with ready-made pieces to create "art." Where, therefore, are all of the great advances in society thanks to progress?

I know what some people are thinking. "This guy sits there and criticizes technology and progress and he probably typed that up on a computer." No, I didn't. I sat at my kitchen table and wrote this book with good, old fashioned pen and paper—the way books used to be written. Now, I'm not knocking legitimate progress. Things like smallpox immunizations have an obvious, long-lasting health benefit. There have been countless lives saved from the use of helicopter ambulances alone. Something we all take for granted such as frozen vegetables have brought healthy foods to many tables. No one denies that genuine progress is valuable. But if what we're told is progress is leading us off the edge of a cliff or actually making our lives harder, we need to pull the plug on it.

Part of the way we've been sold on the idea of progress is by being told we can't exist without it.

In fact, for most of the life of the human race, humans got along fine without the following: cell phones, televisions, computers, vitamin water, professional sports, microwave dinners, computer games, and the constant need for music to be playing. Those are but a handful of things technology has brought to us. If some major cataclysm happened tomorrow and removed all of these things from the equation, there are still several functioning societies on this planet that would be unaware it was gone.

They never had any of it.

In this modern age, they exist without any of it and, according to the anthropologists, appear to be much happier than those who have it. Progress was supposed to bring us more happiness. So where is it? Anti-depressant medication use goes up every year, so we can see that progress is not able to make good on its promises.

Progress is the reason the government says it needs to create more agencies and pass more laws. Corporations say progress is the reason why they need higher profit margins and higher growth. Both of them tell us this progress is necessary for our own good. The way they've sold it to us is by putting forth the notion that we cannot exist without them.

Of a truth, during the American Frontier period, many Americans and smaller American communities had little contact with the federal government at all. Nor were they reliant upon any corporations for things. Yet, this is the time-period most heavily romanticized in books and movies. The government itself unwittingly invokes this era, apparently unable to understand the most attractive thing about it was the absence of government poking into peoples' lives.

If we get any more progress, we'll soon need to acquire government permits to exist as human beings. In a sense, that's what a Social Security number has become. Everyone asks for that number, from banks to all levels of government. But how many people know that when the concept of the Social Security card was being created way back when, it was stipulated by the government that it was never to be used as a form of identification? Did you know that? Soon, the pizza delivery guy will be asking for a Social Security number to find which pizza is yours. They'll call that progress.

People think Space tourism will show progress! That's hilarious! To do what? Pay what, a hundred grand to half a million to see five minutes' worth of what you can see in a good observatory or planetarium? Right, let's ride a ballistic missile with wings so we can see what we've already got pictures of. Not to mention corporations are spending years and billions to develop space vehicles the United States Air Force built in the 1950s and NASA built in the 1970s. They call this progress? Genuine progress would be devoted to spending these resources on solving the very real problems on this planet.

People that believe in alternative energy often think that alternative energy can replace what we have now. They call this moving towards progress. Do any of them realize that wind farms and solar panels are not going to replace coal-fired power plants, hydroelectric dams, and nuclear power plants at the rate

American use electricity? If you can cut consumption, that'd be progress. Not to mention all the green energy advocates among the celebrities that live in a forty-room mansion with a heated Olympic-sized swimming pool. And there's one person living in the entire house! The mansion uses enough electricity in a day to power a remote Moroccan village for a month, but this person will lecture us about progress we need to make with alternative energy. Progress is finding ways to unplug some of the electronic gadgets, not inventing more to plug in or trying to get the wind and the sun to pick up the slack.

So what is the point I'm making here? That progress and technology are evil?

No.

What I'm saying is that instead of progress and technology being the means to an end, they've become the end itself. We don't use technology to build a better way of life. We use technology to create more technology and very little of it has any necessary value. Progress is no longer a course of action leading to a beneficial result for humanity, but a word invoked to justify declaring eminent domain on the house of an elderly couple so it can be demolished and a strip mall built there. The way forward is not forward. The way forward is backward.

Some people are getting it. There's a grass-roots movement afoot towards simplicity and minimalism. But, take heed, lest this get co-opted and Wall Street sells us minimalism. It isn't about becoming attached to a concept and carrying it around with us the way political beliefs and dietary choices, for example, are paraded around. It's about recognizing that we're being deceived every step of the way by the government and Wall Street. Therefore, we build a life of our own without involving ourselves with them any time we can avoid doing so. If we aren't attached to some unrealistic expectation of what we think we ought to own or possess, we won't waste this precious life chasing after those things.

Minimalism is not learning how to bake your own bread then

taking photos of it and posting it on social media and watching it go stale on the counter. It's inviting friends and neighbors over to sit at your table and share that bread with you. But, again, we don't want to get trapped by the word minimalism and let it become another bumper sticker.

What we mean to say is we've seen this society has little to offer, therefore, we should create a new one amongst ourselves without the government and corporations telling us what it should look like. This isn't some new philosophy. It's the way backwards. Back to a time people lived as a community and made time for one another. When there was nothing wrong with have-enough and not feeling the need to pile up more possessions. When joy was to be had with home-baked bread, home-made pickles, hand-sewn pillows, hand-carved wooden crafts, and time was more important than money. People say it isn't possible. I say it is. I'm living it.

I got rid of my television over twenty years ago. I've never missed it. I've pared my possessions down to a few books, tools, two longbows, arrows, arrow-making tools, a small one-foot by one-foot shrine, a backpack, a small number of personal items that would fit into the backpack, and my clothes. That's it for personal possessions. Am I sitting here in sackcloth and ashes, lamenting having so little?

No, on the contrary, I am rejoicing.

When I need something, I usually make it or I trade for it. When I have money, I want to buy some kind of wonderful food with it. Or a gift for my wife. Obviously, we have household possessions, but very few of them were new when we got them. The house has no television, no massive stereo system, in fact, has no stereo system at all.

I'm not stuck marching in an endless parade of technology. I don't have a use for most of it. I have a cell phone that sits home gathering dust. I only have it because there weren't landlines where we used to live. I don't have any computer games. I don't even have any power tools I use when making arrows. I'm immune to marketing because I don't have a television to see it nor do I read magazines where it's advertised. But more to the point, I know that anytime they're trying to sell me something I've never once thought of buying and have no real use for, it's a scam. I don't want or desire endless piles of possessions. To do what with? Display it all like hunting trophies? That's what some people do with all this crap they buy. It goes up on the wall or on a shelf and you'd think it's some famous safari hunter up in there showing off the rhino he shot over in Africa.

There was a bumper sticker back in the 1980s that said "He who dies with the most toys wins." No, he who dies with the most toys leaves this world without any of it and half of it ends up in the thrift shop and the rest goes away in an estate sale.

Wins?

Wins what?

This is how we got into this mess thinking we needed more and more crap to show everyone we had more useless crap than they did. I won't win any such contest because I wouldn't even enter into one in the first place. Okay, you've got far more crap than I have, you win, are you happy now?

You can do more with less than you can do less with more. You'll spend more time enjoying a few meaningful possessions than the time you'd spend enjoying a house full of them and working two jobs to pay for it all. Think I'm making this up? "How can I do more with less?" Because you'll have to learn how to do that. There's an old archer's proverb: "The man with but one bow and six arrows is an excellent archer with great accuracy."

But with twenty bows and a hundred arrows for each, you cannot even get one arrow consistently on target. You can't do even the less with more. People can't sit down and not eat the whole bag of snack chips. The bags of them get bigger to encourage that so people will buy more. That's one reason we have an obesity epidemic. That and everyone sitting in front of the television or a computer game for hours on end.

I don't vote, I don't get involved in politics, and I don't care who gets elected. Whoever is elected will deliver what he or she swore not to and stubbornly refuse to do what was promised. They don't need my participation to accomplish that and I'm not giving my approval to either one of them in an election.

I don't get involved in social justice causes but I'll march in an anti-war march when one's happening. If I want to help the homeless, I find one and give him food and clothing. They're not that difficult to find in this country. When I want to help my community, I go help hand out fresh fruits and vegetables to people through a local food bank program. When I see people that need help I stop to help them regardless of what I'm doing or where I'm going. I don't need to join or create some social justice or political movement to accomplish any of that. I don't need to force my beliefs on others by using government to pass laws. I don't need anyone to believe what I believe. I don't care who marries whom, how many guns they own, whether they eat meat or not, or what they smoke.

The law is not there to be used against one another like a weapon. The government is not supposed to run our lives. If you need that, hire someone as a personal assistant so the rest of us can live without the government reminding us to brush our teeth before bed or otherwise get dinged on our tax return.

I couldn't care less about the economy, corporations, Wall Street, or the stock market. The economy is fixing to fall flat on its keester once again and people attached to it as if it's their own flesh and blood are about to be deeply disappointed when it does. I'll go out of my way to avoid buying anything from a major corporation when I don't need to.

And I'd rather learn how to juggle live rattlesnakes than participate in the stock market. Images I've seen of the traders on the floor of the New York Stock Exchange make me think that's what it must have looked like in Hitler's bunker in 1945 Berlin with the Soviets closing in on them. The looks on their faces are probably the exact same as the Germans officers in the bunker who have just been told Red Army tanks are now only a block away, so they haven't got much time left to shoot themselves. If anyone hasn't noticed that Wall Street will sink in a fashion that makes the Titanic look like some kid's toy sailboat turned over in the tub, they're deluding themselves more than those stock traders.

Actually, they probably know it's about to crash but they're too busy playing Russian Roulette to walk away from it. None of this will fail to happen because I purchased a shopping cart load of overpriced trinkets I really couldn't afford in some misguided notion of helping the economy. Therefore, there is no use worrying about it. I wouldn't be a bit surprised if Wall Street crashed and the government bailed them out again after millions of Americans lost their houses and 401K plans and savings of course.

The end of the story is this: when you eliminate the responsibilities to that for which you are not responsible, your life will be simpler, happier, and less complicated. There is only one thing you can truly change, and that is your own life.

Until you do that, you cannot help change the lives of those around you. They're waiting to see if the proof is in the pudding with you first. Life doesn't have to be as complicated as it's made out to be. Life is not better because we've got fifty choices in toothpaste.

Unplug yourself.

There. No ads, no politicians scaring you about people three thousand miles away, nothing to run out and buy, no medicines to take, no economy to sit on pins and needles over, no texts that needs instant replies, and no constant demands on your time and wallet.

That's regime change you can believe in.

Jack Perry

EPILOGUE

SOME PEOPLE ACT as if they don't know for certain the government is corrupt. They're waiting for some big, world-shattering scandal to be reveal the proof. Excuse me, but ample proof has been revealed. Just pay attention to the events since World War Two. How many whistle-blowers have told everyone what's going on, and people still act like not one of them has spoken?

There is more than enough evidence to prove that the entire political system is corrupt. If the Iran-Contra scandal didn't convince people, nothing will. The less a person has to do with this corrupt entity, the better. There is a lot to be said for just wanting to be left alone and minding one's own business.

Some people act if they don't know for certain our entire economic system is corrupt, unjust, and incompetent. Some think corporations and Wall Street are smarter than the government. However, these are the same corporations that need thirty staff meetings, a fact-finding mission, ten teleconferences, twelve plane trips with hotel expenses and ten more meetings just to decide on new chairs for their offices. These are the same corporations that will gladly spend five thousand dollars over five months if they can save a nickel today and lay off fifty workers in the process. These are the same corporations whose fluctuating stocks prices look more like cardiac arrest than a healthy stock market.

Speaking of which, look at footage of the New York Stock Exchange with those traders. It more closely resembles the antics of hysterical primates flinging dung and food than the behavior of people in an allegedly civilized society. And these are the same corporations and banks that sank the country in the Great Depression and almost did so once again in the Great Recession of 2008 and 2009, not to mention all the recessions in between.

People continue waiting for evidence revealing them all to be fools in the night. In fact, plenty has been revealed, but people choose not to see it because it would reveal that our entire economic system is a farce built on children's play money and worthless stock as fictitious as a pulp romance novel.

And not even nearly so believable.

Along the same lines, some people believe Wall Street is going to pull a rabbit out of its hat some day and save us all. Wall Street doesn't even possess a head to have a hat for. The only thing they'll pull out of their hat is more layoff notices, false economic predictions, government bribes and bogus stock. How anyone can have faith in that cabal of carnival midway brokers, snake oil hucksters, and real estate swindlers just goes to demonstrate the power of Wall Street propaganda.

A person would do better to trust ten rattlesnakes in a small, dark room with than to trust Wall Street. Yet, amazingly, people rely on this entity to chart the economic destiny of the entire country! Had it been Wall Street at the helm of the Titanic, upon striking the iceberg, they would have continued full steam ahead to find another one to hit. That way, in their thinking, it would rip another hole in the ship and let water out that came in from the first hole.

There is a lot of eerie similarity between the sinking of the Titanic and the actions of Wall Street. Such as, knowingly plowing full speed ahead into a dangerous area they've been warned about, just to get there quicker and look good. And when their mistake results in the sinking of the ship, the guy that ordered the ship to go full speed jumps into a lifeboat and escapes his mistake.

Everyone else pays for it, and people that had nothing to do with it at that. But the guy responsible, he gets away with it. Look at the Wall Street execs that got bonuses in the Great Recession of 2008-2009. Wall Street rewards failure.

Think about that one.

Do you suppose the government can prevent another economic collapse? We're already on the Titanic and we are already in the iceberg field going full speed ahead.

We need to shed this lottery mentality that says the one percent chance we might get rich someday justifies this economic system. You're probably not going to get rich, just like you're probably not going to win the lottery. The lottery is another rigged game like the government and our economic system. You're more likely to lose money at lottery then to win it. And you're more likely to lose money in our economic system than to amass lots of money in it. You are statistically more likely to be struck by lightning than you are of becoming rich.

The rags-to-riches fairy tales are just that: fairy tales for children. That's what it is. It's just Cinderella with Wall Street telling it through mass media. It's Wall Street's version of the state government lotteries. Millions upon millions of people playing and throwing their money away and one guy wins the pot. But the suckers still line up to throw away their money on the lottery, just like they line up to throw away their lives chasing being rich. Some people get into this treadmill routine of needing more and more possessions to feel they have enough.

Truthfully, if many people look around, they will see they already have plenty. Some people will say, "I don't have any money so I haven't got any nice things." And that is a true statement in regards to the way a lot of people see things. But for some, if they really looked deeper, it would be revealed that they actually have plenty.

We need to come to a realistic understanding of what "I don't have enough" really means. When a person does not make, or have, enough money to pay for food, rent, clothing, utilities, medicine, medical care, personal hygiene items, childcare if applicable, sufficient transportation, and student loan payments if applicable, then that person does not have enough.

Conservatives say "People like that shouldn't have children, so why are child care costs included in that?" Well, having children is an ancient human trait that dates back to the beginning or we wouldn't be here. Having offspring is a biological imperative, and an instinct of all mammals on this planet. In truth, it defines life itself. No political, economic, or social system can deny that or rewire the human mind. It is a fact of all life to reproduce whether you believe in Creationism or Evolution. Since many conservatives hold up the Bible, they should know that God told mankind to be fruitful and multiply.

There weren't stipulations placed on that. So do these same conservatives get to overrule God because their political and economic ideology isn't meshing well with what the Bible actually says? Having children is obviously a human right. Only an idiot would deny that. But being wealthy isn't a human right. So let's keep our human priorities straight and remember we're human beings, not robots.

Therefore, "enough," what does that mean?

Successfully providing for the necessities required to eat a healthy, balanced diet in a dwelling where lights, water, and gas are on. Where you can bathe, take your medicine if need be, and go to bed with bus fare in your pocket, or gas in your car, or a bicycle waiting to go to work the next day. "But isn't there more to life than that?" Yes, but not really as far as the physical body is concerned. When we define "enough" we need to start with what is necessary to keep the physical body nourished, healthy, and maintained without deficits or shortages of the necessities because there isn't enough money to purchase them.

Meaning, people should not have to sacrifice medicine to buy food because they don't have enough money for both. We need to understand that as human beings, there is a social contract. We have social obligations to one another because we're not wild animals tearing each other apart over a diminishing food supply.

In the economic system Wall Street defined before us, we compete with each other for diminishing jobs and money like wild animals. This is dangerous for society, because a society needs to be based on mutual cooperation, not constant competition and fighting. Once a society falls into competition over food, which is where we're headed with increased poverty, you get a situation like Somalia in the 1990s. Thus, we all have a compelling reason to cooperate and ensure everyone has, at the very least, enough to provide for the physical body.

The mind can be provided for through services in the community like public libraries, recreation centers, and free activities associated with them. We need to abandon the imagined need to be constantly entertained because that's one very effective method Wall Street uses to enslave us. People wrongly think they need all of this expensive electronic gadgetry. However most of human history was lived without even electricity itself.

We cannot, and shouldn't, include entertainment in discussions regarding having "enough." There are just too many free activities out there for anyone to conclude he hasn't got enough if he can't afford a new CD player. The spirit can be nourished for free. That doesn't cost any money. Most churches will give a person a Bible for free, if they haven't got one and can't afford one. Church services are free.

There are Islamic charities and other groups that will mail a person a Quran for free. As far as I know it doesn't cost money to attend a mosque. There are Buddhist meditation groups in most communities that are free. There are groups that give away Buddhist sutras for free, too. Prayer and meditation don't cost any money. God hasn't got a vending machine you have to put a dollar into in order to pray. If a spiritual practice has a price tag attached to it, it probably isn't worth the asking price.

Now having said all of that, none of that means companies get to penny-pinch and pay the bare minimum people need to get by. My reason for pointing that out is to establish the absolute beginning of what a wage should be, and what every human being actually needs.

Companies exist to make profit. That is to get more money above the actual value of their product. If it costs them one dollar to make the product, they expect to sell it for two dollars. Thus, one dollar covers the cost and one dollar is profit. That's capitalism. If a company says they deserve to make a profit, so should their employees so deserve. That's also capitalism because labor is the product the employee is selling. A profit is what the company has after they've paid the expenses in producing the product. A profit is also what an employee should have after he or she is paid the expenses in providing the labor for the company. The employee expenses are what maintain his physical body. Therefore, workers deserve a profit just as much as the company they work for. That is what capitalism is supposed to be. If you deny that the workers deserve to make a profit, you don't have capitalism—you have a type of corporate feudalism.

But that does not mean everyone deserves to run out and accumulate endless piles of possessions, either. We've got to come to realistic interpretations of what this planet can continue to provide. The planet is finite. Our natural resources are limited and some take billions of years to replenish. We can't keep on acting like spoiled children demanding everything we see at the store. That's why people live in poverty. For all of us to have plenty means a lot of people won't have enough.

We have to understand this dynamic and behave responsibly. We need to learn how to say "I have enough." There is lot of power in that phrase. When we can say "I have enough," we don't need to run ourselves ragged chasing after more. We can enjoy what we already have and it has deeper meaning in our lives as a result.

We don't need to chase after satisfaction and happiness outside of ourselves, in material things and consumer goods. We don't need to log endless miles trudging around in vast shopping malls, searching for happiness in that new possession the television promises will bring joy.

Have any of these things held you when you were sick?

Made you a delicious dinner?

Loved you back?

Everything we need is right here, waiting for us to love and appreciate.

We don't need to create suffering so we can be happy.

We don't need to push people down during a Black Friday sale to get it.

We don't need to lay off five thousand people to acquire it.

We don't need to go to war with some small, poor country to take it away from them.

We don't need to build a wall around our country because we fear people might take it away from us.

What happens here is what we do to one another. This isn't a foreign nation doing these things to us. We have a choice in how we act towards one another. Our choices today are what'll create the future we'll have to live in. It's not someone else's job to create it. It's yours.

I have enough.

I don't want more if it costs some poor man his job to get it.

I don't want more if it takes a bombing raid that levels a city to have it.

I have enough. In fact, I have plenty.

I have Jesus, a loving wife, good food to eat, clean water to drink, a Bible to read, clothes, a bed and a whole beautiful world to live in when I look beyond what the politicians tell me about the world.

I have plenty.

Who knows what wonderful things tomorrow will bring?

I shall enjoy today first.

It is enough.

www.ingramcontent.com/pod-product-compliance
Lightning Source LLC
Chambersburg PA
CBHW022330280326
41934CB00006B/595